Critical Psychology

Critical Psychology

Voices for Change

Edited by

Tod Sloan

First published in Great Britain 2000 by
MACMILLAN PRESS LTD
Houndmills, Basingstoke, Hampshire RG21 6XS and London
Companies and representatives throughout the world

A catalogue record for this book is available from the British
Library.

ISBN 0–333–79452–4 hardcover
ISBN 0–333–79453–2 paperback

First published in the United States of America 2000 by
ST. MARTIN'S PRESS, INC.,
Scholarly and Reference Division,
175 Fifth Avenue, New York, N.Y. 10010

ISBN 0–333–79452–4 (cloth)

Library of Congress Cataloging-in-Publication Data

Critical psychology: voices for change / edited by Tod Sloan.
    p. cm.
    Includes bibliographical references and index.
    ISBN 0–333–79452–4
    1. Critical psychology. I. Sloan, Tod Stratton, 1952–

    BF39.9.C76 2000
    150.19′8—dc21

00–041508

This book is printed on paper suitable for recycling and made from fully managed and
sustained forest sources.

10   9   8   7   6   5   4   3   2   1
09   08   07   06   05   04   03   02   01   00

Printed in China

Contents

Acknowledgments

Were it not for Frances Arnold this volume might not have seen the light of day in a timely manner. Her open-minded support and dedication to quality helped us maintain momentum as we worked to produce a maximally effective set of chapters. The contributors to this volume deserve credit for donating their royalties to the Ignacio Martín-Baró Fund for Human Rights and Mental Health, as does the publisher for assigning a portion of their proceeds for the same purpose. University of Tulsa doctoral student Caroline Pyevich helped extensively with copy-editing and the preparation of the bibliography and index.

TOD SLOAN

Notes on the Contributors

Brian Bishop is Associate Professor at Curtin University, Perth, Western Australia. His prime interests are in rural development and community resilience, resource allocation issues, community-based ethics and justice, and contextualism. He has been involved in a broad range of research activities such as rural community development, resource allocation, indigenous issues, self-help and social assessment. He is married to a Jungian clinical psychologist, which does not create any tensions, surprisingly.

Colectivo Contrapsicológico Esquicie consists of the following:

Josep Alfons Arnau, born in Barcelona, took part in the resistance against Franco, and continued in the resistance when he worked to create spaces for freedom in institutions housing people labelled as 'mentally ill'. But that is tiring work, especially if one is working alone, so he was a major force in the founding of the Colectivo. He is now called a social educator and does therapy through the Colectivo. He writes poetry and short stories and, when he is restless, he is accompanied by Trotsky, Marx and Miguel Hernandez.

Pep Requejo was born in Barcelona while Franco was still alive. As a young man, he travelled to France to try to learn something about the strange behaviour of human beings. There he studied Lacan and became a contra-psychological psychologist. He does therapy through Esquicie.

Yolanda Nievas is a contra-psychological psychologist and an exploited worker. For reasons of logic and feeling, she is an untiring trade unionist. She also collaborates with a counter-informational free radio station. She loves continuous conversation and learning.

Jesus Monteagudo is from Barcelona. He has suffered psychiatric violence in the flesh on several occasions. He works to end all forms of oppression, through denunciation, occupations, taking risks. He is also a juggler and a chef.

Victor Jorquera is from Barcelona. He decided to study psychology and found himself learning to diagnose rather than to understand and accompany suffering/knots in life. He is currently finishing his degree heroically. If you are lucky, you might get to hear him play guitar.

Conchi San Martín is from Barcelona. She is the person who had the pleasure to prepare these short bios for the others in the Colectivo. She is a contra-psychological psychologist, struggles to continue learning, and does therapy at Esquicie.

Many other people collaborate with and support the Colectivio Contrapsicológico Esquicie: Doblas, Rosa, Judit, Teresa, Heinrich, Imma, Miguel Angel, Pepe, Josep and . . .

Natalie Contos is an Australian of English and Greek ancestry, who spent her childhood on a farm in rural Western Australia (WA). She currently works with the National Native Title Tribunal where she mediates between Indigenous Australians and stakeholders with other land interests toward the recognition of native title. She is in the final stages of a PhD programme at Curtin University, Perth, WA. Her research with a community in WA's Southwest focuses on social justice and reconciliation between Indigenous and non-Indigenous Australians.

Neil Drew spent his childhood years in Papua New Guinea until that country became independent. His partner is a clinical psychologist and they have two daughters. Neil lectures at Edith Cowan University, Perth, Western Australia, and his research interest includes social impact assessment, the decline of deference, social justice and procedural fairness. He recently coauthored two chapters for a statistics manual. In his spare time Neil tries to revive his career as a rock musician.

Hakan Durmaz is a research student and part-time lecturer in the Department of Psychology, Bolton Institute, UK. His research interests are Marxism and dialectical logic, 'activity theory', socio-historical psychology, the body, intimacy and the cinema. He is currently writing his PhD on the transformation of discourses of the human body and intimacy in late capitalism. The social, cultural and political life in Brazil and Brazilian Portuguese have recently dominated his interests. E-mail: <hakandurmaz@hotmail.com>.

Barbara Duarte Esgalhado was born in New York City and lived most of her bi-cultural life between the United States and Portugal. She received her PhD from Columbia University in New York, where she had a fabulous time. She would have remained quite happily in New York City, had it not been for a teaching offer from her existential-phenomenological, Lacanian, feminist, poststructuralist, postmodern colleagues in the Department of Psychology at Duquesne University in the post-industrial city of Pittsburgh, Pennsylvania. She is now having a fabulous time in Pittsburgh.

Dennis Fox is on leave from his position as Associate Professor of Legal Studies and Psychology at the University of Illinois at Springfield. Co-editor of *Critical Psychology: An Introduction* (1997) and co-founder of the Radical Psychology Network (<http://www.uis.edu/~radpsy>), his most recent publication is 'Psycholegal Scholarship's Contribution to False Consciousness About Injustice' (*Law and Human Behavior*, 1999). Now in Boston mulling over his plans for the future, his periodic walks in the direction of cheap spicy food help him avoid his computer for days at a time – but he can still be reached at <fox@uis.edu> or <http://www.uis.edu/~fox>.

Stephen Frosh is Professor of Psychology at Birkbeck College, University of London, and consultant clinical psychologist at the Tavistock Clinic, London. He has long been interested in trying to develop more 'progressive' forms of thinking in psychoanalysis and psychology and has written several books on the subject, most recently a second edition of *The Politics of Psychoanalysis*. He has no hobbies, but lots of family and community commitments, plus students, trainees, patients, teaching loads, administration, and so on. He would like to have time to think and write, but is employed as an academic and clinician.

Brenda Goldberg is a Research Fellow at the Discourse Unit, Manchester Metropolitan University. She is of working-class

background and is interested in the influence of 'cultural capital' on educational aspiration and achievement. Her research is
influenced by the work of Foucault, French psychoanalysis and
feminist theory. At the moment she is exploring how the construction of certain spaces allows for, or prohibits, the production of particular identities and behaviours. She is author of
'Spatial Transitions: Contesting the Limits of Social and Psychic
Space' in *Psychoanalysis and Contemporary Thought* (1999) and co-
author of *Challenging Women: Psychology's Exclusions, Feminist
Possibilities* (1996) and *Psychology Discourse Practice: From Regulation to Resistance* (1996).

Angel Gordo-López has broad research interests centring on
qualitative methods in poststructuralist theory, the sociology of
sexuality and the relations between technological discourses
and practices and psychological theories. He is a co-author of
Psychology Discourse Practice (1996) and co-editor of *Psicologías
Discursos y Poder* (1996) and *Cyberpsychology* (1999). He has also
contributed to books such as *The Cyborg Handbook* and journals
such as *Theory and Psychology* and *Archipiélago*. In addition, he
has attempted to open new sites for publication including the
journal *Sexualities*. He is currently working with Gill Aitken in a
book on *Queer Andtherness*.

Dan Heggs is completing research on fantasy and superhero
comic books. His particular speciality is in the development
of discourse analytic methods to visual texts. He has written
and presented articles and papers on discourse and visual
representation, 'cyborg-heroes' and cyberpsychology. He is an
associate member of the Discourse Unit at the Manchester
Metropolitan University and Bolton Institute.

Wendy Hollway is Reader in Gender Relations in the Department of Psychology, University of Leeds. She has been involved
in the critique of psychology since the 1970s, developing alternative theory and methodology from her PhD on. She has
researched and published on questions to do with subjectivity,
gender, sexuality, methodology, parenting, anxiety, the history
of work psychology and gender relations in organizations. Her
published works include *Changing the Subject* (1998, 2nd edn,
with Henriques, Urwin, Venn and Walkerdine), *Mothering and*

Ambivalence (1997, coedited with B. Featherstone), *Work Psychology and Organizational Behaviour* (1991), *Subjectivity and Method in Psychology* (1989).

John Kaye is Professor of Psychology at the University of Adelaide. He is a leading proponent of narrative approaches to therapy and is the organizer of the biennial conference on 'The Discursive Construction of Knowledge'. He practises clinical psychology, sex therapy, and, in his spare time, collects fine Australian wines.

Rebecca Lawthom lectures in the Department of Psychology at Manchester Metropolitan University. She is of Welsh working-class origins and has interests which combine class, gender and 'race'. Her primary research interests focus upon the relationships between feminist theory and the actions of women from a variety of subject positions in the context of work. She has written and published in the area of critical psychology and the psychology of women. E-mail: <R.Lawthom@mmu.ac.uk>.

Elizabeth Lira studied psychology at the Universidad Católica de Chile and then worked in educational programs for *campesinos*. After the military coup that overthrew Allende, she completed a masters in social science and worked with a human rights organization offering support to victims of human rights abuses. She was one of the principal founders of the Latin American Institute of Mental Health in 1988, which focused on issues in mental health and human rights. She has also trained mental health professionals in clinical and psychosocial aspects of human rights abuses, not only in Chile but also in El Salvador, Australia, Peru, Croatia, Ecuador and Turkey. She has written and coedited numerous articles and books among the latter *Derechos humanos, todo es según el dolor con que se mira* and *Psicología del miedo y de la amenaza política*. E-mail: <elira@reuna.cl>.

Kareen Ror Malone is Associate Professor in the Department of Humanistic and Transpersonal Psychology at State University of West Georgia. She is also on the Women's Studies faculty. She is co-editor with Stephen Friedlander of *The Subject of Lacan: A Lacanian Reader for Psychologists*. As an undergraduate she was trained as a behaviourist but read Marx and Freud, later moving on to phenomenology. The difficulties of false consciousness (desire) and of gender sent her back to study psychologists who work with social criticism and post-structuralism.

Terence McLaughlin is an independent consultant in mental health and education. His current research is concerned with psychology and mental health politics and the history of the Hearing Voices Movement. He is particularly interested in developing the Martín-Baró Fund for Human Rights in the UK as a strategy for developing critical psychology practice as independent advocacy in the face of increasingly repressive mental health practice. He is co-author of *Deconstructing Psychopathology* (1995). E-mail: <handsellpublishing@compuserve.com>.

John Morss was born in London, England, and educated in Sheffield and Edinburgh before working in the North of Ireland and subsequently Aotearoa/New Zealand. He was until recently Senior Lecturer in Education at the University of Otago, Dunedin, New Zealand. He is the author of *Growing critical: Alternatives to Developmental Psychology* (1996). He is currently 'resting' and endeavouring to remember what the backup plan was. He can be contacted at <m.nichterlein@xtra.co.nz>.

Bame Nsamenang is Senior Lecturer at the University of Yaounde I, École Normal Supérieure of Cameroon. He received his doctorate in child psychology at the University of Ibadan in Nigeria and, in the late 1980s, conducted research at the National Instititute of Health in the USA. In 1995, he founded the Human Development Resource Centre in Bamenda, Cameroon. He is the author of numerous articles on cross-cultural psychology and the book *Human Development in Cultural Context: A Third World Perspective* (1992).

Ignacio Dobles Oropeza is a social psychologist at the University of Costa Rica, where he has served as psychology department chair and director of the Institute for Psychological Research. He is an avid basketball player and a fan of the Kinks. E-mail: <idobles@cariari.ucr.ac.cr>.

Edmund O'Sullivan is Professor of Education at the Ontario Institute for Studies in Education at the University of Toronto. He is co-director of the Transformative Learning Centre, which promotes both research and graduate programmes that emphasize a global-planetary vision combining ecological literacy, social justice and human rights concerns, diversity education that deals with issues of race, gender, class, sexual orientation and ableism. Professor O'Sullivan has been a professor at the Ontario Institute for thirty-two years and has taught courses in child development, educational psychology, critical mass media studies, critical pedagogy and cultural studies. He is the author of eight books and over a hundred articles and chapters in books. His latest books are *Critical Psychology and Critical Pedagogy* and *The Dream Drives the Action: Education and Transformative Vision for the 21st Century* (1999).

Isaac Prilleltensky is Professor of Psychology at Victoria University in Melbourne, Australia. He was born in Argentina, where he spent the first sixteen years of his life. He then moved to Israel, where he lived close to nine years prior to moving to Canada, where he lived from 1984 to 1999. With Dennis Fox, he co-founded the Radical Psychology Network and co-edited *Critical psychology: An Introduction* (1997). He is also the author of *The Morals and Politics of Psychology: Psychological Discourse and the Status Quo* (1994). He enjoys writing newspaper articles, playing pool with his son, and discovering vegetarian restaurants. E-mail: <iprillel@wlu.ca>.

Edward Sampson is Professor of Psychology at California State University in Northridge. Living in Berkeley and teaching in Los Angeles, some 400 miles away, makes each week an adventure in driving. The real challenge, however, is to meet the university's teaching expectations of eight courses per year while continuing to read, write and live. He continues a lifelong project of trying to transform psychology's understanding so that it might someday become more responsive to the real issues confronting real people. No matter how many years he has been working at this task, it seems still to remain much more than 400 miles away from home.

Ernst Schraube is Wißenschaftlicher Mitarbeiter (that's comparable to the American Assistant Professor) in the Institute for Critical Psychology at Free University Berlin. His research interest focuses upon the changes of human subjectivity in a technoscientific world and his recent book is *Auf den Spuren der Dinge. Psychologie in einer Welt der Technik* (On the Trail of Things: Psychology in a World of Technology) (1998). He spent the academic year 1998–9 as a visiting research scholar at the Department of Science and Technology Studies, Rensselaer Polytechnic Institute, Troy, New York. E-mail: <schraube@zedat.fu-berlin.de>.

Lois Shawver is a clinical psychologist and therapist in Oakland, California. She is the author of the book *And the Flag Was Still There*, as well as of a number of recent articles introducing postmodernism to psychoanalysis. She also owns and manages an active internet list (or community) called PMTH (Postmodern Therapies) which welcomes therapists, graduate students, academics and scholars with an interest in postmodern theory. E-mail: <rathbone@california.com>.

Tod Sloan is Associate Professor and Chair in the Department of Psychology at the University of Tulsa, where he has taught since 1982. He is the author of *Life Choices: Understanding Dilemmas and Decisions* (1996) and *Damaged Life: The Crisis of the Modern Psyche* (1996). He has been a visiting professor in Venezuela, Nicaragua, and Costa Rica, where he also studied the impact of rapid capitalist modernization on personality and identity. On weekends, he plays guitar and keyboards, works in the local green movement, and tries to help his teenage son figure out what there is to do besides spend money. E-mail: <tod-sloan@utulsa.edu>.

Christopher Sonn is a South African of mixed ancestry who lives in Australia. His partner was born in Chile; they have two daughters. Chris lectures in cultural and community psychology at Edith Cowan University, Perth, Western Australia. His main research interests include sense of community, community resilience, and cultural diversity. He recently co-authored *Sense of Community: Community Resilient Responses to Oppression and Change*. In his spare time he enjoys playing soccer.

Janet Smithson is Research Fellow in the Department of Psychology and Speech Pathology, Manchester Metropolitan University, UK. Current research includes projects on the reconciliation of future work and family for young people in Europe, discourses surrounding gender, family and work. Her recent publications include, 'Is job insecurity changing the psychological contract? Young people's expectations of work', *Personnel Review* (1999, with S. Lewis). Her many non-academic interests are travelling, windsurfing, salsa, travelling, and green politics. E-mail <j.smithson@mmu.ac.uk>.

Thomas Teo is Assistant Professor of Psychology in the History and Theory of Psychology Option at York University, Toronto, Ontario. He received his PhD from the University of Vienna and worked as a research scientist at the Max Planck Institute for Human Development and Education in Berlin. Research areas and publications in history and theory of philosophical and critical psychology, epistemology and ethics of psychology, concept of race and racism, psychology of liberation, and developmental psychology.

Jane Ussher is Associate Professor in the Centre for Critical Psychology at the University of Western Sydney, New South Wales. She has previously worked in the psychology department at the University of Sussex and at University College London. Her most recent book is *Fantasies of Femininity: Reframing the Boundaries of Sex* (1997). When not working, she swims at Bondi Beach, cooks and eats seafood in the company of friends, and is writing a novel.

Editor's Introduction

The voices collected in this volume argue passionately for critical psychology. Together they tell us that urgent tasks await those who begin to glimpse the undesirable social and political consequences of contemporary modes of psychological theory and practice. As one might expect, however, these voices differ with regard to their diagnoses of the field's malady and their prescriptions for change. For some, the project of critical psychology implies a thorough critique of psychological theory and practice that must be pursued until the discipline is radically transformed, rendered obsolete, or totally transcended. For others, critical psychology requires a consistent dedication of our efforts as psychologists to larger political projects aiming toward the elimination of oppression and economic exploitation. Still other voices argue for profound philosophical and linguistic critiques that would subvert accustomed ways of understanding self and society and thereby alter social relations. This diversity is healthy, for it is certain that psychology has failed in numerous ways to rise to the sociopolitical challenges of the twentieth century, and it has done so in part because it has not listened well to its internal dissidents and its external critics. There can be no single path toward one ideal form of psychological theory and practice. So, as we rethink the fundamental purposes of psychological inquiry and practice in light of contemporary social realities around the world, the multiple voices in this volume invite and deserve open-minded listening from many different angles.

How this book came to be

The idea for this project came to me early one cold morning in February 1998, when I awoke for some reason with a painful awareness of the isolation experienced by many of the psychologists I know who are, in various ways, dedicated to social and political transformation. In my travels to international conferences, I have sought out and met many such progressive and radical psychologists. With a few exceptions, most report that their critical point of view is not shared by anyone else in their university department or mental health clinic. We (for I include myself in this lot) thus feel compelled to prepare conference papers, articles, and books that address and confront mainstream positions, rather than reaching out to like-minded colleagues to build alternative approaches. We may also work locally on psycho-political issues of various sorts, but such work is relatively hidden and there are few natural forums for discussing it with others in far-off places. This situation has not encouraged awareness, dialogue, and debate among the varieties of critical psychology that are sprouting up all over the world. A body of common understandings that would guide alternative modes of work within or beyond psychology has been slow to form.

I decided that a small step toward reducing isolation and encouraging dialogue would be to send out an international call for personal statements on 'critical psychology'. This rubric, as this volume testifies, has been used over the past few decades to signify all sorts of positions in psychology. It does, however, seem to have a certain momentum now, so I thought the project might attract plenty of people who would be willing to raise their voices for a critical psychology of one sort or another. In so doing, they would get a chance to argue in favour of one form of critical psychology or another, and thereby help move a somewhat incoherent intellectual movement in directions they favour.

After twenty minutes of such rumination, I leapt out of bed and posted a call for chapters to various e-mail discussion lists, for example, APA Division for Theoretical and Philosophical Psychology, Psychoanalysis and the Public Sphere, Radical Psychology Network, Social Theory, Society for the Psychological Study of Social Issues, and so on. Perhaps fifty people from around the world showed interest initially. Those published in this volume are those who actually produced a manuscript in time to get this off to press in a timely manner.

The following excerpts from the original e-mail call for chapters should give readers a sense of the challenge that was posed to each author.

The rubric 'critical psychology' encompasses a wide variety of theoretical approaches and practical strategies. This variety reflects the diverse origins of the critical impulse: for example, radical psychoanalysis, neo-marxism, liberation theology, human rights work. It also stems from different agendas: reform of the mental health system, critique of positivism in scientific psychology, labour organizing, community mobilization, anti-poverty work, green or socialist organizing, empowerment of marginalized populations, and so forth.

Given this diversity of origins and purposes, and the pressing challenges of social transformation in whatever form we envision it, we who work under the general banner of critical psychology do not hear from each other enough. We tend to be isolated or to work only in small groups. A sense of affirmation tends to be rare. Furthermore, we have too little time to document what we do, to share basic ideas and lessons learned in practice, to argue about basic principles. We thus suffer from a lack of cross-fertilization. This volume aims to fill this need and thereby contribute to the vitality of the critical psychology movement in general.

The book will consist of two or three dozen brief chapters (not more than 4000 words each) structured in response to a few basic questions – note that these questions may be challenged if necessary to make one's point:

- In a nutshell, what does critical psychology mean to you?
- What brought you to critical psychology? Mention relevant influences, experiences, people, etc.
- What do you see as the basic principles of critical psychology? Justify your position.
- What are the big debates in critical psychology? What issues remain to be resolved?
- What have you done, or what to you do, that exemplifies these principles? How do you practice critical psychology?
- From your standpoint in critical psychology, what are the most pressing general problems to be addressed? 'What is to be done?'

The essays subsequently submitted by individuals and groups from around the world are published here in slightly revised versions. Our intention was to preserve as much as possible the tone of informality that would have characterized personal interviews using these questions as a guide. Of course, many of the academics in the bunch could not resist turning this into a more formal exercise. This, in fact, expresses one of the tensions that often finds expression in debates about critical psychology. Is critical psychology primarily an academic revolution, or does it necessarily work to break down the barriers between academia and the rest of society? But we are getting ahead of ourselves here. The essays are presented in no particular order, except that I exercised a bit of editorial prerogative to place Edward Sampson's chapter first. Among North American psychologists, his steady, critical work over three decades has served as a solitary beacon in the darkness for me and many of the generation that followed his. Following his essay, the order mainly seeks to maximize a sense of variety as one moves through the book, by hopping from continent to continent, from an academic approach to an activist one, from an isolated voice to a description of a collective effort.

Due to some vague anti-authoritarian principle, I was originally reluctant to provide a concluding chapter or an epilogue. But as the essays flowed in and as I read them closely, I began to see that there are some things I want to say about this collection of essays, given my vantage-point as editor, and I would be abdicating a certain responsibility if I were to silence myself. So, at the end, you will find an epilogue in which I indicate some of the trends that are apparent in these pages and develop the beginnings of a critique of the current state of critical psychology. I do hope, however, that readers of the volume will also publish their own reactions either on the new Critical Psychology Network website or in print.

On a personal note

It is only fair, since I asked the contributors to this volume to do so, that I should say a bit about how I came to critical psychology myself. Since I have said most of what I have to say about the current state of society and psychology in *Damaged Life: The Crisis of the Modern Psyche* (Sloan 1996a), I will focus here on the making of this particular critical psychologist rather than delve into my positions on various issues.

I suppose the beginnings of my critical bent could be found in the fact that my father's work took my family all over the world during my childhood, especially to Asia. These travels helped me see that there are different ways of organizing societies, with immense consequences for the well-being of their citizens, and also left me feeling quite alienated from my 'own' culture in the USA, since I kept returning to it as an outsider every few years. Added to this was an element in my mother's faith, Mormonism, which spoke of the primitive communism and simple living practised by the pioneers who crossed the North American plains to Utah. As a teenager, I wondered why the Mormons hadn't continued that noble experiment rather than sliding into individualistic and consumerist lifestyles. During high school, in late 1960s California, I witnessed from a distance the anti-war protests on campuses and in the streets, and learned vicariously that even if it is hard to change the order of things, one nevertheless has an ethical duty to speak out and work for change.

I started college with the strange idea that I was supposed to be an engineer, but I gradually drifted toward the idea of helping people more directly (employing that common projective device that allows one to focus on how others need help when it is actually oneself who is feeling that need!). As I saw it, clinical and counselling psychology offered the most obvious forms for helping individuals. I had received no political socialization to speak of, so I was unable to consider politics or law as possible paths, nor to imagine solutions beyond the individual level. So, I swallowed the standard psychology curriculum with glee and occasional boredom (in social psychology and experimental psychology in particular). I found myself especially attracted to personality theory, especially the existentialist versions, in part as a replacement for my rapidly crumbling religious worldview, but also because of their emphasis on human possibilities and agency. I wondered why more people were not able to explore their options and choose alternative modes of selfhood. But most of the answers to my questions, I now understand, were not to be found in psychology *per se*. Meanwhile, the research training I received as an undergraduate left me cold. Not only were the questions addressed not very central to real problems in living, but it was also clear that the data could be used to buttress anyone's favourite idea. There was also very little one could point to as accumulated knowledge, especially in social and personality psychology. The field felt more like an ever-growing pile of concepts, with a bit of attached empirical support for each. This bothered me especially in my favourite subfield, personality theory. Chapter after chapter in the textbooks – on Freud, Jung, Maslow, Bandura and others – laid out a model and provided pieces of evidence for it. Textbook authors usually pointed to the strengths and weaknesses of theories as well as a review of the evidence for them, but something essential was missing. That something essential was the angle I would come to recognize as *ideology criticism*. But it would take me a few more years before I found that angle.

My first introduction to the practice of critique related to ideology criticism was during my doctoral studies at the University of Michigan in George Rosenwald's (see Rosenwald and Ochberg 1992) course on personality theory in 1975. For the first time in my educational experience, I was asked to evaluate various core concepts in psychology on grounds other than empirical evidence. In the seminar, we examined ethical, political, practical and aesthetic aspects of basic concepts like development, learning and identity and were introduced to the emerging interdisciplinary *human science* perspective. I found this practice of *critique* difficult because I had been taught to accept published facts, concepts and constructs as established once and for all.

During the next few years, I began training as a psychotherapist and became increasingly aware of the critical potential of psychoanalytic theory and the practice of psychoanalysis. I suppose I might have even gone on to become a psychoanalytically oriented psychotherapist had it not been for a fateful encounter with critical social theory, particularly the Frankfurt school, to which I was introduced by fellow graduate students Randy Earnest and Gary Gregg. Earnest had come over to psychology from political science in order to do psychoanalytically informed studies of ideology (see Earnest 1992). Gregg had been reading widely in the anthropology of the self and brought a strong cultural and social class analysis to personality research (see Gregg 1991). We were all doing dissertations based on depth interviews, so we met to listen to interview tapes and to discuss our readings of Adorno, Foucault, Habermas, Deleuze and Guattari, and others. Gradually, I began to see the utter necessity of ideology criticism. For example, I had been infatuated with Heidegger for some time, especially with his concept of authenticity. While interviewing research participants about what they meant by authenticity as they made important life choices (see Sloan 1996b), I ran across Adorno's *The Jargon of*

Authenticity (1973). I finally understood that ideology is more than a set of values that keep us a bit off-track as we go through life. I glimpsed how profoundly social systems produce individual character structures and ideational patterns in a manner that makes it very difficult to imagine that a social order might be arranged in a less exploitative or oppressive manner. The concept of ideology, defined in this *critical* manner, became a compass for all my subsequent work, since it provided not only the method – ideology criticism – but also the purpose that was missing in the psychology I had previously encountered. That purpose is *to challenge and confront ideological processes and the unjust social orders that they sustain.*

At another point during my doctoral work, another Michigan faculty member, Barnaby Barratt, was extremely influential. Barratt was working out a critical epistemology for psychoanalysis (see Barratt 1984, 1993) and required his students (in a psychology course!) to wade through large chunks of Hegel, Husserl, Lévi-Strauss, Heidegger, and Lacan. My discussions with Barratt reinforced my interest in the connection between Adorno's negative dialectics and psychoanalysis. I have yet to find a combination that works as well as a basis for ideology criticism, although I sense that others get to roughly the same place through Foucault or Derrida (or even Lacan plus Marx and Hegel, as in the case of the Slovenian scholar Zizek).

Since those heady days, the question has been how to put these insights into practice. After finishing my PhD, I took a position as a psychology professor in Tulsa, Oklahoma, which cut me off from the progressive urban centres in the United States. I wandered for quite awhile. I did some local disarmament organizing, published a few articles on critical personality theory, and, looking for inspiration, travelled to meet Marxist theorists Lucien Sève, Gerard Mendel and Slavoj Zizek in Paris and Klaus Holzkamp in Berlin. A bit later, in the mid-1980s, there was some obvious political work to do when Reagan's CIA was hurling the Contras against the fledgling socialist Sandinistas. That experience prompted a phase of work in which I tried to examine possible progressive roles for psychologists in the Third World (see Sloan 1990). To make a long story short, I concluded that there is very little to be done as long as we continue to work within the framework of what is known as scientific psychology. There is, however, an immense challenge awaiting anyone who wants to work in solidarity with Third World struggles for democracy, human rights, and economic justice.

Over the past decade, I have been trying to learn from Latin American scholar/activists in social and community psychologists. I was fortunate to meet and learn from the examples of Ignacio Martín-Baró, the social psychologist who was assassinated by US-trained Salvadorean troops in 1989; Maritza Montero, in Venezuela, who exemplifies scholarly and socially committed community psychology; Ignacio Dobles and his colleagues in Costa Rica, who deal with scarce resources and logistical nightmares to conduct psychosocial action research that really makes a difference for communities and influences public policy; and Elizabeth Lira and her associates in Chile, who work tirelessly to develop psychological theory and practice that address the collective and individual suffering caused by state terrorism, torture, disappearances and other human rights violations.

My Latin American colleagues have awakened me from a slumber induced by the relative comforts of academia and the absence of a vigorous progressive movement in the USA and helped me see that carrying critical psychology through to its practical implications is more a matter of courage and commitment than a matter of having obvious opportunities for action. Oppression and injustice are all around us, within a mile or two of our universities and clinics as well as in remote corners of the globe.

I urge readers to allow themselves to resonate to the spirit and energy of the voices in this volume, and then to find their own ways of moving forward, against, or sideways! These voices tell us that we must keep our eyes open and think beyond the ideological blinders that constitute mainstream psychological practice. We must seek out and join with others who see the same problems and work with them to challenge and transform the institutions that reproduce domination. These voices convince us that psychology can be transformed, and perhaps transcended, in ways that will make our collective work directly relevant to global and local struggles for social justice. I trust that there will be many readers who are ready to listen and to act.

1

Of Rainbows and Differences

Edward Sampson

What does critical psychology mean to you?

Critical psychology is 'critical' in two senses of the term. First, it is critical of the field of psychology. Critical psychology asks pointed questions about nearly every aspect of the field: its methods (too experimental and oriented to experimenter-defined laboratory rather than real-life tasks); its samples (limited mostly to young college students, primarily from the United States); its choice of research problems (driven by momentary fads, governmental financing priorities, and the need to fit a quantified lab paradigm); its evaluations of its findings (typically fails to examine the social and political implications of its work). Critical psychology believes that psychology has adopted a paradigm of inquiry that is ill-suited to understanding human behaviour and experience.

The second sense of 'critical' is based on the value commitments that characterize critical psychology: its concern with human betterment, with the social transformations needed to achieve such betterment, and with its belief that helping provide voice for those persons and groups heretofore denied such voice is an essential element in bringing about the societal transformations needed to achieve human betterment.

Psychology occupies a key position in today's society. It helps to organize and legitimize the understandings that people and social institutions require in order to function. Psychology, thereby, could make a major contribution to human betterment through the kinds of understandings it encourages, yet, more often than not, psychology contributes to some of the very problems it purports to be addressing.

Societal problems of prejudice and human exploitation, for example, cannot be adequately addressed by the current mainstream paradigm of psychological inquiry. Its tendency to individualize its understanding of the roots of social problems, by wresting them from the kind of sociocultural context needed to understand them, robs psychology of its potency as a serious player in helping resolve social problems. A critical psychology is cognizant of the necessity for 'psychology' to be a genuinely historical and sociocultural discipline – that is, to see the sociocultural and historical as intrinsic to the psychological.

So that my comments will not foster a misunderstanding, let me clarify another point about critical psychology. It is not simply critical, parasitic of the mainstream, but also represents an affirmative attempt to achieve a better life for people who have been oppressed and without their own voice. As such, critical psychology is more likely to be aligned with the causes of people of colour, with feminism, with gays and lesbians and with Third World cultures and nations than with the dominant western worldview.

What brought you to critical psychology?

I will be brief, having developed a far lengthier response in several other publications. In a nutshell, I rapidly grew disenchanted with both psychology and psychologists shortly after I began my professional career as a professor (actually assistant and later associate professor) of psychology at the University of California at Berkeley. It seemed to me that too many of my highly rated colleagues failed to comport themselves decently in the classroom and in departmental meetings, leading me to wonder about just what this field of mine was actually hoping to accomplish if some of its major practitioners were unable to apply their knowledge to their own lives. They were masters at displaying their arrogance – they and only they had the truth – in putting down everyone who held a contrary opinion, and, especially, in avoiding commitments that would make their psychology as political as it seemed to be. Their goals were primarily self-oriented, designed to advance their careers and gain as much power in the academy as they could for themselves. Where, I wondered, were the people whom psychology was purported to serve?

Meanwhile, my students were seeking an education that could help them address the problems they saw around them: civil rights, war and peace. I could not in good conscience simply continue being and practising as I was taught and as I saw modelled around me. I sought an alternative framework of psychological inquiry that would give new focus to my teaching and help me feel that I could contribute to resolving the pressing issues of my time.

I found hope in the critical psychology I began to encounter: at first, the Frankfurt School's accounts; later, the emerging postmodern approaches. Both offered a psychology that could be responsive to ongoing social issues while providing its practitioners with a way of opening themselves personally to the diverse world around them. Traditional psychology had become much too arrogant; its practitioners pontificated from on high, while people's lives remained ensnared in institutional forms that stole their very souls. I wanted to have nothing to do with this kind of field, even as I wished to remain a psychologist.

My only hope, it seemed, back then as it does now, was to move from the centre to the margins, all the while hoping that what was marginal today would be at the centre tomorrow. I cannot say that I or we have been successful here: with few exceptions, our field continues on its merry way while Rome burns.

What are some of the basic principles of critical psychology?

I hesitate to term them 'principles', but here are some of the key ideas that continue to animate my own work: (1) Social reality is constructed by socially organized communities; its designs give expression to the perspective of its creators rather than to any independent 'reality-in-itself'. (2) Because of this socially constructed nature of reality, it is important to try to uncover the vested interests often concealed in the prevailing forms and to engage in a relentless historical and cross-cultural examination of alternative constructions. (3) In addition to unmasking those possibly concealed interests, however, critical psychology is also dedicated to helping provide voice for those whose versions have rarely been accorded the kind of legitimacy they deserve; these typically are groups who have been systematically exploited and whose voice is not generally sought. This places critical psychology invariably at odds with the dominant society and, obviously, with a scientistically oriented psychological paradigm.

What are the big debates in critical psychology?

For me, one of the continuing issues involves the assumption that because reality-in-itself does not provide the touchstone necessary for evaluative judgements, critical psychologists appear to be caught in a Never Never Land of extreme relativism, unable to tell good from evil. I have never been persuaded that this is a genuinely central issue, although I do agree that it has taken up a lot of journal space, with critics arguing against the apparent relativism of critical psychology and its advocates attempting to defend their position from such critics.

This is a pseudo-issue in so far as it is framed entirely from the perspective of the dominant paradigm. To buy into that paradigm is already to lose the debate. I believe we do best not to accept the idea that evaluative judgements must be grounded in anything eternal or transcendent of any and all human communities, but rather to accept the notion of truth and evaluation as an ongoing process in which people engage and in which the more diverse are the perspectives involved, the more likely are the judgements to be persuasive. In other words, rather than assuming we cannot make informed evaluative judgements unless they can be grounded in some eternal verities, we must be prepared to render evaluative judgements without this rock-solid certainty underpinning us. Further, we must be prepared to persuasively defend our judgements, not by claiming god-like omniscience but rather while admitting human-like fallibility.

How have you practised the ideas of critical psychology?

I am primarily a teacher, and primarily of undergraduates entering psychology, often as a future career. I take it as one of my cardinal tasks to present then a critical perspective so that, perhaps, they will be influenced not to buy into the mainstream without questioning it and without reflectively examining the consequences of their roles.

I used to be more street-active, but that seems to have faded as I have moved away from youth toward retirement. I remain, however, active in my hope to reach and shape students' minds through my teaching and perhaps even my writings. And, for some naïve reason, I continue to believe that one's life and practice as a psychologist should not be removed from one's life as a person and citizen in the world. This belief has posed many dilemmas for me, especially in my teaching and in my current collegial relationships. Unlike many of my current colleagues, for example, I simply cannot teach without conviction and find their willingness to teach what they do not believe both astounding and sad.

What do you see as the pressing social problems that need to be addressed?

I would like to avoid getting into a ranking game, identifying any particular problem as more worthy of transformation than another. For me, however, one of the most pressing of current problems involves the difficulty we all seem to have in dealing with differences and otherness in a celebratory manner rather than an oppressive one.

Historically, whenever a community encountered differences, it sought various ways to repel the differences and install its way as the normatively approved way. At times, this involved physically destroying those who were different; often it involved transmuting the difference into a deficiency and treating those who differed as lesser beings. As single term useful to describe this well-known historical tendency is 'exclusionary': those who differed were removed (that is, excluded) from the community.

One of the most pressing current problems involves moving toward greater inclusiveness: that is, bringing into human community a veritable rainbow of differences, excluding none, nor arrogantly elevating any one form into the esteemed norm. I continue to believe that a critical psychology can make a contribution to this inclusionary ideal, even while non-critical forms of psychology tend to encourage a furtherance of the exclusionary model.

2

Critical Psychology in the Mainstream: A Struggle for Survival

Jane M. Ussher

What does critical psychology mean to me?

To talk of a singular discipline of 'critical psychology' is a misnomer – for there are many different critical psychologies. To me, today, critical psychology is about addressing the relationship between subjectivity, embodiment, the cultural and political forces that shape our lives, and power, at both a discursive and a material level. To be more specific, I am concerned with a critical feminist psychology: with questions such as: What does it mean to be 'woman' or 'man'? How are sexuality and desire represented, shaped and experienced?; why are women more likely to be diagnosed and treated for 'madness' than men? What does it mean as a woman to be 'mad' (or to recover from this state)? How can we understand myths around the reproductive body, in particular pre-menstrual syndrome?

What makes these questions part of a 'critical psychology' agenda is the approach: this is work that is undoubtedly 'psychology', yet it challenges mainstream psychological orthodoxy, while being informed by a diverse body of theoretical and scholarly work, including psychoanalysis, cultural theory, feminism and more recently, spirituality. I am committed to action-oriented research that takes the accounts of my participants seriously, invariably from a qualitative perspective. This means that my research and scholarship acts to question dominant social and psychological truths, and to provide alternative ways of conceptualising or intervening in women's lives (as well as questioning whether intervention is appropriate at all).

To me, critical psychology can never be cloistered in the academy – it must always look to the day-to-day experience of people's lives, and the way in which psychology as a discipline or profession intervenes in or acts to regulate these lives. As a critical clinical psychologist I am committed to developing a practice that offers help to those who seek it, but does not pathologize or medicalize the individual.

The most pressing social/political problems, to me, are about gender and sexuality – the continued marginalization of the interests of women, and of gay and lesbian groups. However, I would also stress the importance of social class and of economic issues, at both a discursive and a material level. The question, 'What should be done about these issues?' is a big one: put simply, I would argue for a greater understanding of the issues, combined with political and social change.

The big debates I'm interested in are the perennial questions around the relationship between body, mind and spirit (Ussher 1999a), the questions around how we can develop genuinely critical theory and method in psychology (Ussher 1996), and questions of the role of gender and sexuality in the development of subjectivity (Ussher, 1997a). That there are many other debates raging, I recognize. These are the ones that seem most vital to me.

What brought me to critical psychology?

At a theoretical and epistemological level, this was a disenchantment with the dominant positivist-realist accounts in mainstream psychology. In particular, I felt frustrated with the way in which the dictates of 'science' precluded the examination of issues that seemed to be of central concern in any attempt to understand how we live our lives. My interest in feminist critiques and, latterly, psychoanalysis and spirituality, also encouraged me to gravitate towards 'critical psychology'. These are schools of thought very much absent from the mainstream, in anything other than a watered-down, anodyne version.

I was drawn to critical psychology as a subdiscipline that is recognized at an institutional level, for a more complex (if familiar) set of personal and professional reasons. For most of my academic and professional life I have worked in mainstream psychology departments, attempting to develop and teach more critical ways of thinking and working, yet be accepted as a legitimate equal among my peers at the same time. Today, I have given up that particular struggle, and work in a department of critical psychology. My colleagues and students are all critical psychologists. My interests are at the centre, not marginalized or dismissed. In many ways I have found my home. My relation to 'critical psychology' has shifted substantially during this journey. This is the story of how and why – which addresses the questions posed to contributors to this volume along the way.

What brought me to critical psychology and how I practise it: a personal narrative

Emerging from the mainstream

I entered psychology through a traditional training: a standard mainstream undergraduate degree at Exeter University, completed in 1983, and a PhD in cognitive psychology, focusing on cognition, physiological arousal and performance in the menstrual cycle, completed in 1986. I hadn't heard of qualitative research, never mind critical psychology, until 1985. When I belatedly 'discovered' critical feminist psychology, during the latter stages of my PhD (see Ussher 1999b), it is not an overstatement to say that my life was changed as a result. I questioned the epistemology, the methodology and the very topic of research I had thus far been enthusiastically engaged in. I wanted to change tack at this point. I wanted to ask women about menstruation, rather than wiring them up to machines to measure their galvanic skin response. I wanted to look at the cultural construction of female reproduction, rather than analyse the results of daily mood questionnaires. I wanted to present my work at conferences where sociologists, feminists, and other cultural theorists would be interested in the subjective experiences of women, rather than at psychology conferences where the size of my t-scores or the level of statistical significance in my multivariate analyses were the issues of most pressing concern. I was interested in forms of knowledge that were not restrained by the dictates of positivism-realism, and that could have some impact on women's lives.

Major influences and key people

This is what first brought me to critical psychology – reading feminist work in the early 1980s, and realizing that there was a whole world out there that I hadn't even known existed. Scouring the shelves of the numerous feminist bookshops that had sprung up in London (many of which are now closed – a sign of the times), I devoured any feminist writing – fiction and non-fiction – I could get my hands on. But it was the work of feminist psychologists that was most powerful in terms of my academic thinking. I was strongly influenced by the work of Janet Sayers, Valerie Walkerdine, Wendy Hollway, Phyllis Chesler and Carol Vance, in particular. I came across Janet's book *Biological Politics* (Sayers 1982) in the women-only feminist library in Hungerford House, on the Thames. It was a revelation – a scholarly feminist critique of research on reproduction that was also a page-turner. I remember sitting in the library transfixed and filled with excitement – both at being in such a place and in finding such a gem. Along with Phyllis Chesler's book *Women's Madness* (Chesler 1973), and Carol Vance's collection of writings on sexuality, *Pleasure and Danger* (Vance 1985), it showed me that I could legitimately study topics that interested me, in a critical feminist way. Slightly later, reading *Changing the subject* (Henriques *et al.*, 1984), in particular the contributions of Wendy and Valerie, introduced me to post-structuralist and psychoanalytic critiques of subjectivity that both challenged and highly influenced on my own thinking. Seeing each of these women talk at conferences was also an inspiration – they were 'critical psychology' made flesh, proving powerful role models at that stage in my career.

What was a sea change for me was the fact that I would have read this critical feminist literature for pleasure – it certainly didn't feel like 'work'. This was because all the questions that had brought me to psychology as a discipline in the first place, as a naïve undergraduate who thought that Freud, subjectivity and sexuality would be part of the agenda (and found that rats and behaviourism were the staple diet instead), could suddenly be addressed. Still a postgraduate student at the time, I was so excited and energized I almost burst with the possibilities of it all. But my supervisor brought me down to earth with a bang.

Split career – split self

A mainstream cognitivist, he encouraged me to finish my orthodox experimental PhD in the way it had been planned. I was nearly finished and he assured me I could go on to do more critical work afterwards. I followed his advice (which was the best I could have received at that point), gained the PhD, presented conference papers and submitted journal articles on the results, and began a life of dual identity, split between mainstream and critical psychology, which I have only recently given up.

While I continued to conduct 'straight' empirical work, in order to maintain my institutional position in psychology, my energy, my 'authentic self', was driven by my concerns with critical feminist psychology. I channelled this in a number of directions. I began writing in what might be described as a more polemic style, certainly a more critical and political one. Meeting Valerie Walkerdine at a conference in 1986, I was asked to contribute a book to her Critical Psychology series, published by Routledge. This book, *The Psychology of the Female Body* (Ussher 1989), contained all that was left out of my PhD: a critique of traditional psychological approaches to understanding menstruation, pregnancy and the menopause, and a plea for a more cultural and historical analysis. Being asked to write it was a turning-point in my career – it gave me the confidence to believe that *I* could have a voice in this sphere. I trained as a clinical psychologist after my PhD and adopted a similar stance in this arena. My second book was a critique of the way in which psychiatry and psychology had conceptualized and treated women's mental health problems *Women's Madness: Misogyny or Mental Illness* (Ussher 1991). I also coedited a number of volumes arguing for attention to critical psychological issues in clinical psychology (Ussher and Nicolson 1991), in women's health research (Nicolson and Ussher 1992) , and in the field of sexuality (Ussher and Baker 1993; Ussher 1997a) and reproduction (Ussher 1997b). Reconciling a critical perspective with daily clinical practice was too difficult a task at this time, so I gave up clinical work, and joined the ivory veneered tower of academia.

Organizing for change within psychology

Another key factor in my critical psychology career was my involvement in organizing within the British Psychological Society (BPS) to get feminist psychology on the mainstream agenda. This culminated in 1988 in the formation of the Psychology of Women Section of the BPS, continued with involvement in BPS committees and sparked friendship with the other women involved in this endeavour that still exists to this day. This group of feminist psychologists, in particular Jan Burns and Paula Nicolson, became my primary support, and my main influence, over the next decade. I would never have withstood the isolation and continuous discouragement meted out to me as the sole feminist psychologist in a mainstream psychology context without support of other women in similar situations. Going against the grain in one's academic thinking or research is not popular with the powers that be. As a junior academic, I was also attempting to conduct my pedagogic practice differently. In my teaching and supervision, I wanted to avoid the formal remote style of teaching and supervision I had experienced as a student, and instead to acknowledge that students were people, that they could bring ideas and views to the enterprise we were jointly engaged in, and that the power differential between us could be eroded to some degree, or even worked in the students' favour. This too was frowned upon by my more traditional colleagues. But I persevered.

During this period, I was committed to critical psychology in order to change psychology as a discipline. I was still in my late twenties, full of the energy and confidence of youth, with a degree of self-belief that proved a powerful force which fuelled me for years. I became a vocal advocate for staying within the system and attempting to effect change. In an edited volume, *Feminists and psychological practice* (Burman 1990), I was one of the few voices arguing for staying in psychology. Indeed, I was asked to contribute to the volume late in the day because the series editor was concerned that the contributors were too negative about psychology as a discipline. She knew I wasn't. I titled my chapter 'Choosing psychology: or not throwing the baby out with the bathwater'. Over a decade later I have changed. I might now advocate throwing out the bath as well as the bathwater (baby with it).

In a nutshell, the reason for this is that while I had I wanted to be a pioneer, to change the system, to do things differently, what actually happened is that to do it I had to sell my soul. I took on too much and got burnt out. Delusions of grandeur are always dangerous. But I only had myself to blame.

Institutional contexts for critical psychology

I started off my academic career in an interdisciplinary department – like many of my critical psychology colleagues who had found comfortable niches in social psychology, cultural studies, or women's studies departments. After working for three years in this context, where to my chagrin my work was far more 'straight' in every sense of the word than that of many of my non-psychology colleagues, I left to join the big league: a highly respected mainstream psychology department that prides itself on being one of the most prestigious in Britain. At the time I rationalized it in terms of geography – I was living in London and tired of commuting long distances to Brighton, where I was based, on the train. But if I am honest it was because I wanted to be back in the mainstream of psychology. I felt safer there. I knew my place. To those around me I was radical, critical, potentially a threat. I liked being different, being other. I liked the thrill of the fight. I liked the notion that I could be an outsider, and yet still be accepted as part of the system. This suggests that critical psychology, at an institutional level at least, is a relative concept: in my first job I was not critical or radical enough (I was still conducting empirical work, my knowledge of philosophical or cultural theory was at that time rudimentary and I was still framed within the discipline of 'psychology', which was seen as archaic and reactionary). In contrast, in my second post I was seen by many to be extreme – my work a travesty when judged against the standards of 'good science'. I enjoyed being in that position. How naïve I was. But as with all stories about growing up (and rebellion against the older generation), I can only say this in retrospect.

I joined the new department in 1992 with optimism and openness: I was not appointed under false pretences. I made clear at my interview that I wanted to conduct critical feminist research. I also made it clear I was not an experimentalist, indeed that I had deliberately turned my back on that mode of work. I had decided that I no longer wanted to pretend. I wanted to try to concentrate on work that felt authentic. I no longer wanted to live the dual life that I had lived for the last six years, of attempting to gain acceptance in both mainstream and critical psychology.

To my surprise I was offered a job. But that was only after I had successfully demonstrated that I *could* be an experimentalist if I turned my mind to it, having been asked to design 'thought experiments' at my interview by one of the senior professors on the panel. Those without an experimental background (which I had) might be caught off guard by the question, or indeed be so indignant at being asked that they would refuse to engage in that particular charade. Foolishly, I was not. It made me all the more determined to succeed.

If you knew my family history here you would say, 'That fits.'

Personal motivations – personal attacks

I bring in this side of my story here because the question 'What brought you to critical psychology?' must inevitably touch on something far more personal than our experiences of education or of the orthodoxy of psychology. Why do we want to be pioneers, outsiders, forever destined to be pilloried for criticizing or debunking the established wisdom of the mainstream? Why do we want to live on the edge? Why didn't I follow the advice given to me early on in my career – that I concentrate on a 'sensible' area of research, like memory or perception?

I grew up rebelling against my father, who had very traditional views about gender roles – in particular the position of women. Education wasn't for girls in his view – so I defied him by gaining high grades in my A levels, and leaving for university, rather than setting up in a hairdresser's shop, or getting married, as he expected me to do. So standing up to the dictates of powerful men, forging my own path in opposition to their views, was something I learnt early in life. How many of us act out rebellion against the previous generation, against the symbolic father, through being 'critical' in our professional lives? As being 'critical' always implies a rejection of what has gone before, is it not a natural part of developing our own paths, and casting aside the truths of those who currently hold power?

I had been warned from the start that in this particular psychology department my 'sort of work' was disliked. 'Not psychology', 'not science', 'journalism', were some of the comments made. These critiques were directed initially at my use of qualitative methods, not particularly controversial in many contexts (indeed, frowned on for smacking of 'empiricism' in my previous employ), but heresy here. Yet this was the least of my worries. Two other factors made me more suspect. One was 'feminism'. I was painted as a political activist rather than a researcher or scholar (ironically, I might have liked to be an activist, but was too busy poring over academic papers and books to leave my desk for more than a few hours at a time). The fact that I argued strongly for the legitimacy of critical feminist work was deemed the wrong stance to take – perhaps if I had been silent, meek and mild my approach would have been more acceptable. But I refused to take the path of apologizing for my very existence, or hang my head in shame. I dealt with each round of criticism, the continuous disparagement, and institutional attempts to curtail my research and teaching by fighting back. It gained me some respect – I was publicly described by one of the senior professors as one of the few women who could survive in such a hostile environment. But it also upped the stakes. The second problem was the fact that my research focused on sexuality, raising suspicions about my personal motives, and my personal proclivities, or so I was told. Leonore Teifer (1991) has written about this phenomenon as a reason for sex researchers adopting experimental methods in their research – as 'rational scientists' they attempt to remove their own sexuality from the equation. Wanting to adopt a critical psychological approach, where our own subjectivity is part of the research agenda, I didn't do this. This meant that I was open about my own sexuality and the fact I was then in a lesbian relationship, in analyses of my work, and discussed with postgraduate students the importance of adopting a reflexive standpoint in their own work. In a department of unreconstructed realists, where objectivity was the order of the day, and heterosexuality the norm, this was, in retrospect, ill-advised.

Judgement and performance criteria

It wasn't all roses (or reflexivity). To survive in this bastion of positivism (where experimental cognitive neuroscientists reigned supreme), I had to perform at a high level, being judged by the same criteria as my mainstream peers, as my books and critical feminist work didn't count for much in the psychology arm of the academic review process which takes place in British universities every four years. (The research assessment exercise rates each academic department on a scale of one to five, and government research funding is given out on the basis of the ratings. Each subject has a panel, made up of members of the discipline, who pass judgement. Critical psychology has, to date, fared very poorly in these assessments, while in contrast more traditional experimental psychology fares very well.)

So while on the one hand, I was writing critical feminist work that came from the heart, and attempting to develop and grow academically in this sphere through drawing on psychoanalytic theory, cultural theory, art history and film theory, in my teaching, my graduate supervision, and in a book I was writing on women's sexuality (Ussher 1997b), at the same time I was running three major empirical research grants, having to publish in mainstream refereed psychology journals, running weekly graduate seminars, conducting my undergraduate teaching, and sole supervising six full-time and two part-time PhDs. In retrospect it was madness – few could keep up that level of work for long. But at the time it seemed the only way to survive. I wanted to make a niche for critical feminist work in a highly respected psychology department, and give a generation of PhD students the experiences of group work, of supportive supervision, or mentoring, that I hadn't had. My mission was to make feminist psychology part of the mainstream map – whether they liked it or not. I did for a while, but at a cost – the cost that many women who succeed in bastions of masculine power pay.

Regulation through the personal domain

The next part of this narrative is probably obvious. I became exhausted. I was overworked, overstretched, continuously undermined, and had no support or collegiate encouragement at all. I had created the feminist enclave – but I was the only full-time member of staff within it. This meant that I was on my own, at the top of a pyramid, with all those I was working with looking to me for advice and support, rather than part of some egalitarian system, which is what I had fantasized. For a while it was wonderful – I was fuelled by the pleasure and sense of personal power I gained from working with a close group of women, of being able to do it all, to have it all, as I then thought I could. But eventually I got to a point when I could take no more. I could no longer tolerate the continuous deluge of requests, complaints, and demands for time and attention from those working with me. While I could take a step back and both contain and 'hold' (in a Winnicottian sense) the anxiety and uncertainty which is endemic to postgraduate and research assistant work so long as I was feeling personally strong, as soon as I felt overstretched myself, it became too much. I began to feel as if I was under siege. I was having to cope with criticism and attack from above, and now it felt as if I was getting it from below as well.

The final straw came when complaints made by a disgruntled student, who had been unhappy with criticisms I had made about her work, were used by the establishment as a vehicle to question my whole way of being and working: the subject matter of my work (sexuality was suspect, and I was advised to focus on more 'serious medical' research); my approach to supervision (reflexivity was incomprehensible – it was seen as voyeuristic interest in students' personal lives, and banned); my pedagogic style (I was told I should only talk to postgraduate students about their research, and should not engage in any discussion or socializing with them outside supervision). I was specifically told not to disclose any personal information about myself to students in future (interestingly, a stricture not applied to members of the department in heterosexual relationships). Ironically, at the time I had been relatively circumspect in disclosing my sexuality (although I had informed my head of department that I was in a lesbian relationship, as I was aware

of the way in which gay and lesbian individuals are vulnerable
to persecution and attack at work, the use of innuendo or false
accusations, particularly if they are not 'out'). Since then I have
not been so circumspect. When a complaint that I had 'con-
fessed' to being a lesbian can be taken seriously by university
authorities, and used as a vehicle for constraining my academic
freedom, I can no longer argue that my sexuality is simply a
private or personal matter.

The most benign interpretation of these criticisms is that they
were made in all innocence – from the perspective of those in
authority, my way of working and interests were undoubtedly
unorthodox. The fact that I was at the same time commended, in
writing, for the 'good-quality research' I produced, and encouraged to continue it, might support this interpretation of events.
However the covert hostility underpinning these judgements is
evident in the fact that I was also censured by the authorities, in
writing, for being 'moody'. This was manifested by my having
been openly irritated with students on a number of occasions. It
is true. I was. But who can honestly say that they have never
shown irritation at work? I also could ask the question, 'Who
wouldn't be irritable, in such circumstances?' Or I could reflect
on the irony of a feminist academic who has written critically
about the way women have historically been controlled and
condemned for displaying 'irrational' emotion (Ussher 1989,
1991) being castigated in such a way. But perhaps the most
important point of all is the implication of something so
nebulous being formally levelled against me – for how could
I be certain that I would never be judged to be 'moody'
again, thus risking further censure? My work was not the
object of scrutiny and regulation here, but my very person. It
was this final humiliation that made me decide I had
had enough. Walking away is better than drowning in a
never-ending fight.

In my view, this particular case illustrates some of the pitfalls
of practising critical psychology in the mainstream (or at least,
practising critical feminist psychology in a department popu-
lated mainly by heterosexual male cognitive neuroscientists).
There is no institutional protection of personal or academic
freedom, and so the individual who challenges the establishment is always at risk of their work (or their personal life) being
undermined or scrutinized.

Horizontal violence: tensions between generations of women

In many ways I have sympathy with the student whose complaints were used as a vehicle to constrain my work, although there was a time when I was devastated by what felt like an unprovoked attack. All of the students I supervised were attempting to survive in a critical feminist enclave in a department where their work was under attack from the majority, in the same way that mine was. I had a reputation outside this narrow sphere that could sustain me in my darkest moments. These students only had me (and each other). When I was overstretched (and overwrought), it's not surprising that they felt angry and let down. I'd led them to have such high expectations of me. But I was only human. I probably set myself up by my attempts to be a 'good enough' feminist supervisor: I was told that the worst thing I did was to feign equality, and then use my institutional power (by criticizing their academic work, and retreating to professional mode when I wanted to get on with my own writing and research). This was experienced as both an insult and an abuse – a contravention of everything they believed (or fantasized) about feminism. (See Gallop, 1997 for further discussion of this issue in a broader context, and for an analysis of the problems inherent in feminist PhD supervision, particularly associated with issues of power.) I certainly hadn't intended it to be like this. Isn't it sad how our ideals so often bring us down?

With the benefit of hindsight, I now realize that this is a familiar tale: successful women being squeezed out of male-dominated organizations through professional and personal attack (Nicolson 1996); envy and competitiveness between women destroying ideals of feminist egalitarianism and collaboration, as well as leading to 'horizontal violence', which serves to bring down those who challenge masculine power and authority (Orbach and Eichenbaum 1988; Gallop 1997; Ussher 1997c). I had also overlooked the fact that I had become the older generation – so I shouldn't have been surprised when my students turned their critical energies on me (Game and Metcalf 1996). Hadn't I modelled such behaviour myself, having spent my career criticizing those who came before me?

Re-evaluating critical psychology

This whole experience caused me to re-evaluate my way of working (or at least the place I was doing it in), my academic goals, and my desire to make critical feminist psychology a part of the mainstream agenda. I am now working with Valerie Walkerdine in a newly formed department of critical psychology, involved in setting up and running a research centre and a graduate programme that will provide the context for the critical psychological research and teaching I had wanted to achieve in my previous job, but was impossible there. I am confident that it will work this time. One reason is that I am not alone – there is collegial and institutional support for this venture, which makes research and teaching the pleasure and exciting enterprise I had always fantasized it would be. PhD supervision is now conducted jointly, so there is less risk of the difficulties which are endemic where there is only one all powerful supervisor. Equally, in this context, critical psychology is not an enterprise always having to fight for legitimacy in relation to an ever-present 'other' – mainstream psychology. Instead it is an integrated programme, covering all areas of the curriculum. Analyses of subjectivity (including our own) are a crucial part of the agenda – discussions of our own experiences and how they impact on our work are neither suspect nor secret.

Today, critical psychology means something different to me. It is not about battling for small change, for recognition, for an inroad into the mainstream of psychology. Those endeavours are admirable, and I have nothing but respect for those who wish to pursue that path – for the students we teach it is often the only life line they have in an otherwise straight spectrum. But I don't have the energy, or the inclination, any more. I have come to the conclusion that innovative, meaningful research or teaching cannot be carried out, at least without great personal cost, if critical psychologists are having to justify their existence on a daily basis; if they are having to explain, persuade and cajole, rather than engage in dialogue with others of a similar disposition and intellectual bent; if they are having to watch their backs. The 'big debates' that contributors were asked to outline cannot be even contemplated in a context where the very notion of examining subjectivity is suspect, where experimentalism reigns, and where the critical psychologist is in danger of being perceived as the enemy within.

So the question I will end with, the question of my own that we are invited to design, is this: how can critical psychology coexist with, or remain in relation to, the mainstream of psychology, without personal acrimony, burn-out, or compromise and cooption being the order of the day? I thought I had the answers, but I did not. I'm fortunate to have a new space, and exciting place, in which to develop a different path. I wonder if others can manage to maintain critical in a traditional space and survive – both personally and professionally. I'd love to know how they do it, if anyone honestly can.

Acknowledgments

Thanks to Ann Game for discussions on the tensions inherent in being critical yet staying sane and for comments on a previous version of this chapter.

3

The Critical Psychology Project: Transforming Society and Transforming Psychology

Dennis Fox

In a nutshell, what does critical psychology mean to you? What are the hallmarks of critical psychology?

Critical psychologists follow a variety of theoretical, methodological and political traditions differing in goals, substance, terminology and style. Yet it seems to me that critical psychology overall has two essential components.

First, in common with many self-defined 'critical' approaches in disciplines such as sociology and law, *our ultimate political goal is to help bring about a radically better society*. Using psychological insights to evaluate, synthesize and extend competing perspectives, critical psychology explicitly or implicitly envisions what this fundamentally better society might look like and how we might help bring it about. Our assumptions, conclusions and speculations often take us beyond the relatively minor reforms advocated by politically liberal, mainstream psychologists. Although we may never reach our ultimate goal, it provides a fluid working model today as we try to learn better how to expose and oppose injustice, oppression and other institutional barriers to a meaningful life.

Second and equally crucially – again departing from liberal mainstream psychologists – *we reject mainstream psychology's values, assumptions, and practices as a legitimate framework for our work*. Reflecting the historical and cultural context that spawned them, many of these traditional norms reinforce the *status quo*;

they provide ideological support to dominant institutions and channel psychologists' work and resources in system-maintaining rather than system-challenging directions. And more: psychology itself is a dominant institution with its own oppressive history, often stemming from norms that demand or facilitate measurement, categorization, manipulation and control. So critical psychology aims not just to transform society but to transform psychology, replacing its norms with emancipatory alternatives.

What brought you to critical psychology?

I became interested in psychology as a student in the late 1960s, following an introduction to socialist Zionism during high school that combined psychological and political theory (I recall reading Kurt Lewin on the Jew as 'marginal man'). A course I took at Brooklyn College on 'the psychology of prejudice' impressed me with social psychology's relevance to social issues; other courses during that period of on-the-street 'helping behaviour' research were fun. Clearly, I had not yet developed a critique of psychology to match my Vietnam-era dissatisfactions with modern society.

Two years of early 1970s graduate work at Michigan State University eventually and conveniently focused on social movement participation and value change among members of a group I had helped organize that planned to start a new kibbutz (collective settlement) in Israel. That group eventually splintered, as did my first dissertation and my affinity for much of the Zionist agenda. But my kibbutz-style, small-scale socialist impulses persisted; they were later reinforced by my discovery of anarchist theory, modern communalism and environmentalism, and the work of psychologists such as Erich Fromm and David Bakan, who had understood that the psychological could not be divorced from the sociopolitical. I spent a decade outside academia, working for brief periods in the social security bureaucracy (the basis in part of a later article on the politics of disability evaluation) and other settings while participating in social movements such as the direct-action opposition to nuclear power.

When I returned to graduate school at MSU in 1982, I discovered that, a decade earlier, I had overlooked (or had never been introduced to, or perhaps I had just forgotten) social psychology's late-1960s 'crisis of confidence', during which the field was confronted by persistent critical challenges. Catching up on my reading, I came across something called qualitative methodology and realized I could do a new dissertation based on interviewing people about their values and politics, a topic always much on my mind. Frankly, because I adopted this qualitative approach before I had read much that justified it, I quickly immersed myself in a mostly anthropological, sociological and feminist psychology literature that dissected the political and philosophical ramifications of quantitative 'positivist' research. Frequent calls for a 'paradigm shift' coincided with my own interest in fundamental social change and my growing awareness that the field I was once again pursuing needed changes of its own. During this period I wrote several papers critical of psychology's methods, assumptions, and political affinities, and organized a 'psychology and controversy' student–faculty discussion group that debated critical ideas (an unpublished paper on my website lists the discussion topics and describes the group's experiences).

I was fortunate in having as my MSU mentor the late Charles Wrigley, who had left his directorship of the Computer Institute for Social Science Research because, he said, he wanted to end his career working with people rather than with machines. Wrigley, who taught courses in political psychology and the psychology of social movements rarely offered in psychology departments, agreed with much of my politics (a supporter of the peace movement, he was intrigued that the Michigan State Police Red Squad had kept a file on him for signing a newspaper advertisement protesting against the Vietnam War); trained in philosophy, he encouraged my growing awareness that social psychology had become bogged down in trivia (as did a retired faculty member, my decade-earlier adviser Gene Jacobson). Although impatient with qualitative methods, Wrigley's endorsement kept my dissertation committee from rejecting or mutilating my proposal. Unfortunately, he was unable to persuade the core social psychology faculty to fund my research during the whole three and a half years I was there – unlike my fully funded years in the 1970s, when I still dabbled with statistical analysis and hadn't yet criticized the kind of research my professors were doing.

Wrigley gave me a piece of advice that has stuck with me: to be a 'good' traditional psychologist one should read narrowly but in great depth, writing for the ever-proliferating journals devoted to increasingly narrow and irrelevant topics. But to be a 'great' psychologist, and to publish in journals read by generalists, one should read broadly and demonstrate how different fields of study interrelate, thus introducing psychologists to new literatures. Although I wasn't aiming for greatness, I did follow Wrigley's advice in my first significant paper: combining a critique of centralized authoritarian solutions to environmental problems with a call for utopian speculation, I described how anarchist theory paralleled and enriched psychological thinking on the tension between individual autonomy and a psychological sense of community.

When the paper was published in *American Psychologist* (Fox 1985), the American Psychological Association's primary journal, I realized I could actually present radical ideas to a mainstream audience if I was willing to jump through the necessary hoops (adopting a certain tone, responding to reviewers' and editors' concerns either by revising as they wanted or justifying not revising, recognizing good advice when it was offered, letting go of the small stuff without losing sight of the big stuff); dozens of supportive letters in response to the article made me think it was worth it, both to spread my (admittedly recycled) ideas to people who didn't read political journals and to find like-minded people. Most of my writing since then thus has been for mainstream psychology journals, though sometimes the hoops have remained insurmountable. On the other hand, editors have sometimes solicited or facilitated my work, making me think that real people in mainstream institutions vary among themselves more than their formal gatekeeping roles might indicate.

A final graduate school story: Joel Aronoff, a personality psychologist with his own early kibbutz experience and a broad range of interests, told me that I could not be an academic and an activist at the same time. I would have to choose, he insisted, and perhaps, given the department's refusal to fund me, I would have to choose sooner rather than later. Aronoff's advice foreshadowed a somewhat nastier comment by an untenured psychologist responding to a short polemic of mine that criticized academic publish-or-perish expectations; he suggested in print that 'a competent vocational psychologist might suggest pursuit of a different occupational environment.' Although at the time I found both comments amusing, my inability ever to find a job in a mainstream psychology department and my subsequent career path have since elicited occasional second thoughts. I did find a job eventually, but only after another year outside academe and two years of postdoctoral work in the University of Nebraska at Lincoln's psychology/law programme, where Gary Melton's call for a values-based 'psychological jurisprudence' offered a starting point (and someone respectable to cite) as I began to look at the psychology/law field with a critical eye (for example, Fox 1993, 1999).

Finally, though, I found a real job, in an unusual teaching university that actually encouraged critical approaches. As a faculty member in an interdisciplinary legal studies programme, I spent a decade teaching, writing and organizing. I even got tenure. Unfortunately, the former Sangamon State University, since taken over by the research-driven University of Illinois, has succumbed to relentless efforts to weed out everything non-traditional, paralleling efforts by universities across the United States to cut costs, boost enrolment, eliminate faculty and student power, and persuade legislators and alumni that their university needs more money to teach job-relevant skills (Fox and Sakolsky 1998). Now that I've chosen to go on permanent leave, my department, pressured from above, is seeking to replace me with someone whose work and politics are more mainstream. It is still the case, I think, that academics can be critical theoreticians and sometimes even off-campus activists without extreme jeopardy. But criticizing their own institutions and rejecting traditional research and publication norms makes academic life difficult, and sometimes impossible. In this respect the university resembles other institutions designed to replicate the *status quo*.

What do you see as the basic principles or concepts of critical psychology?

Four premises:

(a) *Psychology's values, assumptions, and practices have been culturally and historically determined*, reflecting among other things the prevailing socioeconomic setting, political affinities, responses to external pressures, and battles over power, professionalism and turf. In contrast, mainstream psychology generally portrays itself as progressing through objective, scientific, 'value-free' progress. (For example, demanding quantitative rather than qualitative methodology cannot be attributed only to the experiment's supposed superiority; also crucial are factors such as an interest in psychology's being perceived – and funded – as a high-status hard science, one that can produce quantifiable results sought by those who seek not just to understand behaviour but also to predict and control it.)

(b) *Modern society is marked by widespread injustice, inequality and systemic barriers to both survival and meaning.* To explain the origins of the unacceptable *status quo* and to justify its continuation, dominant institutions inculcate a psychologized *ideology* and use the process of *false consciousness* to encourage widespread belief in unjustified assumptions about human nature. Societal elites may or may not believe the ideology they disseminate; in either case, it narrows the range of institutional arrangements the society considers possible and desirable and encourages people to accept unjust outcomes. (A capitalist economic system is justified by the insistence that human beings are inherently selfish, competitive and accumulative, and that people who fall behind have only themselves to blame; people learn to expect the worst from others and from themselves. A legal and political system whose essential principles, procedures and styles were created by white privileged men with substantial property is justified by the false claim that today everyone is treated equally; because the law is unconcerned with unjust outcomes so long as approved procedures are followed, *substantive* justice is displaced by the perception of *procedural* justice.)

(c) *In their everyday work, mainstream psychologists too often contribute to complacency at one extreme and oppression at the other.* This is the case whether they are well-intentioned and avowedly apolitical helping professionals or, less commonly, conscious agents of social control. Mainstream psychologists typically overemphasize individualism, the narrow pursuit of personal goals, and either adapting to or bypassing societal norms and expectations; they de-emphasize mutuality beyond the family, justice, and the need for institutional change. Mainstream psychology and critical psychology differ, thus, in their *level of analysis.* (For example, by reducing widespread job or relationship difficulties to 'manageable' personal problems, traditional psychotherapy diverts energy and legitimacy from efforts to transform work, community, or societal institutions; it reinforces the false belief that we can determine our own outcomes if we simply work hard to find the socially appropriate individual solution.)

(d) *Critical psychology seeks to alter, and ultimately provide alternatives to, both mainstream psychology's norms and the societal institutions that those norms strengthen.* Desired values such as social justice, self-determination and participation, caring and compassion, health, and human diversity must be advanced in a balanced way, with awareness that some of these culturally specific values have more potential for social transformation than others. Our ultimate goal is to respect and enhance both individuality and diversity within a mutually supportive just and equal society. (Isaac Prilleltensky and I discussed these points in more detail in *Critical Psychology: An Introduction* – Fox and Prilleltensky 1997; Isaac's ideas are now so intertwined with my own that I can no longer easily discern when I should be citing him.)

What are the big debates in critical psychology? What issues remain to be resolved?

Efforts to devise an internally consistent, clearly defined critical psychology have led to debates among critical psychologists who bring to their work differing emphases and motivations. Reflecting a variety of 'critical psychologies', these debates are valuable. They spark intellectual interest; coalesce new insights into a more comprehensive whole; direct needed attention to issues such as economic class and false consciousness; and motivate both mainstream psychologists and critical psychologists alike to question their own assumptions.

On the other hand, overemphasizing intellectual purity creates a risk common to all movements seeking social change: splintering into factions that devote more energy to distinguishing real but relatively minor differences than to pursuing shared goals by different routes. This risk is magnified by competitive academic norms demanding not just intellectual rigour but also a substantial number of publications and other evidence that one's views are influential. So for me, the big debate in critical psychology is over the importance of theoretical consistency. I don't think we should allow our differing approaches to mask the much more fundamental divide between critical psychology and mainstream psychology.

Having said this, several overlapping issues confront critical psychology, some of which I present here, mostly as oversimplified, forced-choice questions. Having a critical psychology perspective does not require answering them, however, and specific critical psychology projects can proceed without trying to accomplish everything all at once.

(a) *Ultimate allegiances.* Are critical psychologists primarily psychologists interested in theoretical rigour, advocating political goals only when they happen to be compatible with critical theory? Or, perhaps motivated by sources outside psychology such as Marxism or feminism or anarchism, are we really activists primarily interested in social change, using psychology's theory and methods only when they happen to coincide with our politics? We believe critical theory supports political change, but what if we are wrong? If critical theory ultimately justified only an apolitical stance, would we abandon politics, or abandon the theory?

(b) *Methods.* Should we use traditional methods stemming from positivist assumptions to uncover inequality and injustice and achieve political and institutional reform, or should we refrain from methods that strengthen mainstream claims to legitimacy?

(c) *Legitimacy.* Should critical psychologists claim special expertise *as psychologists* to advocate social change, or does rejecting positivist methods reduce our rationale for doing so? And a related issue: Given psychology's historic role as a servant of the state, on what basis can we legitimately advocate specific public policies today? Should our goals be merely to keep psychology from doing more damage and to avoid fooling ourselves about the value of our insights?

(d) *Moral relativism.* Can we advocate our politically preferred values such as equality and empowerment or must we abandon all value preferences because they are culturally determined?

(e) *Audience and style.* Should we primarily write in journals, and use a style that can be understand only by other theory-oriented academics, or should we reach out instead to students, psychologists who don't read critical theory journals, and the general public?

What have you done, or what to you do, that exemplifies these principles? In other words, how do you practice critical psychology in your academic work, activism, personal life, etc?

It's difficult for me to distinguish between activities stimulated by critical psychology and activities reflecting my pre-existing political perspective, and even between academics, activism and the personal. However:

(a) *Academic work.* My most significant critical psychology academic project was organizing and editing with Isaac Prilleltensky the book *Critical Psychology: An Introduction.* With chapters written by two dozen psychologists on three continents, the 1997 book presented a relatively readable overview of critical psychology's approach to different areas of psychology. It's been used as a text in courses around the world, though much more frequently in the United Kingdom and elsewhere than in the US and Canada, where relatively few professors have even heard of critical psychology. (Introductions to the book's chapters are on my website.)

In the past sixteen years I've also published some two dozen articles, mostly in psychology journals, and presented a similar number of conference papers – not an impressive number by US academic standards but enough to get my basic points across. Essentially, all my work is critical of mainstream psychology or of some aspect of society – not because non-critical work is never interesting or worth doing, but because enough people already do it. None of my articles is based on original empirical research; instead, they range from comprehensive synthesizing essays through pointed polemics to short rebuttals; as a body of work they pursue in different contexts several themes I've noted in this chapter.

These themes also appear in my teaching, where I've tried with mixed success not just to teach critical subject matter but to use a critical pedagogy, encouraging students to think about the connections between their studies and their lives. I'm always energized by the relative few whose horizons are indeed transformed by what they discover. I'm also repeatedly awed by the example set by colleagues whose creativity in the classroom consistently demonstrates higher education's critical potential, a potential we should defend against efforts to turn universities into mere suppliers of state and corporate workers and data.

(b) *Activism*. Beyond anti-nuclear, anti-war, and other direct-action movements over the years, I've focused on issues related to my workplace (for example, faculty and staff unionizing, campus free speech) and to psychology. I think it important not just to oppose injustice and oppression around the world but also to turn a critical eye toward my own institutions.

From 1993 to 1999 Prilleltensky and I coordinated RadPsyNet: The Radical Psychology Network. RadPsyNet evolved from a discussion group we had organized at the 1993 American Psychological Association (APA) convention on the topic 'Will Psychology Pay Attention to Its Own Radical Critics?' We had proposed that session after realizing that even though journals such as *American Psychologist* published our articles, our work seemed destined to have no impact; the well-known and mostly long-gone psychologists whose work we repeatedly cited had published in the same journals and had written many books and had even received lots of awards, yet not many people followed their advice. Perhaps we were all just a novelty, serving only to justify the mainstream's claim to openmindedness. So, partly to avoid the lure of armchair radicalism, we decided to move from writing to organizing.

RadPsyNet now has over two hundred formal members in more than two dozen countries (including many students), an active e-mail discussion group run by David Nightingale, and a website with reading lists, conference notices, position papers, teaching materials, and much more (see http://www.uis.edu/~radpsy for membership information). Coordinating the group, editing its original newsletter for two years, and maintaining the website for the past three years have taken a lot of time. However, providing a forum for critical psychologists to find, support and debate with one another has seemed to me more useful than adding more publications to the proliferating literature (though I am glad to report that three graduate students in three countries have recently taken over most of the coordinating tasks).

Coordinating RadPsyNet has clarified for me the degree to which people have differing perspectives on what it means to be a radical or critical psychologist. RadPsyNet has received some criticism for not having a clearly defined theoretical approach, but as a loose network there has been little member interest in excluding people willing to join a group with 'radical psychology' in its title. *Radical* psychology has as many potential meanings as does *critical* psychology, and for many of us they mean the same thing.

On the academic–activist borderline, I created a second website designed to disseminate my own perspective beyond journals read only by other academics and to draw connections between my academic activities and other aspects of my work and political life. This project has led to a slow but steady stream of e-mail, mostly from students and psychologists around the world, some of whom have since joined RadPsyNet or made other critical psychology connections.

(c) *Personal life*. These days I live a fairly conventional middle-class life, a sometimes uneasy compromise between my ideals and my reality. With varying degrees of both success and failure, I've tried to implement my values in raising my children, interacting with family, friends, and colleagues, making a living, and engaging in community and other activities. I'd like to think that someday we will all create a world where our compromises are harder to get away with, as well as less necessary. Awareness that 'the personal is political' may help clarify certain issues, but it doesn't always help resolve them.

On a different personal note, an admission: despite my politics, I sometimes fantasize that I am not a critic but a true participant in the institutions around me – fitting in rather than struggling against. After thirty-five years of being 'critical', at fifty I'm more tired of confrontation than in the past, perhaps reflecting academic and activist burn-out at least as much as a fatiguing disability that's required simplifying my life. But inevitably, the yearning for calm is overcome by the impulse to point out what should be obvious, to place things in context, to try to get 'to the heart of the matter' (as I was recently told when I asked simple questions about the parent–teacher organization at my daughter's school).

And when I do step forward I'm almost always reinforced. I don't think there's ever been a time in my life that others didn't tell me my questions or criticisms matched their unvoiced concerns. I appreciate this positive feedback, but I appreciate even more those who move to active collaboration. As critical theorists and radical activists we need to focus more attention on how to remove systemic barriers to voicing opposition. Within psychology, for example, we could do more to disseminate information to students and faculty about how to pursue critical perspectives within mainstream institutions, or about how to find alternative institutions, or we could create alternative institutions. One loud individual can always be dismissed as a crackpot, two as some bizarre pair. But three critics are the beginnings of a movement, with a mailing list, and a future.

From your standpoint in critical psychology, what are the most pressing general social/political problems? What should be done about them?

Critical psychologists should create an effective coalition that seeks to raise consciousness about, and opposition to, the societal ramifications of mainstream psychology's values, assumptions, and practices. Groups such as RadPsyNet (centred in the US and Canada) and Psychology Politics Resistance (in the United Kingdom) are a start.

This coalition should foster efforts to end class and other forms of inequality, oppression, materialism, the degradation and homogenization of social life, and the destruction of the environment. Because all these problems are exacerbated by the power of multinational corporations to reshape the political, economic, and natural environment, removing the vestiges of corporate society is especially crucial to achieve our aims. There already exists a widespread but struggling movement against corporate power; its mostly sociological, environmental and economic analysis could be broadened by critical psychologists who can focus on the psychological consequences of life in corporate society and on the psychological assumptions and methods undergirding the *status quo* (Fox 1996).

The ultimate long-term goal is to create a truly better society, the kind many now dismiss as utopian (Fox 1985). In my view, such a society would reject capitalism's individualistic assumptions about a conveniently selfish human nature and abandon efforts to find technological solutions to social and political problems. The future society should foster decentralized socio-political institutions that rely on mutually derived, environmentally benign arrangements and enhance our ability to seek, and perhaps even to find, meaning and mutuality in our daily lives. The kibbutz and other forms of intentional community are potential models. Despite their flaws and failures, small communities are our best hope of meeting conflicting needs for both individual autonomy and a psychological sense of community. And this I believe: We should state – *as psychologists* – that such a society would be better for most human beings.

But this is my view. Clearly, we cannot – should not – clarify in advance what will emerge from democratic participation. in establishing the future. There will always be many cultures with differing institutions, and no doubt towns and cities as well, though these would likely take new forms to reflect new understandings and priorities. People will always differ and crave different experiences at different times. Rather than restricting us, the future society should allow a wider range of personal experiences and social arrangements than most people around the world can even dream of attaining today.

Note

Several complete papers, summaries of all my work, and related materials are located at <http://www.uis.edu/~fox>.

4

Practising Critical Psychology within a British Psychology Department

Wendy Hollway

I chose psychology out of a desire to understand myself and those around me, both near and far: to know 'what makes people tick', as my mother and grandmother would say. I soon became dissatisfied: the issues were trivial and the means of inquiry consistently missed the point (my point). I have acted on (and acted out) this desire in myriad ways in the thirty years since I embarked on an undergraduate psychology degree. Here I want to talk about effecting some institutional change through one psychology department, where I have worked for almost two years. Although the conditions under which they study are so different these days, that same desire is evident in many of today's students if they are given a space for it. The critical intellectual and political climate of the 1970s and 1980s in the UK formed my understandings and helped to provide a form for my inchoate dissatisfactions with psychology as an undergraduate. What will help to develop the critical impulses of the generation – Thatcher's children as they are often called – who are now being formed by a similar curriculum? How will critical psychologies influence this future generation of psychologists?

Here I won't be talking about the project of critiquing the 'rational unitary subject' of psychology. That project was set out in 1984, with Julian Henriques, Cathy Urwin, Couze Venn and Valerie Walkerdine, in *Changing the Subject*, before the term critical psychology was in use. Our new foreword for the 1998 edition discusses what we think some of the salient theoretical issues are now, fourteen years later. The question of how to theorise a 'psycho-social' subject in the face of many dualisms is as pressing as ever, and all of my work approaches it in one way or another, preferably with some kind of empirical material to rescue me from the giddy heights of philosophical abstraction where I don't function well at all. My own trajectory has increasingly drawn on psychoanalysis (of the British rather than the French type) as a way of not losing sight of psychological questions, of not falling into the many versions of social constructionism which are dominant in contemporary critical theory, including critical psychology. (In the face of perspectives which rely on a socially constructed subject, I find myself championing the cause of a subject whose motivations, actions, and experiences are best understood by the idea of unconscious intersubjectivity. For example, the concept of projective identification for going beyond the assumptions about unitary rational subjectivity is rarely appreciated in critical uses of psychoanalytic theory, nor in its applications in the research process.)

While my critical psychology has been defined by the above theoretical trajectory, for the purposes of this chapter, my definition, is any project which opposes the elements of psychology that reduce people; that rob people of their complexity, for example their imagination and their emotions. Psychology can do this at a number of levels, namely in the way it represents the individual (and therefore how it influences ways of understanding ourselves and others), the methods of inquiry it uses and how it legitimizes and institutionalizes ways in which people are treated. The ways in which psychology so often ends up with reductionist constructions of the human subject have both theoretical and methodological causes, intimately connected over psychology's history as a science (cf. Hollway 1989). I briefly discuss methodological issues in defining critical psychology below.

For the last two years, then, the main beam of my critical impulse has been turned on working in an ordinary psychology department in the UK. I chose to move there, ambivalently, after twenty years of working in higher education locations which were emphatically not psychology: women's studies, social policy and social work, organizational and management theory, Third World development. All these developed my analytical breadth but in some respects diverted me from the psychological questions around which my intellectual passions have always revolved.

What are the forces that are producing psychology graduates in the current higher education climate in the UK? We may be relieved that an older generation of psychology teachers is retiring, but are not the behaviourists being replaced by the cognitivists? Isn't it fashionable now to be an evolutionary psychologist, not a critical one? In my optimistic moments, I can see the evidence that positivism is suffering from a crisis of confidence that it deserves, after more than two decades of sustained critique from feminist theory, environmental activism, post-structuralism and post-modernism. But psychology thrives in the wider world where modernism still offers the reassurance of prediction and control, and psychological measurement gives simple answers in the service of regulating people and populations: employers appear to like psychologists' research skills and funders like the simplicity of measurement and scientific answers to market questions.

Let me first give a vignette to illustrate my personal experience of the changes that make it worth working in a psychology department, rather than in a potentially more critical context.

On the train I finish reading an undergraduate project which I have supervised. My pleasure mounts as I read this young gay man's inquiry into the relation between coming out and identity. He cogently critiques the psychological and sociological literature before turning to psychoanalytic theory. He discusses his relation to the theme and the data based on his own experiences of coming out. He explains why he left aside two other interview transcripts in order to concentrate his analysis on one in-depth case study. He analyses the transcript in detail, insightfully. As I write the grade – first class – on the mark sheet, I have a fantasy – indeed it is soon a plan – that this project will be submitted for the undergraduate prize: gay, qualitative, and psychoanalytic/psychosocial. How significant that would be. I hope it will raise consciousness about other (critical) approaches to psychology. I check the second marker – a colleague who is qualitative – and gay. I only need worry about how the psychoanalytic interpretations will be received. I send up a message of thanks to the colleague who has so sensitively allocated second markers. What the external examiners will make of it remains to be seen.

Later I discover that a batch of about eight projects has gone to the external examiners who will award the prize. What were the criteria for selection, what was the procedure? I point out that five quantitative psychologists got together and assumed their competence to evaluate qualitative projects. These are new differences within the department, where everyone until recently took it for granted that one methodology was correct. I put the matter on the agenda for the next relevant meeting. I wonder about the symbolic value of this prize – is it worth fighting over?

This is the stuff of institutional change. But this student's achievements (and he was not the only one) depended on the provision of an intellectual climate within the degree where he could develop that interest in a critical psychology which I think is present in most students. It also depended on my provision of sufficient reassurances that those who took the risk (as they understandably saw it) of doing the kind of research which seemed to break all the rules they had been taught up to that point would not find themselves penalised when it came to assessment. In this respect, my seniority in the department (next in the hierarchy after four male professors) helps me to get innovations accepted. Providing this kind of environment for students involves holding on to a paradox: making challenges to the status quo (as above) but generating a non-threatening and cooperative climate with my colleagues. I remember making some resolutions before I started in this job: one was 'don't hesitate to regard my mode of inquiry as legitimate and worthy of equal respect. Don't be defensive, thereby conveying that I position myself as on the periphery. Psychology has no centre.' I think this has worked well.

My first contribution on joining the department was organizationally simple: most of the academic staff are expected to offer a final year module in their area of interest. In the current market-driven higher education climate, everybody is pleased if a course entitled 'Psychoanalysis, gender and sexuality' attracts eighty students, including some from other resource centres who therefore bring in extra income to the department. Colleagues whose options attract ten students don't mind if it's me, not them, who is saddled with a huge marking load as a result. There is almost nothing in the preceding curriculum that prepares students for this course and I spend the first session talking historically about the relations between psychology and psychoanalysis, in order to give them a position outside of positivism from which to see the development of psychology as a discipline. I have been amazed at the transformations in their thinking that this course affords some students. One of the external examiners, while noting that this was the course she (yes, a woman for the first time) knew least about, was happy with the quality of work and interested in the non-standard forms of assessment (a learning journal and a seen exam). I think liberal academic traditions of respecting diversity are strong enough to support innovation where the formal power of the external examiner might otherwise work against it.

The British Psychological Society (BPS) has considerable institutional power, including over the core undergraduate curriculum as it is taught throughout Britain, since this is the basis for the further qualifications that permit professional membership. The core subject matter (largely taught in the middle year) is scrutinized by the BPS and our accreditation is seen as essential to attract our undergraduate applicants. Nonetheless, it was acceptable to the department that I teach critical social psychology as a part of the social psychology core: the power of an institution like the BPS is not monolithic: they are wary of infringing on the academic freedom of university teachers. Their committees largely consist of academics and their positions are subject to change, not least by market forces.

Predictably, the BPS places heavy emphasis on the acquisition of quantitative and experimental research skills and no psychology programme will earn accreditation without these. During the teaching of critical social psychology, one student, genuinely confused, came up at the end of a session and asked 'what can you do if you don't measure things?' My continuing close encounter with psychology reminds me that its edifice is built, not primarily on a theoretical commitment to the unitary rational subject, but on its methodological commitment to positivism. The consequent methods narrowly define what questions can, and cannot, be asked. In this sense, psychology does have (or has had) a centre and the teaching of research methods which until my arrival was overwhelmingly quantitative in my department, is central to undergraduate psychology training.

What is the relation between critical psychology and a critique of positivist methods in psychology? It is often assumed that quantitative methods are *per se* antithetical to critical psychology and that, conversely, qualitative methods are *per se* critical. I do not agree. However, the dominance of quantification, given that it has been underpinned by positivist principles, has contributed more than anything else to the reduction of the human subject within psychology. The appropriate use of quantification can only be developed alongside influential and healthy qualitative alternatives. Likewise, qualitative methods have suffered from being subordinated to a powerful and dogmatic commitment to positivism in psychology and in the social sciences more generally, especially in the Anglo-American tradition. They have not in general been well taught, partly because there has been so little space to develop and teach them at all. Moreover, in the polarized climate of challenges to positivism, it has been hard to be self critical about our uses of qualitative methods. Yet they can be a vehicle for producing what the researcher is already looking for and wanting to find and, when not used with sufficient theoretical ballast can be irredeemably descriptive, and in that sense uncritical.

For all these reasons, the programme of practicals (assessed by writing laboratory reports) seemed the most important place for change in the undergraduate psychology programme. I convened a working group to introduce qualitative methods teaching into the curriculum in a staged way. I have two – women – colleagues whose work is also entirely qualitatively based and one of these had already succeeded in introducing three qualitative lectures into the second year methods course. As a result, this year I designed and taught one first year practical (students do eight in the year) and one second year practical (out of four in the year) to introduce qualitative methods to about 150 students in each year. Three or four demonstrators – doctoral students – are assigned to help and not one of them has experience of qualitative research, so they need to be trained and their marking supervised. It is still a small proportion of students' methodology training, but, from their first semester, they now get experience of an alternative to measurement. The interest and commitment among many of them was impressive and as a result, more students come asking if I will supervise their third year projects (the demand is already high on the three of us who do out of an academic staff of twenty).

There are other, more 'bottom line' sources of institutional power which encourage psychology's adherence to principles of positivist science: science funding arrangements which pay the university considerably more to train a psychology undergraduate than, for example, a sociology one. The Funding Council (Higher Education Funding Council for England) recently reviewed its funding arrangements for psychology, perceiving an opportunity to cut its costs by redefining some psychology teaching as non-science. Every psychology department was obliged to submit an account of the laboratory and related science teaching costs which were involved in its curriculum delivery. The threat was that, if these did not reach a certain proportion, our undergraduate income would be cut by as much as 25 per cent (in our case, maybe five job losses). In one meeting, we were all asked to consider including laboratory work in all our modules, though it soon became evident that this was not only unacceptable to some, but not feasible, since the practicals are organised as separate modules. But what an irony for me: on the one hand my firmly rooted critique of positivist psychology, with all its experimental trappings, and on the other, the institutional reality of resource cuts which would threaten colleagues' jobs and make the teaching load of those who remained a misery. In this case, financial resources dictated the valuing and bolstering of practices which in their turn reproduced orthodox knowledges irrespective of the increasingly influential critique of those knowledges. Some psychology institutions may give up the scientific route and survive on reduced funding, but they will surely be seen as the poor relations of 'scientific' psychology departments, thus reproducing the initial superior status of scientific psychology. Even this form of financial power is not monolithic however. Because I see good qualitative methods teaching – based on the production and analysis of data – as central to critical psychology, it was possible to use the structure and financing of laboratory teaching to introduce these alternatives. (The department stocked up with an extra fifty portable audio tape recorders so that students could go out and conduct interviews.)

I have described two external sources of institutional power which impact directly on the undergraduate psychology curriculum, the BPS and science funding. Other institutions and practices work indirectly to affect that curriculum, and a description of two of these, namely research and teaching assessment, will provide a fuller picture of the many forces which interact in complex ways to produce the present conjuncture. The way that research assessment is conducted influences who gets appointed to academic staff positions, and this affects who is most likely to be interpreting the curriculum which produces future psychologists. Teaching assessment has given more consumer power to students over the curriculum.

The Research Assessment Exercise (RAE) was introduced over ten years ago in order to assess, for the purposes of differential funding, the quality of research output in British Higher Education. It followed the unification of the 'old' universities with what were the Polytechnics for funding purposes and was the main instrument in the Conservative government's broader policy of distinguishing research universities from the majority of institutions which could be funded at a lower level, whose staff would be mainly engaged in teaching. The bureaucratic exercise which followed had first to define its units of assessment and, despite intellectual and institutional trends in the direction of inter-disciplinary work, it used disciplinary categories for this purpose. Over the course of three rounds of assessment (the last in 1996), universities' and departments' attempts to maximize their research income by performing well in the RAE has profoundly affected academics' research output. If, for example, it becomes known – or even suspected – that the psychology panel rate highly publications in certain reputable (read scientific) journals, submission rates to those journals go up and waiting lists become even longer. Publication in non-refereed journals is not a good RAE strategy and, importantly, neither is publication in a journal not recognizably fitting into the unit of assessment to which your department will submit. My journal publications for the next round will probably include *Qualitative Inquiry, Sexualities, British Journal of Sociology* and *Clinical Child Psychology and Psychiatry* (the last partly chosen, I admit, because it had psychology in the title!). Understandably, the RAE coordinator will be at a loss what to make of them. Gender Studies, where I would most easily fit, does not exist as a unit of assessment. If I go in under Sociology, what does that say about my 'fit'? All sorts of well-meaning attempts have been made to find solutions to interdisciplinary work, but it has been disadvantaged and marginalized by the RAE. This has accompanied and supported a movement reinforcing disciplinary boundaries in the restructuring of academic units into resource centres. Where resource centers, like psychology, are responsible for their own income and expenditure, interdisciplinary collaboration is discouraged unless it generates income for the resource centre. Instead of collegiality, the logic of accounting means that staff are expected to concentrate on the activities that generate money for the resource centre. This is a clear example of Foucault's claims concerning power-knowledge-practice relations: a bureaucratic procedure, with huge power to influence income, generates practices at university and departmental level that profoundly influence the production of knowledges.

One practice resulting from the RAE has been the strategy, widely adopted throughout academic institutions, to 'cluster' departments' research activity, so that it looks coherent and good value for money. Minority interests in departmental research have been hard to accommodate in this clustering process. For example, my department has four research clusters: biopsychology, cognitive psychology, applied social psychology and health psychology. Not too bad, you might think: I could in principle fit into the latter two. In practice, my research methods and questions are very different. Research 'fit' is now widely used as an essential criterion in academic staff selection, although it is sometimes demoted by the financial interest in appointing people with a track record of large research grants, bringing overheads which will help to offset the looming deficit.

So, is it the case that the outcome of these institutional and financial powers is that psychology departments (and others) will reproduce their already dominant areas of expertise and discourage innovation? If so, these areas are likely to reflect, not just the theoretical dominance of cognitive and biopsychology (the knowledge domain), but also the market forces which buy research of a psychotechnical kind (the domain of practice). A combination of such forces would, according to this analysis, conspire to make unlikely the appointment of critical psychologists, those with an interest in theory development, those whose work is interdisciplinary in nature and those who avoid the role of psychotechnician. I gather one line of opposition to my appointment was that I wouldn't fit in to a cluster (quite so). Selection practices influence not only who will be in a position to research and publish (produce future knowledge) but also those who will train the next generation of psychologists.

However, if the above forces were working perfectly together, I would not be in my current job. Foucault's understanding of power-knowledge-practice relations involved emphasis on a diversity of forces which caused contradictions and oppositions, as well as on the role of conscious resistance.

Several countervailing forces modify the above picture. For example, the government body which funds social research (the Economic and Social Research Council) has strengthened its support for interdisciplinary research. It works independently of market requirements and research proposals are judged by academic peers. It is still possible, therefore, to get grants for work with a central theoretical purpose. As regards the RAE, those of us working critically with the help of theoretical perspectives derived from outside psychology were often successfully publishing in an intellectual climate which saw a blossoming of critical perspectives, alternative journals and publishers with their eye to radical new markets. This looked good in RAE terms as long as there was a recognition of interdisciplinary work and there was plenty of opposition to disciplinary units of assessment, based on widely shared intellectual arguments. Many departments, when asked to name the discipline's most prestigious journals, for RAE ranking purposes, simply refused or put in a comprehensive list: it was not in their interests and against their liberal principles.

Research and teaching have increasingly felt to be in conflict for academics' time and research assessment has had profound consequences for the status of teaching in British higher education. Partly in response, teaching quality has been put on the agenda of higher education policy and, consistent with the times, students have been reinvented as consumers with market choice.

The mechanism which has been put in place to audit teaching quality (the Quality Audit) depends firstly on student evaluation, so that now there is a series of formal procedures which are based on students' opinions about their courses. Whilst I disagree with the proposition (implicit in much student course evaluation) that what the students like is necessarily what is good for their learning, the existence, visibility and consequences (for example, for university 'league tables' and admissions) of student evaluation have meant that psychology teaching is much more amenable to change in accordance with the preferences of the primary consumers – the students. Approximately 75% of these consumers are female (Radford and Holstock 1996). Feminism is one of the intellectual forces which has challenged positivist science and many have identified science as masculinist, both in its history and its desires (cf. Keller 1985). I have argued this case for psychology, paying special attention to the elisions between, on the one hand, man, scientist and control and on the other, woman, nature, to be controlled (Hollway 1989). A linked debate has emerged in a more pragmatic form in the pages of *The Psychologist*, the monthly magazine of the BPS, where male psychologists have been worrying about the preponderance of women psychology undergraduates. One letter writer (March 1997, p. 107) asked 'What action should be taken to make psychology more "boy-friendly"?'. Radford and Holdstock (May 1997, p. 201) replied, regretting the 'loss to the discipline of "masculine" input', and suggesting degree programmes 'which emphasize the male-attracting elements of psychology'. According to Radford and Holdstock (1996), psychology 'appeals more to the interests of females than males and tends to consist more and more of caring rather than hard science elements'.

I too perceive gender differences among the students, though not all the men line up behind 'hard science', nor all the women behind the 'caring' (often qualitative) versions. But when I am reading a qualitative practical report which uses notions of objectivity and statistical sampling to dismiss the validity of a case study interview, or a psychoanalysis learning journal that maintains an intellectualising mode of critique, or a psychology and women essay that fails to talk about experience, chances are that it's written by a man. I can often tell by the tone. When I introduced qualitative methodology teaching to the second years for the first time, the excited buzz of students who came to tell me how and why they'd nearly left the course because of their dissatisfactions with reducing people to numbers were even more predominantly female than the course ratio. Our consumers are powerful in the current climate of evaluation, quality audit and league tables, and those consumers are three quarters women.

As long as students are inspired by approaches to psychology which resonate with their experience; which address complex topics such as intimacy, desire, love, homophobia, racism and misogyny, mental distress, parenting, family dynamics, care, violence and morality, without reducing these issues to responses on a five-point scale, there will be support for critical psychology.

5

Reflecting On Who We Are in a Technological World

Ernst Schraube

What does critical psychology mean to you?

As a German psychologist, I have come to understand critical psychology as a catalyst for self-reflection by virtue of its role as an alternative branch of study within the discipline. Its beginnings can be traced to the student movements of the late 1960s, when psychologists began to recognize the problematic character of traditional psychological theory and practice. In contrast to positivistic, natural-scientific approaches and their 'worldlessness', an alternative scientific understanding of psychology has been developed along with a theoretical language and methodology which reveal together the social and technological embeddedness of psychological phenomena. Critical psychology understands itself not as a kind of social technology, that is, not as a way to control or classify individuals, but as an approach that takes people's psychological issues and the vulnerability of the human subject as paramount aspects of its study. Rather than from an external perspective, critical psychology takes up the *standpoint of the subject* and analyses from an internal perspective the ambiguities and dilemmas of daily life and attempts to provide a better understanding of human experience and action.

What brought you to critical psychology?

In Germany, the main centre for work in critical psychology since the 1960s has been at the Psychological Institute (PI) at the Free University of Berlin. The critique of science and society brought about by the student movements in Germany could be transformed at the PI into a vision of a new 'emancipatory' psychology more than anywhere else in the country. At the PI, an institutional structure was created featuring a challenging curriculum for the critical study of psychology and a democratic process in which different academic groups were equally represented in decision-making regarding departmental matters (see Mattes 1988). The idea of an interdisciplinary, problem-oriented form of critical psychology proved attractive to a number of students throughout West Germany at that time, and it was the opportunity to work in this atmosphere that brought me to the PI as a student in the early 1980s.

One of the most fascinating people there was Klaus Holzkamp, who died in 1995. Trained initially as a traditional psychologist, Holzkamp was a professor who lent a sympathetic ear to the student movement's critique of science and society. His insights into the crisis and limits of traditional psychology, together with his dedication to humanistic thinking, served to bring forth a new theoretical language for critical psychology and made him the most prominent figure in Germany within the field. Holzkamp's work always involved a tight collaboration between theory and practice – a hallmark true of most critical psychologists. He was a great abstract thinker. But even his most difficult theoretical discussions were always related to real human experience. The thread linking his thoughts always wound through the problems and contradictions of everyday life. He once explained that Science

> does not come as the result of somehow trying to apply fixed procedures. It must be seen as a never-ending acquisition of human knowledge, an enduring battle against narrow-mindedness, superficiality, and false knowledge. Science is a permanent questioning of the apparently obvious. It, in principle, means swimming against the stream, which also means swimming against the stream of your own prejudices... Science is *critique* and at the same time *self-critique*. (Holzkamp 1983b: 163)

What do you see as the basic principles or concepts of critical psychology?

A main problem with traditional psychology stems from its insistence on a positivistic, natural-science-oriented theoretical language and methodology, where the variety of human psychological experience is reduced into models of cause-and-effect relationships. In traditional psychology, the world in which we live is made into an abstract form of 'stimulus', or 'input'. In this kind of a scheme, broader understandings of psychological phenomena *within* the world become difficult. Some have come to label this problem a 'worldlessness' in traditional psychological thought – an omission that I think can only be remedied by a fundamental redirection of the discipline (see also Holzkamp 1996; Graumann and Sommer 1984; Bruner 1990).

Diverse though the field of critical psychology may be, there are two traits common to its varieties that are important. The first is its 'real world' orientation, the second its move beyond a mere positivistic understanding of science. Rather than rely on statistical experimental methods, critical psychology asks questions about the kinds of interpretive approaches that can best provide insights into the inner connections between the individual subject and his or her social world.

I would like to discuss a few of the basic concepts and principles developed in Berlin that have proved helpful to me. In order to do this, I need first to elucidate one important point central to the theory and practice of critical psychology. If you want to work in psychology, as in any field, you have to rely on basic concepts and categories to provide you with an initial approach towards understanding things. Since our view of reality is always determined by these basic notions – that is, not just the *what*, but also the *how* – our critical view and continual assessment and reassessment of our categories is of central importance. 'One cannot make psychologically relevant observations without the use of psychological categories,' Kurt Danziger explains. 'These categories define what it is that is being observed' (1997: 7). One of the first tasks of psychological science should be to focus on the discipline's own conceptual framework and terminology. But usually this type of criticism is left beyond the scope of scientific examination. Danziger points out that

> Psychologists have devoted a great deal of care to making their theoretical concepts clear and explicit. But much of this effort has been rendered futile by their complacence about the way in which

psychological phenomena are categorized. The meaning of these categories carries an enormous load of unexamined and unquestioned assumptions and preconceptions. By the time explicit psychological theories are formulated, most of the theoretical work has already happened – it is embedded in the categories used to describe and classify psychological phenomena. (1997: 8)

This contradiction of a scientific psychology omitting to reflect on its own scientific conceptual make-up has been something that critical psychology has been attempting to resolve. Holzkamp devoted a great deal of attention to this, and with a historical approach he reconstructed *das Psychische* from its beginnings to its different forms in the evolution to its specific human shape. Holzkamp's work in turn offers psychology a historical–empirical foundation for conceptualizing the human psyche and solid insights into the deep association between the social world, 'natural' conditions, and individual subjectivity (Holzkamp 1983a). What seemed most important to me in all this was the way individual experience was intertwined with the social world and how this connection called for a psychology that sought to examine things from the standpoint of the subject.

In his historical analysis of the human psyche, Holzkamp pointed out that on account of the societal form of human life, we, in comparison with other creatures, can always create a *changing relationship* to the world which we inhabit. Humans do not live *immediately* within a natural environment, where *meanings* dictate the activities of living beings, but rather in a *mediated* social world, where meanings *reflect possibilities of action* and allow for a *consciousness* of the world. It is this unique relationship that creates our awareness of *being a subject*. Regardless of how determined given conditions in life may be, the individual subject always deals with them in a *relationship of possibilities*. We humans are subjects who can always act.

Life's circumstances do not reveal themselves immediately to us, but rather, again, are mediated through symbolically represented structures of meaning (in forms of thought and language). Since these represent social possibilities for behaviour, they are not 'conditions', as such, but *bases* for individual feelings and actions. Holzkamp saw human action as neither immediately determined by such conditions, nor as simply the result of individual autonomous constructions of meaning, but as *grounded* in life's premises. The concept of *subjective grounds for actions* (*subjektive Handlungsgründe*) together with a concept of *meaning* (*Bedeutungskonzept*) are each critical for a psychological understanding of the mediation between subject and world. If the relationship of the subject to itself and to its world is mediated by subjective grounds for action, the psychological language through which human subjectivity is scientifically researched has to correspond to this specific relationship. Therefore Holzkamp derived – relating to the subjective grounds for human actions – the *'grounding discourse'* (*Begründungsdiskurs*). In contrast to the 'conditions' discourse of traditional psychology, based on its stimulus–response model and on an assumed immediate relationship between subject and environment, Holzkamp posed the 'grounding discourse' as the basis of a unique psychological science that truly addressed its topic. 'We have', Holzkamp explained, 'to recognize the "grounding" discourse as a universal foundation and medium in the language of psychological science' (1991: 12). Since 'grounds' and 'reasons', unlike 'causes' or 'factors', are essentially 'one's own reasons' and are usually expressed in the first person (and, as such, gained from an internal perspective), the adoption of the *standpoint of the subject* is vital for a kind of psychology that seeks to analyse phenomena on the basis of the 'grounding discourse'. Therefore subjects, on or about whom research is conducted, cannot be objects of a psychology based on the subject's standpoint. Since the researcher is essentially a subject as well, the subject's perspective categorically collapses into that of the observer, such that the subject basically becomes a collaborator instead of an object of study. A psychology from the subject's standpoint, as Ute Osterkamp puts it, 'will not tell people the right way to go but help them to recognize the societal preconditions of their problems and hence to voice, discuss and tackle them' (Osterkamp 1999; see also Holzkamp 1983a, 1992, 1993, 1996; Maiers 1991; Tolman 1994). I see each of these ideas – the notion of the subject, subjective grounds for actions, the creation of meaning, the 'grounding discourse', and a psychology from the subject's standpoint – as key conceptual tools in the work of critical psychology.

What are the big debates in critical psychology? What issues remain to be resolved?

Critical psychologies have existed for more than thirty years now. But the issues remaining to be resolved are today more numerous than ever before – especially when we look on the social problems that emerge within the global world of high-tech capitalism. In two areas – in the field of the politics of psychological knowledge and in the field of the psychological study of technology – I see particular issues that need to be addressed further.

There is without a doubt a need for debates within critical psychology dealing with such topics as the clarification of concepts, the search for appropriate empirical research methods, and so on. But in my view, the main debate should not be within critical psychology, but rather between *critical* and *traditional* psychology. Historically there has never really been any significant, open discussion between critical psychology and traditional approaches – no heated discussions like, for example, the 'science wars' at present taking place between traditional scientific understanding and the approaches represented by areas such as 'science and technology studies' (see Ross 1996). It has not been enough, I feel, for critical psychology to have merely scratched at the surface of traditional psychology if it wishes to bring its understanding of the limits of conventional science and the possibilities of other approaches to a wider audience. From the traditional side, critical psychology has never been taken seriously, but rather continually ignored, marginalized or shut out of discussion. This has to change. As we consider a future with fewer resources, in which the sciences will be faced with even greater challenges to legitimize what they do, psychology too will be placed under greater scrutiny with regard to its societal relevance. This is where critical psychologies can reveal their strengths. We should not look to continue keeping our treasure a secret; we should consciously seek to confront the dominance of traditional psychology and its uncritical view of natural-scientific methodology. We could at least discuss whether we are dealing with a bona fide natural-scientific methodology or nothing more than an assumed one (see Holzkamp 1996). In this regard, the inability of traditional psychology to develop a genuinely *psychological* theoretical language and methodology could become a formal topic of inquiry. Other topics could include the fact that academic study of psychology often has little to do with later professional practice, or the fact that traditional psychology seems to contribute little of meaningful substance to the pressing social problems of our time. There are a variety of areas in which the debates of the future can take place. We should make it a point that they do in fact occur and that they are heard.

One of the strengths of critical psychology stems from its concern with the experiences and problems of everyday life. Strangely enough, however, problems with regard to the role of technology in society have remained largely untouched by either traditional or critical psychology. In the future, I think we need to take more time to examine what human subjectivity has begun to mean in an age of high technology – not only because of the considerable role that technical objects play in our daily lives, but also on account of the way scientific and technical innovations adversely push our social lives and ecological environments out of balance.

What have you done, or what do you do, that exemplifies these principles? How do you practice critical psychology?

As I mentioned, a key direction of critical psychological work involves its attention to the categories and conceptual frameworks in which psychological phenomena are being addressed. These categories are like a pair of glasses that focus reality in certain ways. In my recent work, I have moved toward a theoretical treatment of how technology has been conceptualized historically in psychology. In doing so, I, on the one hand, have been investigating the influence of technology on the development of psychological theory and categorization. On the other hand, I have been examining the kinds of concepts and categories used historically in the discussion of the relation between people and technology. The primary psychological discussions of technology have thus far largely taken place on the margins of traditional psychology, in studies that deal with interpretive approaches trying to overcome with the dichotomy of the individual and the social. These treatments can be found in psychoanalysis (see, for example, Freud 1976; Fellman 1991; Barglow

1994), social constructionism and discursive psychology (see, for example, Gergen 1991; Turkle 1995), as well as in critical psychologies (see, for example, Holzkamp 1983a; Projekt Automation und Qualifikation 1987).

I have been interested in developing a psychological concept of technology and a theoretical approach dealing not only with the potential and opportunities afforded by technology but also with the conflicts and contradictions inherent to our human relationship with objects (Schraube 1998). The basic concepts of critical psychology, like the concept of meaning, the notion of the subject, the 'grounding' discourse, and the idea of a psychology from the subject's standpoint are all useful for the study of the relation between people and technology. But the concept 'technology' still needs to be more precisely examined. Technical products are not just tools or means to an end; they are structures that *constitute* our world. They possess potentially political qualities. They can compel, they can prohibit and they can dehumanize. Discrepancies invariably arise in the relationship between humans and technology. The question is to what extent we have constructed a world and reality we cannot appropriately reconstruct. The philosopher of technology, Günther Anders, speaks of a 'Promethean slope' between what we are able to produce and our comparatively limited other abilities as human beings. The scale of things we have constructed around us is simply too great. Today's technological world, Anders explains, is 'like an oversized frock that flaps around our mind' (1992: 7). We are dealing with a contradictory technology which, although *socially constructed*, cannot be conceptualized in practical, tangible terms of human activity and connection. Critical psychology recognizes that the loss of human subjectivity, symptomized by blind, technically driven behavioural compulsion, environments that have no meaning to us, and a feeling of being at the mercy of the world, is synonymous with psychological pain. Dignity and psychological well-being each presuppose a sense of security and the possibility of being able to influence things that affect us. Therefore, critical psychology is primarily concerned with the effort to articulate circumstances that, despite being alien to us, indeed have profound effects on our lives. Critical psychology attempts to deal with how these realities influence our own human subjectivity and the horizon of our abilities. It attempts to articulate the unsaid and the unspoken, including often the unspeakable within words themselves. In such an analytical framework, which tries to make human hardship and suffering transparent, we need to include understandings of the politics of technology, along with the contradictions inherent to our technological way of life. A critical language needs to be articulated that can adequately address the various meanings of technology in our lives and how those meanings can be included within the sphere of our human activity and potential. But we do not have to do this alone. In the other social sciences, including the emerging field of science and technology studies, we find critical studies by such figures as Lewis Mumford, Günther Anders, Langdon Winner, Donna Haraway, Michel Foucault, Elaine Scarry, Manuel Castells and others, who help us understand the social meaning of technology.

In his review of the development of psychology in the nineteenth century, the psychologist William Stern discussed the distinction between an experimental, object-oriented psychology anchored in the natural sciences and an interpretive, subject-based psychology rooted in the humanities. His hope was that the marginalized psychology of the subject of his time would give his discipline 'bread instead of stones' for the twentieth century (Stern 1900). It seems we have been very patient. In the twenty-first century, the subject should finally have its turn.

Translation by Marton Markon

6

In Praise of Unclean Things: Critical Psychology, Diversity and Disruption

Stephen Frosh

In a nutshell ...

In a nutshell, critical psychology is not any specific thing. It is not there, it does not exist, it cannot be located or finally found. It can be observed at work, obviously, otherwise a volume like this would not be possible. It might even be an aspiration ('Let us make a critical psychology'), but no-one can show what it is. This reminds me of something, but as with every object of desire, it's all obscure. One of the conditions for writing in this book is clarity, so I will try to identify this object, negatively at least. It is not:

  an entity;
  an organized system;
  a mode of knowledge;
  a theory;
  a method;
  a methodology;
  a tool;
  masculine;
  feminine;
  a very good way of making a living.

It is, instead, a *process* – something moving, identifiable by its effects more than by its content. It is disruptive and potentially chaotic; within psychology, it is a reflection of a wider struggle over the nature and forms of power.

Let me try a little harder to put some content into this. Above everything else, for me at least, critical psychology is an attack on purity. My starting point for this is a refrain from an odd source, the mystic nineteenth-century Jesuit poet, Gerard Manley Hopkins. 'Glory be to God for dappled things', he writes in *Pied Beauty*, going on to embrace in his gratitude and praise, 'All things counter, original, spare, strange.' 'Dappled things', apparently spoilt, their formal beauty sundered, their perfection humanized. Sylvia Plath (1963) characteristically brutal and fierce, puts her pen exactly and unsparingly on why this dappledness, this spoiltness, is so much better than the dead surface of the truth.

Perfection is terrible; it cannot have children

Creativity, spontaneity, even love (see how critical psychologists can become liberal humanists in middle age) all require fertilization, the breaking of perfection, the disruption of purity. Much of the history of the twentieth century has revolved around a battle between 'pure things' and 'dappled things', between those who believe they possess the 'truth' (and would like to impose it on others) and those who wish to celebrate otherness, multiplicity and diversity. Fascism is the prime example, arising naturally out of narcissism and the denial of difference: make everyone, everything the same it demands, do not let opposition in. This is, of course, always gendered and racialised too. For instance, Hélène Cixous (1976) interrupts her celebration of feminine heterogeneity to comment: 'Their "Symbolic" exists, it holds power – we, the sowers of disorder know it only too well' (p. 255). The 'sowers of disorder' are subversive women, feminists no doubt, full of the infidelities and provocative embodiments that challenge the rule of (patriarchal) law. The context here is a rebellion against the man known as the Master, in real life Lacan, and his statement about what he calls 'The woman':

> *The* woman can only be written with *The* crossed through. There is no such thing as *The* woman, where the definite article stands for the universal. There is no such thing as *The* woman since of her essence . . . she is not all. (Lacan 1972–3: 144)

As ever with Lacan, there are paradoxical implications of this. On the one hand it is a way of recognising the impossibility of the fantasy of the 'perfect woman', fulfilment of man's desire, comprehensively wiping out all loss. This woman (~~The~~ woman) is a fantasy. On the other hand, Lacan wipes out women too, dismissing them; for example, 'they don't know what they are saying' (ibid.: 144). Cixous recognizes the political power of Lacan's formula, the way patriarchy rules through *keeping things in their place*, for instance in the Oedipus complex (known to Lacanians as the gateway to the 'Symbolic' order of language and culture) by prohibitions and ordered structures. 'Sowing disorder' is the critical endeavour here, but it is up against the power of paternal authority.

Racialization operates similarly. Joel Kovel (1995), a genuine radical, tries to prise open the racist psyche by playing with the idea of the 'primitive', valorizing it to make it into an evocation of that which is avoided or potentially lost in personal and social history. He first makes a general claim, that the 'primitive' is identified with the 'polycentric' nature of the mind, 'this being associated with an openness of the psyche to the world and, in primitive society at least, an openness of society to otherness' (p. 211). As modern bourgeois society develops, as modernization and capitalism come to fruition, so this polycentricity can be observed to be closed down in favour of the rationalist concept of the integrated self, the unified personality. In this view of things, western modernity is built on the renunciation of alternative possibilities of being; the drive for profit swamps the impulses for pleasure and enjoyment. Noting the need for a specific, socially located explanation of how this renunciation turns into racism, as what he calls the 'peculiarly modern form of repressive exclusionism' (p. 212), Kovel asks the following question:

> Could it be that as the western mentality began to regard itself as homogeneous and purified – a *cogito* – it was also led to assign the negativity inherent in human existence to other peoples, thereby enmeshing them in the web of racism? (Ibid.)

More precisely and eloquently, he suggests that the focus on reason associated with the advance of modernity has led to a flattening out of experience and a fear of the 'irrational' – the polycentric – which then becomes split off into the being of the derogated racial other. Their physical blackness, marking them as distinct, is merged together with already-existing psychic defences against what Norman Brown (1959) has called the 'excremental vision' to create the ideal object of repudiation. Excrement, mess, animality, anality, polycentric enjoyment, the 'primitive': all these are denounced by capitalist accumulation, and their psychic representation is blackness.

So, getting back to the request to state 'in a nutshell' what critical psychology is about, what its 'hallmarks' are, I say: it is about excrement, about spoiling the purity of the vision of the normative as 'good', about denouncing claims to truth. It is constantly provoking, never-endingly analytic, always trying to see the system in the individual, always prising open the 'natural' to see how it is constructed. It is gendered and racialized, it promotes social and political analysis; it celebrates diversity and otherness. What romance...

What brought you...

There are a hundred ways to skin psychology. My way in came from Freud and Laing, plus the humanizing influence of a psychology degree laced with politics and literature (the University of Sussex was a fine place in those days), so I could see that all those experiments, all those 'elegant trivia', could not serve as a way to understand people. Freud was a source for everything marginal and unexpected; most of all, in Philip Rieff's (1966) phrase, the 'analytic attitude' surprised and attracted me. On the margins anyway through my Jewish background, I identified with Freud early on, particularly with the relentless quest for *what's really happening*, for the underlying, the hidden, the that-which-trips-us-up, 'the skull beneath the skin' (Eliot 1920). But this was Freud socialized, partly through what at the time seemed the radical vision of Laing (before I had understood Peter Sedgwick's (1982) and Juliet Mitchell's (1974) critiques of his work) and partly through the ebullient, searing, brilliantly difficult 1950s Freudian utopianism of Herbert Marcuse (1966) and Norman Brown (1959). Try these lines, for an inspirational start for adolescent critical analysis:

> The Freudian revolution is that radical revision of traditional theories of human nature and human society which becomes necessary

if repression is recognized as a fact. In the new Freudian perspective, the essence of society is repression of the individual and the essence of the individual is repression of himself. (Brown 1959: 3)

Over time, Brown and Marcuse have come to seem limited models for a humane and progressive psychology; still, they made it possible to think differently, to understand that what is on the surface might be a *systematic* distortion of how society works. From the point of view of critical psychology, they also showed up the poverty of the 'individual–social' dialectic as described in mainstream psychology. The debates I had been taught about were individual versus society, socialization processes, conditioning, traits versus situations, nature versus nurture. What radical Freudianism showed was that these debates already assumed what they purported to analyse: that individual and society were separate entities, knocking against each other but not intertwined.

There begin the big questions, which for me centred on ideology. What makes it possible for people to live in what seem to be self-evidently self-destructive ways, through fascism, racism and the like? How can the influence of these ideologies be resisted? Foucault entered here, deconstructing away, demonstrating how discourses have material effects, embodying power relations, making things happen. Althusser, another complex Frenchman, showed a way to think using Marxist theory and Lacanian psychoanalysis with its emphasis not so much on the drives as on modes of representation. And feminist psychoanalytic theory – particularly Juliet Mitchell's *Psychoanalysis and Feminism*, but also the severe translations of Lacan and the wild, wild sexuality of Jane Gallop's writing – showed how psychoanalysis could ask 'critical' questions and could be reoriented to provide radical answers (Althusser 1964; Foucault 1979; Gallop 1982; Mitchell 1974).

None of this would have been enough, I suppose, without some kind of *practice*. In the early 1980s I was part of a group of 'radical' mental health workers, all of us trying to combine our nascent understanding of psychopolitics with our resistance to Thatcherism and wish for a renewed socialist order. Perhaps because of the growing difficulty in working effectively on the political stage, and certainly in response to the shocking realization that people actually *voted* for Thatcher out of what appeared to be their own free will, psychology became both an arena for the perpetuation of conformism and the essential social science for progressives. How could people think that way? Why has authoritarianism such a hold? Is therapy in the sense of changing people's emotional relationship to the world an essential part of political action? We even wrote a book as a collective, only falling out slightly over the order of authors, trying to understand all this (Banton *et al.* 1985). Riddled though it was with jargon and incompatibilities, it nevertheless contained some of the first examples of politically driven discourse analysis, although none of us knew this term. We also worked and thought about our work, offering therapy and consultation, workshops and training sessions, counselling and mental health advice. Was this politics or an escape from political pessimism into individualism?

But I am starting to get nostalgic.

Basic principles

In the section above on nutshells, I have already asserted my view of critical psychology as an activity aimed at subverting the dominant assumptions of mainstream psychology. As such, it is part of a general political endeavour to introduce more dissent and diversity into social and academic life. It draws on the margins (in post-modernism, the margins have become the centre anyway – what is valuable is again what is extreme), it asks about otherness both as something to encounter 'without' (respecting and recognizing the other's subjecthood – see Jessica Benjamin's (1998) invaluable work) and 'within' (for example, coming to terms with the strangeness in the psyche of each one of us, known in psychoanalysis as the disruptive unconscious). It grants privileges to the voices of those usually silenced. Putting this more formally as a set of basic principles, I suggest the following, all beginning with 'critical psychology is...':

> an analytic process, interested in the social underpinnings and effects of psychological theories;
> disrespectful of received wisdoms and assumptions about 'how psychology should work';

interdisciplinary, drawing particularly on politics, feminism, anti-racist theory, critical social theory, literature, anthropology, systems theory and psychoanalysis;

predominantly qualitative rather than quantitative, that is, meaning-oriented;

intersubjectivist, indicating that it aspires to treat human subjects as agents or 'authors', not objects of study;

social constructionist and discursive in orientation, interested in how people's experiences are put together in the social domain;

activist, attending especially to the use of psychology in disentangling various ideological strands in people's lives; marginal;

inconsistent, ironic, subversive and funny;

none of the above, that is, not to be pinned down by any list of basic principles.

It will be noted that my main emphasis is again on the disruption that good critical psychology can produce, how it does not allow anything to be taken for granted. It is, in a sense, classic resistance politics, paranoid much of the time, always asking questions. It is also primarily *negative* in the old Marcusian (1968) sense of always looking for the other side, the underside perhaps, of what is being asserted in social theory. The targets move and change, but the process is to be constantly renewed: as every attempt to pin down the truth is made, so critical theorists of all kinds, including critical psychologists, must be on their guard.

Big debates

I have learnt quite a lot from postmodernism, even though I have also had several arguments with it, particularly as applied in the psychotherapeutic arena (Frosh 1997a). One of the things that has influenced me most has been its resistance to 'grand narratives', its argument against the existence of general theories. In contemporary parlance, this means putting the local before the global: local knowledge, specific modes of practice, are of more help in understanding the world than broad, 'big debates. Indeed, Lyotard, a central figure in the emergence of postmodern theory, writes, 'I define *postmodern* as incredulity

towards metanarratives' (1989: 186). With this in mind, it
is once again hard to talk in general terms about the 'big
debates' in critical psychology and particularly about the
issues that 'remain to be resolved'. *All* issues remain to be
resolved; they are all there to be fought over – that is part of
the point.

Nevertheless, as they always say, it is worth trying to articulate something here. My basic issue or 'big debate' can be
summarized as the relationship between the body and the
word. This is an area of work in which identity politics, including feminism, gay and lesbian studies and 'race', intersects with
the more general interests of discursive psychologists. The
debate concerns the way in which material, non-linguistic features of the world entwine with the constructive processes of
language. It can be seen at work, for example, in the development of Judith Butler's ideas on 'performativity' in the context
of gender. This refers to the notion that identities, and meaning
more generally, are created as effects of language and symbolic
action. Butler argues that gender is itself performative, by which
she means that

> there is no gender that is 'expressed' by actions, gestures, speech,
> but that the performance of gender was precisely that which pro-
> duced retroactively the illusion that there was an inner gender core.
> Indeed, the performance of gender might be said retroactively to
> produce the effect of some true or abiding feminine essence or
> disposition, such that one could not use an expressive model; for
> thinking about gender. (1995: 31)

The difficulty with this position, as Butler recognizes, is that it
leaves gender floating freely in an unconstrained space which is
not only empirically unconvincing, but which needs to be
supplemented by ideas on the coercive power of the normative
'iterations' that determine which performances are allowable.
These and other factors have led Butler to consider the ways
in which gender may not be *reducible* to display, but rather be
a product of what is and is not enacted in performance. She
now acknowledges that 'there are clearly workings of gender
that do not "show" in what is performed as gender, and the
reduction of the psychic workings of gender to the literal performance of gender would be a mistake' (ibid.: 31–2). Specifically,

psychoanalysis shows how the complexity and 'opacity' of the unconscious sets limits to what can be expressed or enacted, and argues, correctly says Butler, 'that what is exteriorised or performed can be understood only through reference to what is barred from the performance, what cannot or will not be performed' (ibid.). There is thus some notion of a limitation to the freedom with which gender can be constructed, suggesting a degree of 'indeterminacy' between the material and discursive aspects of identity construction.

What we have here is an example of a more general tension between the discursive and materialist branches of (critical) psychology. Quite obviously, each is part of the other, two sides of the same piece of paper, inseparable even if distinguishable. But how does it work? In the contemporary strands of psychoanalytic and family systemic therapy with which I am familiar, a great deal of significance is placed on rewriting the client's narratives, that is, on finding with them new discursive constructions for their experience. This seems to me to be an enabling and productive therapeutic approach. Nevertheless, one has to ask what its limits are, how far the material is resistant to the discursive; when does speaking turn to silence? This issue arises similarly in feminist and in anti-racist projects, where the malleability of gender and racialized identity seems heavily constrained. It can also be seen, in a general and theoretical sense, in the current popularity of the Lacanian concept of the 'Real'. This term, as interpreted particularly by the cultural theorist Slavoj Žižek (1991), refers to the underside of experience, the way unarticulated pockets of emotion act to disturb the orders of representation with which we are more easily familiar – those of logic and law, and also of common fantasy. Žižek raises the issue here of what makes for the extraordinary investment people have in their identities, even when this leads to internecine warfare. Writing about the new nationalism to be found operating so particularly virulently in ex-Yugoslavia, he employs the notion of 'enjoyment' in a shocking and unexpected way, to convey the emotional investment that might be sucked into any symbolic position. Indeed, the argument runs that it is *only* through use of this notion of enjoyment that the power of these apparently ('rationally' speaking) arbitrary categories of self- and social-definition can be understood:

To explain this unexpected turn [the self-destructive new nationalism of the ex-communist states], we have to rethink the most elementary notions about national identification – and here, psychoanalysis can be of help. The element that holds together a given community cannot be reduced to the point of symbolic communication: the bond linking its members always implies a shared relationship to a Thing, towards Enjoyment incarnated. This relationship towards a Thing, structured by means of fantasies, is what is at stake when we speak of the menace to our 'way of life' presented by the Other; it is what is threatened when, for example, a white Englishman is panicked because of the growing presence of 'aliens'. It is this eruption of 'Enjoyment' which explains what is happening in the East. (1990: 51–2)

What is being suggested here is that the turn to discourse so enthusiastically and often productively espoused by critical psychologists has also to be able to theorize that which is *not* discursive, that other side of subjecthood which is irrational, affective, intense and sometimes frightening. Showing how theories are constructed is one thing; but employing powerful analytic arguments to make sense of, and potentially influence, political and social practices demands something considerably more potent.

What have you done...

At this point I might appeal to the inconsistencies and fragmentation of the postmodern state, meaning that what I do is not necessarily in line with what I think. For instance, my own identity politics are not quite what might follow obviously from the analysis given above (Frosh 1997b). To the extent that I 'practise' critical psychology, it is in three domains: theory, research and therapy. The *theory* is an attempt both to offer a political critique of psychoanalysis and to employ psychoanalytic insights constructively to advance understanding of subjectivity (particularly the identity issues already mentioned) and to offer a broad-based critique of traditional psychological theory in the process. I will not labour this further here (see Frosh 1987, 1991, 1994, 1997c). In terms of research, my colleague Ann Phoenix and I have been trying to develop a way of working with boys in which their status as agents is respected and advanced *through the process of the research itself.* This fundamentally involves an interview procedure that is reflexive and critical, allowing boys to speak about their experiences (in this case, their sense of themselves as young men) while also identifying with and for them the areas of emotional investment – both aspirational and anxiety-laden – that which inform their narratives. Coupled with a narrative analytic procedure in which we try both to represent what the boys say and to establish its discursive and psychodynamic constituents, we hope this will lead us to a position from which young masculinities can be rethought (Pattman *et al.* 1998).

Finally, therapy is not always thought of as an area for critical work. Indeed, some of the authors I mentioned above as influences have been hostile to any idea of therapy as radical practice; Marcuse, for example, distinguishes between psychoanalytic theory and therapy as follows.

> While psychoanalytic theory recognises that the sickness of the individual is ultimately caused and sustained by the sickness of his civilisation, psychoanalytic therapy aims at curing the individual so that he can continue to function as part of a sick civilisation without surrendering to it altogether. (1966: 245)

Still, that does not always seem such a bad ambition for therapy. Despite its theoretical weaknesses, the discursive or narrative approach to therapy can have democratizing effects, at least in comparison with the 'expert' treatments on offer in most arenas. For instance, the use of 'reflecting teams' in systemic therapy, in which families participate in the therapist's discussion, the aim being to revolve a variety of alternative narratives and to deconstruct the whole process of 'seeking help', is one that brings to the forefront issues of knowledge and control, difference, power and change (see Papadopoulos and Byng Hall, 1997). This is all microsocial stuff; but it is 'critical' in reflecting back on traditional assumptions about therapy and asking what purpose they serve.

And finally . . .

Finally, we return to the 'most pressing general social/political problems'. I have little trouble in identifying these, as should be evident from this whole contribution. They all relate to the emergence of identity politics in the context of a social, economic and political setting in which fascism, nationalism, racism and religious fundamentalism are all thriving. This means that the emotional energy, the 'enjoyment', of identity is being taken up into these movements, irrational and emotive as they themselves are. Hate is on the rise; everyone is to be pure and uncontaminated; every faction owns the global truth. Of course there are hopeful signs, but as the Real breaks through everywhere, it is anxiety that is released – and everywhere there are retrograde movements waiting to receive and contain it. Critical psychology, like all forms of progressive politics, needs to contest this, to keep on analysing and revealing, showing how identities are constructed, how discourse works, how dissent is marginalized, how whenever a truth is found, there is another, alternative one underneath.

7

Bridging Agency, Theory and Action: Critical Links in Critical Psychology

Isaac Prilleltensky

Introduction

The role of agency in critical psychology is often invoked but rarely discussed. This is ironic, for it is we, the actors of critical psychology, who would ultimately bring about (or block) personal and social change. Agency refers to our ability to deal with our subjectivity in such a way that it promotes social ideals. The interdependence of agency, theory and action is such that none of them can exist without the other two: (a) agency without theory is uncertain at best and destructive at worst; (b) action without theory is dangerous; (c) theory without action is futile; and (d) neither theory nor action exist without agency, for it is people who critique the world and try to change it. This is a rather complicated matter, which reminds us how difficult it is to pursue critical psychology's goals.

What is critical psychology, and what are its main objectives?

Critical psychology is a movement premised on four basic assumptions: (a) that the societal *status quo* contributes to meaninglessness and the oppression of the powerless, (b) that society can be transformed to promote meaningful lives and social justice, (c) that mainstream psychology upholds the societal *status quo*, and (d) that psychology can contribute to the creation of more just and meaningful ways of living (Bulhan 1985; Fox and Prilleltensky 1997; Ibáñez and Iñiguez 1997; Martín-Baró 1994; Parker and Spears 1996; Sullivan 1984; Tolman 1994). Hence, critical psychologists assume a critical position with respect to society and with respect to the profession of psychology. But critique is not enough. Following Paulo Freire, the renowned Brazilian educator and leader of popular education, critical psychologists need to engage in annunciation as much as in denunciation (Freire 1975, 1994, 1997). Whereas the latter concerns itself with exposing what is wrong with society and psychology, the former is an effort to adumbrate the way ahead. Hence, my plea for complementing discourse with action, and for understanding agents' limitations in amalgamating the two.

My chapter is concerned with the relationship between agency, theory and action. It does not purport to offer recommendations for blending them, but rather to present reflections based on grounded experience. I don't feel ready or qualified to prescribe recipes for the integration of subjectivity, conceptual sophistication, and commitment to moral and political aims; but I do feel ready to share with others experiences that may nourish the process of integration. If nothing else, these reflections may help others to see that we share similar dilemmas. With this objective in mind, I will elaborate first on agency, then on theory and action, and will conclude with praxis.

Agency: personal trajectory towards critical psychology

Personal histories shed light on why we become involved in critical psychology in the first place, and why we can or cannot articulate clear objectives and act on them. In my case, growing up in a Third World country, living in a country at war, joining a radical youth movement, feeling out of place as a minority and as an immigrant, learning from role models in psychology, and searching for a niche as a psychologist are some crucial events that drew me towards critical psychology.

Argentina: growing up in a Third World country

Only those who did not want to see could ignore the brutal repression that was taking place in Argentina in the 1960s and

1970s. Death squads and paramilitary units terrorized the population. Abject poverty, oppression and government-sponsored killings were fertile grounds for the development of radicals. If you were even remotely critical of the regime, developing a mistrust for authority was a natural way to survive. In my case, this suspecting attitude towards the establishment was extended to any type of academic or political discourse. The professions were not viewed as necessarily helping those in need, but those in power. Universities and professors were seen as either supporting the social order or challenging it; there was no middle ground. Those who challenged the regime faced great personal risk, and those who supported it came to personify all that was wrong with the professions in Argentina: the pretence of neutrality, exclusion of dissenting voices, support for the interests of the rich and powerful, and endorsement of repressive US foreign policies designed to 'clean' South America of 'troublesome' activists and liberation movements.

In this context, developing a critical attitude towards authoritarianism and the institutions that enforced it was only natural. Asking how psychology upholds the societal *status quo* was just part of asking how the social sciences and university professors represented the interests of the powerful. Under these repressive circumstances, a slight inclination toward dissent made you a radical. I believe that my analysis of the relationship between psychology and the *status quo* began twenty years before I published my first article on the topic (Prilleltensky 1989).

Jewish and leftist: developing critical consciousness in a youth movement

'Be a patriot, kill a Jew' was a piece of graffiti I would see on my way to school every day. Anti-Semitism and oppressive regimes are good prescriptions for the development of critical consciousness. Unless you were totally oblivious to your surroundings, you could not help but wonder what was wrong with society. Some light about the sources of suffering of Jews was shed by the teachings I received in a leftist Jewish youth movement. The movement provided a sense of community and identity and clarified for us (even if somewhat dogmatically) what was wrong with society. From the age of about eleven we would

spend Friday night and part of Saturday discussing politics and
dreaming about our socialist future in an Israeli kibbutz, a
collectivist farm. While most kids would be dancing we would
be reading (or hiding) leftist literature. My dissenting identity
began to form about twenty-five years before Dennis Fox and I
formed the Radical Psychology Network (for information, see
internet web page <www.uis.edu/~radpsy/>).

Immigrant once, immigrant twice: feeling out of place in Israel and Canada

In Argentina I was a Jew, in Israel I was an Argentinean, and in
Canada I am an immigrant. I moved from Argentina to Israel
when I was 16 years old, and from Israel to Canada when I was
24. At the time of this writing I have been in Canada for 14 years.
Feeling out of place forces you to inspect the culture with special
lenses. Feeling marginal and somewhat inferior due to lack of
command of the language, or ignorance about 'basic' cultural
facts (like hockey or musical legendaries), is not uncommon
among immigrants. I sure felt them, wherever I lived. I still do
today. Feeling discriminated against, even just mildly peripheral
to the mainstream, sharpens your senses about disadvantage
and oppression. I think there is a connection between this
history and my writings on oppression with a political scientist
(Prilleltensky and Gonick 1994, 1996).

Freddy, George and Seymour: learning from role models in psychology

I studied psychology in Israel and in Canada. I completed my
PhD at the University of Manitoba in Winnipeg, in a department
in which all previous dissertations were of an empirical nature.
Mine was titled 'Psychology and the Status Quo' and was theoretical in nature. I had multiple difficulties negotiating acceptance of a conceptual dissertation, including vehement
opposition by some members of the department who were not
even in my committee. Freddy Marcuse, my adviser, was, and
continues to be, a brilliant radical mentor who instilled in me
confidence to pursue critical notions. George Albee, who was

my external examiner for the PhD, was, and continues to be, a long-distance but much appreciated mentor. Seymour Sarason, whom I invited to a conference while I was a clinician at the Winnipeg Child Guidance Clinic, was, and continues to be, a role model for me in psychology. Freddy, George and Seymour did much to show me that there is a place in psychology for critical thinkers. Consolidating a critical stance within the mainstream would have been much harder without their support. Like them, I try to bridge between critical and mainstream psychology, in order to ensure that our notions reach beyond a small circle of people.

Identity: searching and creating a niche for critical psychology

Lacking a clear-cut identity within a specialty in psychology makes life hard. It sure makes it hard to find a job. Although I had training in child clinical psychology and in the field of personality, most of my writings concerned critical psychology. Establishing an identity as a critical psychologist was an important part of my development in this field. I owe much to Dennis Fox for helping us affirm our identity as critical psychologists. Dennis and I coedited a book on the topic and cofounded the Radical Psychology Network. I also received vicarious long-distance support from similar efforts in Europe, primarily by Ian Parker. Geoff Nelson, my esteemed community psychologist colleague at Wilfrid Laurier University, also helped me feel at home at the university and in community psychology in general, a field that is very receptive to critical psychology. Associating with like-minded psychologists attenuates the feelings of isolation and insecurity that come about from being placed at the periphery of a profession.

Cuba: learning from a collectivist society

Che Guevara, who also grew up in Cordoba, was a childhood hero. He represented many of our youthful ideals of courage and determination that would lead Cuba to become a bright star in the Americas. For us, young socialists, Cuba was a beacon of hope. Since an early age I wanted to visit Cuba, which I did for the first time in 1997. Collaborating with psychologists on research and teaching has taught me a great deal about being a psychologist in a collectivist culture. It has broadened my horizons immensely, and it helps me affirm my identity as a critical psychologist in the individualist society in which I live.

Integrity: living with contradictions and limitations

I believe we have enough of a foundation to practice critical psychology, but I am not at all sure that my personal, professional, and political efforts do justice to what we know or what we should do. I always thought that it takes much more than writing to do critical psychology. Although I am involved in community actions to advance the tenets of critical psychology, I feel often the discomfort of being primarily a writer and an academic.

Theory: conceptual bases for critical psychology

What are the main pillars of critical psychology? What is unique about it? What makes it a worthwhile endeavor? I believe that its foundations lie in its values, assumptions and practices (Prilleltensky 1997). This three-part framework helped me articulate the building blocks of critical psychology. The main values of critical psychology, as I see it, should reflect the aims of a good or just society and a good or just life. Of course there isn't a single list of values that can reflect the prerequisites for the good or just life, or the good or just society. We are obviously limited in our value-preferences by our history, social location, and subjectivity (Burman *et al.* 1996; Gordo López and Linaza 1996; Henriques *et al.* 1984; Richardson and Fowers 1998). The best we can do is take into account the values prescribed by community members, researchers, philosophers, and critical theorists and apply them judiciously for the benefit of those who suffer from injustice. This type of analysis has led me to identify three types of inter-related and complementary values (Prilleltensky 1997).

Personal values reflect critical psychology's concern for individual self-determination, health, and personal liberation from oppressive relationships and social structures. Self-determination or autonomy refer to the ability of the individual to pursue chosen goals without excessive frustration; while personal health is a state of physical and emotional well-being that is intrinsically beneficial and extrinsically instrumental in pursuing self-determination. These values uphold the rights of the citizen to be different than others but still to enjoy the same resources as everyone else.

Social values complement individual aspirations, for the attainment of personal objectives requires the presence of social resources. Distributive justice, or the fair and equitable allocation of bargaining powers, resources, and obligations in society, is a key social value. Without fairness there is domination and oppression.

Support for societal structures that advance the well being of the entire population is also crucial if everyone is to have her or his needs met. The procurement of free and accessible public services, like health and education, is vital for the quality of life of all community members, rich or poor. Sense of community and solidarity is yet another social value that is needed to pursue both the good private life and the good society.

Mediating values concern the harmonization of personal with collective values. Personal aspirations need to be harmonized with social aims. Mediating values such as collaboration and democratic participation ensure that private and collective goals be achieved in tandem and not at the expense of one another (Habermas 1990). Conflicts among values abound, as is the case between self-determination and distributive justice. Too much self-determination degenerates into individualism and disregard for the well-being of others. This is why collaboration and caring for the dignity of others are indispensable.

Respect for human diversity is another mediating value of high importance. This principle seeks coherence and harmony without violating the identity of minorities (Fowers and Richardson 1996; Taylor 1992; Young 1991). This protects the powerless and affords them an opportunity to develop their identity without fears of reprisals or pressures for assimilation.

A delicate balance between personal and collective values is needed to promote a society in which the good of the private citizen is not inimical to the good of the society. This is why we should promote mediating values and processes that are supposed to bring a measure of collaboration among groups with varied interests. Good and just societies cannot thrive but in the presence of the three groups of values. The absence of social values leads to the competition we are all too accustomed to in capitalist societies, whereas the absence of personal rights leads to the debacle of collectivist communities.

These values capture the main ingredients for balancing personal with collective well-being; they can be applied to social problems and to professional and ethical dilemmas. In situations of conflict, we ask: What values are being privileged and what principles are being neglected? Whose interests are being upheld and whose are being denied? What resources do the poor have to uphold their basic rights? What societal changes should take place to achieve a more equitable allocation of resources in society? And, how does psychology contribute to the advancement of values for the entire population?

In addition to identifying the main values of critical psychology, I set out to explore how psychology promotes or inhibits these values, and who benefits the most from psychology: the psychologist, the client, society's power holders? To answer these questions I proposed checking psychology's stance with respect to some basic assumptions concerning the nature of knowledge, the good life, the good society, professional ethics, and power in relationships (Prilleltensky 1997). Based on that analysis, I recommend that: (a) the pursuit of knowledge in critical psychology should serve the interest of the oppressed, (b) the good life should take into account mutual self-determination and not just autonomy, (c) the good society should concern itself with justice and not market-driven survival, (d) the power imbalance between psychologist and community members should be rectified, and (e) the current restrictive notions of applied ethics should be discarded in favor of participatory principles (Prilleltensky 1997; Prilleltensky et al. 1996). Critical psychology differs markedly from mainstream psychology in its stance on these five assumptions (Prilleltensky and Fox 1997). The values and assumptions help us delineate the concerns of critical psychology and provide direction for theory and action.

Action: practical tools for critical psychology

How does critical psychology define mental health and social problems? What role does the client have in critical psychology? What role does the helper have? What type of interventions do critical psychologists favour? The way we answer these questions will determine what type of practice we follow. I propose (a) that we define emotional and social problems in holistic terms that take into account economic and political power as well as biological, psychological and sociological forces, (b) that we provide clients and community members with an opportunity to be active participants in the helping process, (c) that we assume the roles of collaborators as opposed to experts, and (d) that we promote macrosocial and political interventions to complement the usual emphasis on intrapsychic therapies and microsocial solutions.

Tools for holistic definitions of oppression and mental health problems derive from interdisciplinary explorations of all the aspects of a person's life. Political (for example, class status, globalization), environmental (for example, urban stress, pollution), occupational (job insecurity, unemployment), and cultural factors (for example, violence, discrimination) pose serious mental health risks for a growing number of people. Embracing holistic views of wellness that go beyond intrapsychic dimensions is a good antidote against the psychological reductionism that has plagued the parent discipline for so many years.

Participatory techniques can facilitate the active involvement of the client in the helping process, but these have to be complemented by a process of depowerment of the expert (Huygens 1997). Participation is closely tied to control. Meaningful participation and ownership happen only when the person in charge (read the psychologist) is willing and able to share power and control of the helping encounter. The concept of partnerships for solidarity with oppressed people captures the essence of the egalitarian relationships that critical psychologists ought to pursue. Although technique is important to elicit client participation, commitment to the philosophy of partnership and solidarity is even more crucial, for without them a technique is just an empty exercise.

Vehicles for the promotion of macrosocial and political interventions include consciousness raising, coalitions with labour

and grass-roots organizations, support for social justice movements, public education and community mobilization (Prilleltensky and Nelson 1997). These ventures, which typically
occur outside the mainstream establishment, have to be accompanied by work within dominant institutions, for much can be
accomplished by changing public policies concerning unemployment insurance, health care, welfare, taxation and child
care. Social change is too big of a job to accomplish with single
focus strategies. Having said that, it is crucial to be clear on
the nature of the work. Minor changes in policies, however
important, do not shake the foundations of inequality. This
type of work, helpful as it might, is to be distinguished
from long-term efforts at eradicating poverty, oppression and
exclusion – projects more transformative than ameliorative in
nature.

Praxis: integrating agency, theory, and action

In this section I hope to combine agency, theory and action. By
drawing from actual work in which I have been involved, I
discuss some the challenges and possibilities involved in imple-
menting critical psychology's values, assumptions and practices.
Based on this grounded experience, I identify dilemmas, contradictions and some lessons for the future.

Action research: defining and refining professional ethics in Cuba and North America

Along with two colleagues and several graduate students we set
out to explore the lived experience of ethics in the mental health
professions (Prilleltensky *et al.* 1996). We wanted to explore how
clinicians in two vastly different cultures define and experience
applied ethics. We worked with several organizations in North
America and with colleagues from various provinces in Cuba.
Although it was our intention to collaborate with all the agencies throughout the entire process, we were more successful
with some than with others. We have described elsewhere
how issues of organizational politics, subjectivity (of researchers
and participants) and power all interfere with the implementation of processes that promote ethical dialogue in a climate of

safety (Rossiter *et al.* 1996; Walsh-Bowers *et al.* 1996). We gained great insight into how possibilities for (a) speaking about ethical dilemmas, and (b) pursuing what is good for the helper and good for the client, are severely limited by fears of being seen as a troublemaker or a 'boat rocker'. People's fears, vulnerabilities, personal agendas and prejudices are very closely related to how people define ethics and what they are prepared to do when faced with moral dilemmas pertaining to their jobs.

As a critical psychologist and action researcher I had to constantly ask myself whose interest I represent here: the workers', the clients', the managers'? I had also to ask what legitimacy do we have to interfere with agency life, even if we were given permission to do the research and offer recommendations. A lesson I derived from this action research is that collaboration requires a constant process of renewing informed consent between researcher and agency. Permission to participate in an agency's life should be renegotiated every time the researcher feels that his or her action can have negative repercussions on the organization or some of its workers. Consent should be seen as a dynamic process and should not be assumed to apply as a blank cheque. Decisions about what report to write, who should read it first, and what recommendations not to prescribe are painful decisions that should not be taken lightly. Close collaboration among researchers and research participants should be a priority. Scrutinizing all players' subjectivity is an indispensable part of promoting respect, caring, compassion and appreciation for human diversity and justice.

In one of the organizations we were quite successful in having our recommendations placed high on the institutional agenda. This required close attention to the value of collaboration and democratic participation with an advisory committee, respect for the organizational culture (even when we disagreed with many practices) and appreciation of our limited view of the problems by our social location as 'outsiders'. Attention to these principles brought about some humility, which paradoxically allowed us to speak freely at the end of the process about changes that should be pursued in the organization.

Our research team learned a tremendous amount about ethics, cultural diversity, and collectivism by collaborating with colleagues from Cuba. We interviewed clinicians in Cuba and later on conducted interpretation of our findings together with two Cuban psychologists. This collaboration challenged our preconceptions about the good life, the good society and professional ethics, and forced us to reconsider what is just or good about our own society, about Cuba, and about our professional practices. It was a successful exercise in bringing diversity home. The challenge of working cross-culturally, however, remains. We are still working out the details of bridging between our interpretations and their reality. For this, we continue to collaborate with our colleagues in Cuba.

Our work in Cuba demonstrated the importance of attending to personal, collective, and relational values. In the Cuban collectivist context, which I philosophically endorse, I met many people who are discontent about the state of personal freedoms. In the Cuban solidaristic society, which I feel strongly attached to, I met many people who are unhappy about the lack of recognition of their personal efforts and about the undeserved recognition of others. Contradictions, in Cuba and in North America, are helpful in shattering idealized visions of societies. Throughout this process of cross-cultural work I am reminded that regardless of the organizational or societal structure in place, power differences are omnipresent and people are reluctant, for different rewards or punishments, to challenge them. Whether in Cuba or in North America, people in position of authority can turn insensitive to the needs of others with less power.

The micropolitics of the workplace are not all that different in Cuba and in North America. Though the context is different, power dynamics and their attendant injustices prevail in both places. A striking difference I noted though was that in Cuba people seem more articulate about naming processes of injustice, a product perhaps of better political education.

At a personal level, I risk in my exchange with Cuban colleagues to feel like a benefactor. Cubans' appreciation of our material and educational contributions to their country is such that I can easily feel full of myself. Many of my encounters with Cuban colleagues are marked by mutual embarrassment: I feel embarrassed about the material resources I have, they feel awkward about their material deprivation. This is a healthy annoyance that reminds me of my privilege.

Wellness: promoting mental and physical health through counselling, consultation and collaboration

It was very important to me when I was a school clinician to establish egalitarian relationships with parents and teachers. I found that a child's wellness depended so much more on collaboration among adults than on some test results. I found that the values of caring, compassion and respect for the unique circumstances of parent, teacher and child were absolutely vital in the helping process. I felt that what was typically needed was a caring problem-solver more than an expert (Prilleltensky et al. 1997a). I ached at the sight of clinicians confusing parents with psychological jargon that made them feel stupid. Although this was years before I would formalize some precepts concerning values in mental health, I always appreciated as a clinician the importance of respecting clients' dignity, uniqueness and integrity. For me, it was a manner of advancing justice at the micro level of the counselling encounter.

Wellness entails more than psychotherapy, but some clinicians are too invested in therapy to see the need for prevention and for attending to non-psychological factors (Prilleltensky 1994). This view presented a challenge to some colleagues and myself when we were asked to review the mandate of a children's mental health agency (Peirson et al. 1997; Prilleltensky et al. 1997b). As declared preventionists, we were questioned about our investment in pushing for preventive models at the expense of therapy. This threatened some people at the agency. As consultants, we had to be clear about our own values, which we stated openly on the first page of the proposal and at the first meeting with the agency; but we also had to be mindful of workers' interests. A measure of conflict between us and some clinicians was inevitable, however, and we had to live with it. We differed with some of them with respect to problem definition, time and type of intervention. The tension we generated was at times unpleasant but not fatal. We negotiated our differences quite successfully with an advisory committee that helped us remain loyal to our values without violating the agency's principles.

Wellness is of course not just psychological but also physical. A few years ago I cofounded a self-help group for immigrants from Latin America. We embarked on several initiatives, including

Spanish classes for the children, parenting courses, advocacy workshops, and liaison with schools. One of our projects was to help prevent smoking in children and youth. The process of planning, conducting and evaluating the project was highly collaborative and participatory in nature, driven mostly by a steering committee consisting of local residents and Latin American professionals living in the area. As a middle-class professor I felt the power and authority ascribed to me by the group. I was invested in having as participatory a process as possible, but I struggled with input that seemed to me would derail the process. I was afraid at times to be too outspoken for fear that they would accuse me of arrogating too much power by virtue of my 'status' as a professor. Like them, I was an immigrant, but unlike most of them, I was well off financially and had a secure and 'prestigious' job. At one point the micropolitics of the group were such that a few people were hurt and left. I lost some of my close allies in the group because of the actions of other members. After about five years of close collaboration with the group, I needed a break. It was not without mixed feelings that I took a break, for I felt the group could use my input, but I needed distance. My departure caused me to question my commitment to the project. Although the community was involved in some social action, like children making a presentation to city hall on the risks of smoking, and display of anti-smoking art in public spaces, most efforts were not transformative but rather ameliorative. Sometimes I feel stuck in this mode. This feeling led me to form a coalition of children's rights that would be involved in political action and not just on ameliorative actions. The coalition is too young to have accomplished much yet, but several newspaper articles I wrote sparked interest in the community to politicize children's issues.

Conclusion: the struggle for integrity

Values obtain their meaning in lived experience. I selected a few passages of my work to show how values influence and are influenced by assumptions, practices and subjectivity. Values and ideals interact with subjectivity, and it's very hard to make progress toward personal accountability without support. Perhaps the very concept of personal integrity belies an individualistic conception of personhood that I think I oppose. But on the other hand, I can't renounce the role of personal agency in promoting critical psychology. It is a dialectic, it is not one or the other. Commitment to a cause requires lucid goals, practical tools and periodic scrutiny of one's aims and interests. The values, assumptions, and practices of critical psychology may serve as a guide towards higher levels of integrity. Solidarity may help us reflect on our imperfections without losing hope that we can attain higher congruence between our words and our actions.

To further this congruence, I challenge ourselves to engage in annunciation and review our praxis in light of critical psychology principles. I submit that critical psychology would have made gains when our concern for personal wellness would be matched by our concern for collective wellness, when our devotion to empathy and compassion would be equalled by our fight for social justice, when our interest in others' subjectivity would be rivalled by worry with our own privilege, and when our speculations about deconstruction would be balanced by constructive political action. To achieve these objectives, I propose we ask ourselves to what extent our praxis promotes the following:

I.   *The expression of care, empathy and concern for the physical and emotional well-being of clients and others in positions of disadvantage.*

II. *The ability of clients and others in positions of disadvantage to pursue their chosen goals without excessive frustration and in consideration of other people's needs.*

III. *Respect and appreciation for diverse social identities.*

IV. *Peaceful, respectful and democratic processes whereby clients and others in position of disadvantage have meaningful input into decisions affecting their lives.*

V.   *The fair and equitable allocation of bargaining powers, resources and obligations in professional, interpersonal and political contexts.*

8

Reflections on Critical Psychology: The Psychology of Memory and Forgetting

Elizabeth Lira

It was my own experience in the practice of psychology with people in conditions of poverty, violence and political oppression that led me to question psychological knowledge. This persistent questioning has influenced my clinical work and the manner in which I have approached my teaching and research in psychology.

Currently I am conducting a historical, political and psychosocial study of the process of reconciliation in Chile and the role of memory in this process. This study is a continuation of the human rights work I began in 1977. I believe my work is a form of critical psychology in the sense that the extremely difficult social and political situations in Latin America have challenged us to construct answers where psychological knowledge reaches its limits.

Critical psychology is the critique of a psychology that pretends to have theoretical and practical answers to the problems that affect the lives of human beings but does not really have them. From another angle, critical psychology is a psychology developed in 'critical' areas of life, that is, where the humane production and reproduction of life is threatened. Both ways of understanding critical psychology imply an ethical notion that is inseparable from psychological practice. What I have written here is an attempt to make this ethic more explicit.

The intelligence of the poor

My critical encounter with psychology dates back to the beginnings of my professional training. When I was a second-year psychology student at the Universidad Católica de Chile, in a course on psychological diagnosis, they took us to an institution at the edge of the city where they kept children without families, children who had been picked up by the police because they were living on the streets, and were thus called 'children in irregular situations'.

I was to interview Vicente. He was 9 years old and had been living in the streets for 3 years. I had to give him a test to measure his IQ. The results on the Raven test showed that he was at the 5th percentile. The majority of the children tested very low. The professor explained to us that poverty affected the capacities of children and that these children and their families were poor because they were not intelligent. We students argued that these children had other skills that the test could not measure, for if they had survived in the streets, it was unlikely that they were not intelligent. Furthermore, children with high scores on the Raven might not be able to survive a day in the streets. We suggested that the concept of IQ should be rethought. We heard the usual refrain that 'the tests measure intelligence and therefore these children are not intelligent.' Any other argument was wrong, including our own evidence. Psychology seemed to be based on concepts of intellectual capacities that had little to do with the situation of millions of poor, unschooled Chileans, perhaps the majority of the population. They were, of course, the people on whom we could practise the administration of IQ tests. And these tests gave evidence, according to the professor, that the poor were poor because they were not intelligent.

This example is not meant to demonstrate the ignorance of such professors. It is meant to show the impact of prejudices that become theoretical presuppositions. The same prejudices are expressed by the powerful in Chilean society, and attributed to psychologists.

Vicente was a street child, outside the system, poor, unschooled, homeless. The test results 'demonstrated' that he was not intelligent and that he could not be, and the academic in charge would not consider the possibility that his theories and instruments were inadequate measures of Vicente's capacities. Thus, it was assumed that Vicente did not have the capacities that are universally called normal intelligence.

Violations of Human Rights

Manuel

Manuel was a *campesino* leader who participated actively in the unionization of *campesinos* and agrarian reform in Chile. In 1973 he was detained and tortured barbarously. He was 49 years old. As a result of the torture he had cerebral damage and presented symptoms of severe epilepsy and psychotic reactions. He committed suicide in 1994, when he was almost 70 years old, on the day when Eduardo Frei was elected president. He had received psychiatric treatment at la Vicaria de la Solidaridad, a human rights organization created by the Catholic Church in Chile, and psychotherapy between 1978 and 1980, and from 1984 to 1987, from the Social Aid Foundation of Christian Churches (Fundación de Ayuda Social de las Iglesias Cristianas, FASIC), an ecumenical human rights organization. Manuel had been dedicated to political and union work for more than twenty years. He had a wife and eleven children, the youngest of these being born in 1972. All the children were younger than 16 in 1973.

The focus of his treatment from 1975 on had all the advantages and risks of a traditional approach. He was treated in family therapy, which in the 1970s was quite new and implied bringing together the best professional and technical resources in an act of solidarity. His family was diagnosed as dysfunctional and he was labelled a 'peripheral' father and as 'absent' for many years from his traditional role as provider. During treatment, Manuel stayed at home, after being freed from prison. He could not find work, and he lived on a disability pension and occasional donations. The economic situation of the family was thus quite precarious and they barely kept food on the table. Manuel was an alien to his family and he felt like an alien among them. The initial treatment did not consider the political repression that existed in the country. It failed to take into account the fact that his 'real family' for twenty years had been his political party. Nor did it consider that agrarian reform had been a 'cause' that Manuel had deeply felt because he hoped and dreamed that it would end the exploitation, misery, dependency, marginality and sociopolitical exclusion of Chilean *campesinos*.

Because of Manuel's background, the family harboured enormous resentment against the political work that had kept the father out of the house for so many years and now had brought him back completely destroyed. The treatment, as it was initially conceived, had left out important problems such as his political participation and the meaning of the repression he had experienced, even though these were clearly central elements of conflict within the family and for Manuel himself. Despite the treatment he received, Manuel remained depressed up until his death. We must wonder what the course of treatment might have been if the professionals he worked with had worked with a more precise conceptualization of the family problematic. If the impact of the political context, if the repression, the persecution, and poverty had been considered from the beginning, linking them to the neurological and psychiatric sequelae of the torture, if the conflict with the family had not been separated from the meaning that being a political militant held for Manuel, then perhaps Manuel could have lived and died in a different manner. Of course, his experience reflected the larger national problematic because torture was official policy, even though it was denied by the government, and the government sought to discredit those who denounced the practice in public.

For the victims, torture and related political repression as public policy meant individual trauma. Public policy became individual trauma, but a trauma unlike other traumas precisely because of its political context, its intentionality and its subjective meaning for victimizer and victim. In other words, the objective of political repression was to destroy those defined as enemies. This repression engendered a perception of inescapable threat and fear that defined the relationship 'victim–victimizer', crystallizing anguish to the breaking point, and making manifest the risk of death and annihilation. To understand the development of therapeutic techniques for the treatment of torture victims, it is first essential to frame the political context of this type of trauma.

María

When María arrived in Santiago, she was lost even to herself. She had lost her memory. Someone sent her to la Vicaria de Solidaridad near the end of 1979. María didn't know her name, but she insisted that she be called María. María didn't remember if she had children, but she insisted she had many. María didn't remember how she lost her memory. No one knew how to retrieve it for her. Someone who knew her told her who she was and spoke to her of her past, but María had forgotten everything so the story she was told had no meaning for her.

María became my patient and I invited her to invent the past that she had forgotten and María recounted what was actually her own past. I had no idea that she would be able to do this, but I did know that she was very troubled that she had lost touch with her past. Her story went as follows: Some 'rich people' in a small town in southern Chile decided that she, her husband, and three other men were subversives and should die. She was the mayor of the town, appointed by President Salvador Allende who had been overthrown and assassinated. Five men came wearing vampire masks, kidnapped María and the others from the town jail, and took them on a long rural road to a bridge to be executed. María says that every two kilometres she saw a clock. 'I had never seen them before in my life, but that night I saw them. I saw the clocks without hands.' When we arrived at the bridge, I stepped forward to tell my husband, 'This is as far as our life goes, no further.' María somehow survived the execution but forgot everything. For six years she wandered past houses and through towns and then one day she came to a Catholic church, and listened to a mass given in the name of the detained and disappeared. It was October, 1979. Outside it rained torrentially. She waited for the priest and then told him an incredible story: she had been a disappeared person for six years.

Not many Chileans come back from the shadow of death. There are many who would prefer to have lost their memory. I was impressed by her description of the clocks. They have no hands with which to tell the minutes and hours. Do they represent the anguish of a timeless death? Or perhaps the multiple losses María suffered both politically and privately? How can we understand María's suffering?

Poverty, political repression, human rights violations and their traumatic effects at the individual and societal levels create enormous challenges for psychology. When individual and collective processes of suffering, loss and traumatization are combined, it is especially difficult to understand how the different levels interact.

In the case of María's loss of memory, a deeper understanding would mean trying to understand, even if only at a metaphorical level, the sort of protection that a person can develop when pushed aggressively toward death. It would mean understanding how memory and amnesia are two opposite aspects of survival in the face of death.

With these tough questions in mind in the 1980s, we found Ignacio Martín-Baró, first through his writings (see Martín-Baró 1994) and later through personal dialogue. He helped us think our way more directly toward a psychology that would address the problems we faced in Latin America: civil wars, military dictatorships, political repression, and masses of poor people. We became more clearly aware of the limits of a clinical psychology that had always ignored the specific social, political and cultural contexts of those who sought therapeutic attention. These days, some of these factors are finally beginning to be taken into account at least in a general way, so it seems that our discussion over the years have not been totally in vain.

Nevertheless, some of the problems we have been discussing for so long are still with us. Near the end of the 1970s, we questioned the idea that 'neutrality' is essential in psychotherapy. We challenged the concept from ethical and ideological perspectives. Since we were trying to develop forms for working effectively with people who had been persecuted or tortured, or who had family members who had been abducted, disappeared and executed, we had to ask what sense could neutrality have in the context of such human rights violations? Neutrality is not ethically possible in such cases. However, while recognizing the ethical commitment of a professional in a specific political situation, it is important to maintain a very clear distinction between 'neutrality' and 'abstinence', both concepts that originated in psychoanalytic practice. These terms refer to limits on the forms of involvement and to the technical and ethical safeguards that are necessary in general clinical practice. The debate about 'neutrality' has helped us pay attention to the

risks of paternalism and the importance of distinguishing
between emotional and ideological overidentification and genuine compassion.

Professional confidentiality is a related concern in such circumstances. Just imagine how many psychologists in Argentina,
Chile and Uruguay were persecuted during the periods of state
terrorism and had to go into exile because of the confidential
information they received from clients. How many feared that
they would not be able to keep these confidences under torture?
And how many psychologists now in Peru live in fear because
they work in human rights organizations in solidarity with
victims of political violence? How many have encountered the
limits of their professional knowledge as they try to work with
such victims or with indigenous *campesinos* who have lost their
land and are forced to live in our enormous cities, marginalized
and stigmatized for their poverty, their language and their suspected contacts with revolutionary groups? One could ask the
same questions about the situation of psychologists in Colombia, El Salvador and Guatemala. What effects do such instances
of massive suffering have on professional practice and the social
responsibility of psychologists?

Questions such as these have emerged in our work in relation
to political violence with other psychologists in Latin America.
We have had to go far beyond the domains of clinical and social
psychology for answers. In fact, we have been working to
establish an interdisciplinary field of human rights studies that
integrates the historical, cultural, legal, societal, psychosocial
and clinical dimensions of these problems. This is particularly
important as we move through the 'transition to democracy' in
so many Latin American countries. We see numerous residual
consequences of terror and torture in one sector of society and
other effects on daily life and political process in general. We
are very concerned about the themes of social peace, the
need for truth and justice with regard to past human rights
violations, the proper functioning of democratic institutions,
the impunity that is maintained because the victimizers cannot
be brought to trial, and so on. Truth commissions in various
countries (Argentina 1983–4, Chile 1990–1, El Salvador 1992–3,
Guatemala 1995–8) have aired some of what occurred in the
past. The official reports show how brutally the popular movements were suppressed. The names of martyrs fill hundreds of

pages. Clandestine cemeteries have been discovered and bodies disinterred for identification. Nevertheless, either amnesty laws that guarantee impunity or fear on the part of new authorities have affected not only the political process but also victims' hopes for justice or family members' hopes of finding out what happened to loved ones who disappeared.

In this period, we hear calls for national reconciliation, especially in those countries that were gravely fractured by divisions that led to civil war and dictatorial governments. Such calls lead to debates about truth, justice, forgiveness, impunity, memory and forgetting at the social, political and psychological levels. A new psycho-ethical-political field has emerged, which we could call the psychology of memory and forgetting, or the psychology of the process of political reconciliation. Memory is not identical to history and does not imply a critical perspective. Memory is the reconstruction of past emotions, feelings and perceptions associated with historical events that have traumatically affected everyday life.

The strategies of forgetting and memory in relation to political violence raise even more questions about how to study collective processes that are also individual ones. They can be interpreted in light of old psychological or psychoanalytic theories of memory and repression, but they are also subjective and collective expressions of a political battle for the future. In the Chilean case

the battle for control of social memory and official history is taking place on a bulldozed political topography, a battlefield reshaped by the armed forces before the 1990s transition to civilian government. The military regime's policies and practices were founded on fear. An internalized every-day caution, a psychological and social 'distancing' by many individuals from public view and from controversial political action, came to characterize public behavior. Few Chileans would risk 'another September 11' to defend *any* political program or policy. The armed forces and their civilian allies sought to protect the new institutionality due to fear of the rebirth of subversion. This socio-psychological and politico-cultural legacy now frames and infuses the Chile of the 1990s. (Lira and Loveman 1998)

This legacy of internalized fear (*along with* the historical authoritarian political culture of Chile) is captured in Sergio Marras'

(1998) bitingly sarcastic *Carta Apócrifa de Pinochet a un Siquiatra Chileno* (Apocryphal Letter from Pinochet to a Chilean Psychiatrist).

In my opinion, it is exactly this sort of historical situation that makes it necessary to rethink political processes in a manner that includes their subjective moments, not only during the period of violence, but also during 'normalization'. This concern would also apply to attempts to understand and address the enduring horrendous socioeconomic conditions of the masses. A subjective and collective interpretation of memory implies the acknowledgment of suffering that has been experienced by vast sectors of society as well as their hopes and dreams. The exclusion of these experiences from public acknowledgment has often been a major latent factor that contributes to ongoing social antagonism. An interdisciplinary reformulation of our fragmented and fragmenting discipline in the light of other forms of understanding would bring us closer to a psychology that responds to some of the dilemmas of the contemporary world. Perhaps this would be the major role for a critical psychology at the end of the century in this corner of the world.

Translated by Tod Sloan

9

Critical Psychology: A Sub-Saharan African Voice from Cameroon

Bame Nsamenang

Although my initiation into critical scholarship came through Supo Laosebikan (1982, 1986) at the University of Ibadan, Nigeria, I only became aware of the subdiscipline of critical psychology in late July 1998 through Colleen Loomis, a doctoral student at the University of Maryland, Baltimore County. She handed me the 'call for chapters' for this volume on critical psychology and challenged me to submit an African voice for it. In spite of limitations in this field, my effort is in consideration of the non-representation of African voices in international discourse on psychology. African psychologists face the challenge of demonstrating the relevance of the discipline to Africa. Accordingly, my primary focus is on the challenge to Eurocentrism in psychology and the calls for its relevance to all human beings. In doing so, I am seeking, like Nsamenang and Dawes (1998), to give voice to the intellectual endeavours of African psychologists, whose attempts to evolve an appropriate psychology for Africa are fraught with difficulty. At this point it is reasonable to examine the state of psychology in Africa and its contribution, if any, to the discipline.

Africa has been a major recipient of alien influences that have been largely imposed rather than solicited (Nsamenang and Dawes 1998). The continent has always had to adjust to intrusive frames of reference and systems of knowledge instead of relying on its remarkably different versions. An important influence on contemporary Africa is academic acculturation. Scientific psychology is a German invention that was cultivated in the Western world, particularly the United States, before being exported to the rest of the world. Acculturation to scientific psychology in Africa has not simply been an imperialist domination, but also a self-imposed emulation of imported models (Nsamenang 1995).

Scientific psychology arrived in sub-Saharan Africa during colonization in the context of anthropological research. Like many a colonial import into the continent, psychology is still imperialistic and racist in outlook (Bulhan 1990; Moffitt and Owusu-Bempah 1994). As a result, the models driving training, research, and practice on the continent are Eurocentric (Bulhan 1990; Nsamenang 1995). Thus, academic psychology largely fails to incorporate many aspects of African social reality and mental life because its theories and methods cannot capture them. Compared with its position in other world regions, the status of scientific psychology in *Afrique noire* (that is, sub-Saharan Africa) is inchoate, with virtually no impact on the discipline. Nevertheless, it is gradually developing into a professional discipline, a fledgling science that still occupies only the fringes of academia and society (Nsamenang 1995). For instance, very few sub-Saharan Africans know the meaning and value of psychology (Eze 1991).

The tools of scientific psychology were constructed to suit, reveal and constitute the post-modern person (Ingleby 1995). Accordingly, psychologists still have to consider what humanity in *Afrique noire*, as in other regions of the world that comprise the Majority World (Kagitcibasi 1996), portends for the science. How, for instance, do psychologists feel about the exclusion of '95% of the world's children' (Zukow 1989; 3) from the literature of developmental psychology? If this is true, then psychology is a science standing insecurely on scattered facts, strung together (White 1996), ostensibly to discover universally applicable principles, from only 5 per cent of humanity. Whatever the reasons, this should alert gatekeepers of the science to reconsider the rationality in excluding 95 per cent of their discipline's subject-matter from its knowledge base, yet claiming the status of a science for it!

In consequence, Tyler (1998) has characterized contemporary psychology as an exemplar of an imposed etic enforcing Western cultural hegemony and Eurocentric paths to psychological development worldwide. In this sense, not only does contemporary (read Western) psychology constitute one version of human psychological knowledge in a world that exists to be discovered, but also it is intrusive in imposing its images and biases on the study of behaviour and mentality throughout the world.

What is critical psychology?

I regard critical psychology as a subdiscipline of scientific psychology that is emerging from the realization that the epistemologies, paradigms, theories, methods and so on – as well as the ideology that undergirds a Euro-American discipline – are inadequate or insufficient to study or understand the diversity that characterizes human psychological functioning in its global context. The ultimate goal of critical psychology, then, is to inspire a revision and a formulation of broad-based frames of reference that can permit and foster the development of paradigms, epistemologies, theories, methodologies and so on. that are sensitive to all forms of psychological reality. Because the scientists active in the field came to it from various ideological and ethical positions, with varying professional and practical experiences, they have brought a rich variety of theoretical approaches and practical strategies to the subfield.

The human being, the source of psychological knowledge, has worth and possesses a dynamic, humane spirit, a crucial fact that critical psychologists would benefit from not ignoring. A central idea for psychology is the fact of human embeddedness in a 'community' of other humans. The 'human "animal" becomes humane by virtue of its incorporation – humanization via care and socialization – into the human community' (Nsamenang 1992a: 75). Itard's account of the *Wild Boy of Aveyron* highlights the value of the community in human life. From this perspective, studying individuals as de-contextualized entities (Trickett 1996), implies critical theoretical and empirical shortcomings. Sensitivity to the power differential inherent in the research relationship is equally crucial. Paranjpe (1997) has cited an instance of power differential becoming epistemic as the erroneous view of researchers as knowledgeable and the treatment of research participants only as 'objects' of knowledge. These issues compel a consideration of both the context and the perspectives of the research participants. This calls for

participatory and interpretive approaches to research, wherein
the participant and researcher enter into dialogue that focuses
on understanding situated meanings (Greeno 1998; Serpell
1993a).

In so far as psychological knowledge primarily is generated
through the construction and interpretation of the mentalities
and behaviours of others by psychologists, psychology is a subjective science. In fact, psychologists are engaged from the
beginning in an enterprise of translation and selection. Thus,
cross-cultural psychologists, for example, perhaps more than
anthropologists, should 'be aware of the difficulties and dangers
of extrapolating the terms and concepts of their "own" cultures
into the representations of other cultures' (Beattie n.d.: 8–9).
With calls for prudence, a plausible approach would be one
that figures out and charts a systematic process of how best to
articulate to capture the 'reality' constructed through the subjectivity rather than lay claims to a non-existent value-free psychology. The process of pursuing science itself is motivated and
value-laden. Scientific choices tend to be consistent with the
intentional worlds of scientists and their sponsors (Ingleby
1995; Nsamenang 1992b).

Becoming involved in critical psychology

I realized from my graduate years at the University of Ibadan,
Nigeria, that the social reality and goals of human development and education presented in standard textbooks in education and psychology were somehow different from my
perception and experience of them in African societies. In contrasting the images that emerged from those books and the
messages I received from my professors with childhood experiences in my cultural community – the Nso of Western
Cameroon – I became wary of their relevance to African realities.
The images in such books are different from the social reality
and world views that frame life in African cultures, a fact that
carries serious implications for education, psychology and
development work in Africa. These apprehensions were reinforced through wider exposure to psychological literature and
discourse on psychological reality as a Fogarty Fellow (1987–90)
at the National Institutes of Health (NIH).

The major influences on my value orientation as a budding critical psychologist have come from a number of sources. Three of the most influential ones are Supo Laosebikan, my dissertation adviser at the University of Ibadan, Michael Lamb, my mentor at NICHD, and Robert Serpell at the University of Maryland, Baltimore County. Whereas personal experiences and Laosebikan's creative and critical mind nurtured my critical spirit (Laosebikan 1982, 1986), Lamb's disciplined research mentoring and supportive collaboration effectively initiated, sustained and oriented me into context-relevant research (Lamb *et al.* 1992). Serpell's (1993b, 1994) impact came by way of his seminal work on indigenous Zambian precepts and effective networking within the international psychology community. Others who have influenced me include Moghaddam (Moghaddam 1987; Moghaddam and Taylor 1985), whose authoritative reviews of the state of psychology I found informative and insightful. Over the years, I have been inspired by the work of Patricia Greenfield (Greenfield 1966, 1997a and b), Barbara Rogoff (1990) and Michael Cole (1996) on the role of context on human development. A more recent influence was Colleen Loomis, whose sharp-tongued articulation expresses an incisive mind that tends toward a creative and intriguingly delightful critique of the field. Furthermore, participation at international conferences and involvement in forums on international discourse on psychology have deepened my understanding of some of the enduring debates and fallacies that impede progress in psychology.

Sensitivity to these shortcomings prompted me to challenge psychology's Eurocentric nature and to question its purported relevance to all human beings. Consequently, in *Human development in cultural context: A Third World perspective* (Nsamenang 1992a) I took issue with the assumptions and fallacies that undergird research and scholarship in psychology, including the lack of clarity about whose mind and behaviour psychology studies and developmental stages based on biological maturation. The book's editors have characterized it as the first by a psychologist from a less-developed country 'to provide a comprehensive, systematic account of human development which is sensitive to the needs, interests, and ecologies of nonwestern cultures and individuals'.

I am also part of a network that is developing strategies to create opportunities for African psychologists to interact with and interstimulate each other and to participate in forums of international psychology (Nsamenang 1995). Thus, I focus effort at interesting international psychological associations not only to understand but also to empathize with the inhospitable research environment in Africa in order to provide support and assistance. Part of my effort on the editorial boards of the *Journal of Psychology in Africa, International Journal of Behavioral Development, Journal of Cross-Cultural Psychology, Human Development*, Sage's new series Culture and Cross-Cultural Psychology, is directed at sensitizing editorial expansion of visions to the multicultural sources of psychological knowledge. Besides involvement with publications, I am also involved in the Human Development Resource Centre (HDRC), Bamenda, Cameroon. The HDRC was founded on the principle of providing indigenous, culturally appropriate and relevant resources to families, as well as providing facilities for participatory action research that is systematic, collaborative and contributes to sustaining psychological research on the continent.

Some basic principles of critical psychology

Diversity in the human condition breeds variability in psychological functioning. It is futile to consider the diversity an aberration in search of a solution; diversity is in the nature of the human experience. Human beings acquire culture (the vast majority in multicultural environments) during ontogeny, hence the need to understand how multicultural contexts shape psychological development. This necessity derives from the fact that 'Between our universal humanity and our special individuality lies the large part of each of us that is created by the culture handed down to us by our society' (Maquet 1972: 5).

We see the basic principles of critical psychology as deriving from three major sources, namely, (a) the notion that the human person is a basic animal that gains humanity through the acquisition of culture, (b) the diversity in human nature, and (c) science has universal applicability. From these basic points, we may identify the following nine principles:

1 *Diversity* shapes both the content and form of the mentality and behavioral patterns that emerge as human beings

develop in their varied contexts. Human variability begins with genotype through physiognomy and extends to the content, structure, resources and dynamics of developmental environments.

2 *Multiculturalism* is the most acceptable way to handle human diversity; it is the only way by which the whole of humanity can be greater than the sum of its parts. It prevents us from being churned into a monocultural 'melting pot'. This requires us all to acknowledge, tolerate and work with different interpretations of the things we believe in or cherish. Some of these things are cultural heritage, which include the frames of reference within which researchers and participants 'construct' psychological reality.

3 *Ideology and motives* play a determinant role in the process and outcome of science. The work of creating, pursuing and generating scientific knowledge is not at all value-neutral. Psychologists look from their positions using their sentiments and values (Redfield 1959). Although such values pervade at all levels of the research process, they are usually not acknowledged or identified as possible limitations.

4 *Psychology is a representational science.* A universal problem that applies equally to all humans always is that human experience of the world is as re-presented, not as presented (Cole 1996). Neither 'psychology nor any other science deals with a complete real world. The content of science is an abstraction' (Poortinga and Malpass 1986: 20). Psychological knowledge is a 'constructed' representation of what exists as reality; it is not the reality itself (Cole 1996). Scientific psychology has grasped only some aspects of what psychologists have been able to measure as mental life and behaviour; its bulk remains inaccessible to the methods and tools of the science.

5 *The generative nature of the human being is a distinguishing factor* between us and other animals; specifically, human beings have the capacity to create and communicate experiences across generations. Human beings have from infancy an intrinsic disposition to gain knowledge from others, thereby showing themselves to be intrinsically social and cultural (Greenfield 1997; Trevarthen 1980).

6 *Interactional and social characteristics of human beings* effect the development of individual minds and personalities. As a

'situated' entity, individual behaviour and cognition are better understood within 'larger systems that include behaving cognitive agents interacting with each other and other subsystems' (Greeno 1998: 5). It is therefore an egregious error to develop a science of psychology without reference to the role of the social network in the individual's life.

7 *The interdisciplinary nature of psychological reality.* Psychological reality is rooted in ethnographic, sociological and linguistic dimensions of communities, hence the need to borrow wisely and creatively from the models and methods of other social sciences, notably anthropology, sociology and linguistics, and to interact with them.

8 *Distinction between physical and psychological science reality.* Psychological reality is different from physical science reality. Unlike physical phenomena, psychological reality is said to be 'capricious and unstable across time and setting' (Weisz 1978: 2), hence the value of cultural-historical approaches to psychology (Cole 1996).

9 *Universality of science.* Scientific disciplines are universally applicable. The current theories and methods of psychology are inadequate to study the mental life and behaviour of all people throughout the world. A unified psychology is needed, but it will come to life only as a cooperative enterprise, when psychologists together will develop inclusive models and procedures that are sensitive to human diversity and how it is expressed.

Addressing persisting issues and enduring disputes in psychology

Western scholars may be accused for being obsessive in presenting Western ideas as if they were the only rational and universally valid ones. When Western psychologists, for instance, elect to listen to, say, Africans or to observe their behaviour, some of them decide a priori what they want to hear or see and how it should be said or seen. African and authors in less developed countries are under considerable pressure to address the international community, implying Europeans and North Americans, from this perspective rather than speak to their people.

Psychology suffers from an identity crisis. At the root of the crisis is uncertainty about psychology's subject content. Tyler (1998: 1) is inviting us to consider how 'A science's content does not exist until exemplars are provided for identifying and abstracting it. A science's laws cannot be tested until there is a content against which to test them.' The uncertainty about the content on which to test or apply psychological laws arises from the lurking doubt about whose behaviour is implicated in the definition of psychology as 'the science of human behavior'. The issue comes out poignantly in concerns about whether psychology actually applies itself equally to all humans. For instance, do the so-called minorities around the world and their majority peers receive comparable attention as knowledgeable participants in psychological research? Categorization is an integral part of science, but many category labels, like those identified above, are stigmatizing the people whose social identities they address. Some categories do not present the persons so identified as bona fide citizens. Furthermore, the apparent limiting of the scope of psychology to 'aspects of behavior conveniently available to investigators in highly industrialized nations with a history of scientific endeavor' (Triandis and Brislin 1984: 1006) is suspect.

A persistent debate relating to the role of nature versus nurture in shaping the human mind has riddled the discipline since Wilhlelm Wundt 'discovered' it in 1879. As researchers explore the impacts of heredity and environment on human development, issues pertaining to their dichotomous influences inevitably arise. Divergent thinking on the matter is not productive (Nsamenang 1992a), as nature and nurture may be instigating different developmental processes that probably contribute parallel rather than competitive influences on development (Segall *et al.* 1990). In other terms, nature and nurture act in synergy to produce developmental change. Thus, culture and human development are inextricably intertwined (Greenfield 1997b), with culture comprising the humanizing component of human nature. The active acquisition of cultural knowledge by human beings constitutes the interface of culture and human development. This way of thinking breaks down the enduring dispute between biology as nature and culture as nurture (Greenfield and Suzuki 1998). This assumption may inspire the search for basic principles and appropriate methodologies by which to investigate how culture and mind make each other (Cole 1996; Shweder 1991).

Current psychological paradigms claim universality on the basis of intrusive but unvoiced assumptions and scattered ethnocentric data sets derived predominantly from middle-class white college students. The discipline has thus come to be dominated by theories that value individualism and the split between cognitive and social development. This is typical of European-driven cultures (Mundy-Castle 1974), particularly that of the United States. But the split between the cognitive and the social is not normative in all cultures. In African societies, for example, cognitive and social development are tightly integrated, with cognitive development *subordinate* to social development (Wober 1974; Dasen 1984). Research in cultures that do not value cognition in itself, but as a means to social development, could generate data to inform the discipline about what are, or are not, universal aspects of psychological functioning.

African psychologists who have focused on indigenous precepts, among them Eze (1991), Eweka (1993), Loasebikan (1986), Nsamenang (1992a), Serpell (1993b) and Tape (1993), are beginning to make such a contribution. For instance, whereas Serpell (1993b) and Tape (1993) have described the role of indigenous concepts on the cognitive development of African children, Nsamenang (1992a) has sketched a typology of nine stages of human development in West African cultures. According to Serpell (1994: 18–19), Nsamenang's (1992a) 'characterization of ontogeny as a cumulative process of social integration within the community and clan differs in theoretical focus from the more individualistic accounts proposed by Freud, Erikson, and Piaget'.

Psychologists calling for a liberation of psychology from Eurocentrism need to be reminded that science is a creation of the Enlightenment, and is thus inescapably a Eurocentric product (Nsamenang and Dawes 1998). This historic truth does not and should not justify arrogance and disciplinary domination by the West. It alerts psychologists, however, to intense ethnocentrism and casts doubts on the scientific status of a discipline that has failed to attend to the bulk of its subject matter. A liberatory project may focus on:

1 a retreat to indigenous psychologies (Kim and Berry 1993),
2 a rejection of the discipline as it now stands, and its replacement with a 'distinct science' (Moghaddam 1987) that has its own epistemology and rules of practice, or

3 acceptance, with the sensitivities this engenders, of contemporary psychology as derived from a set of Western ethnothe-
   ories and models, to constitute a platform from which to
   launch a project to evolve a truly universal psychology. The
   primary objective of the project would be to transcend the
   integration of non-Western perspectives to develop inclusive
   frames of reference that permit the study of human diversity
   and its expression worldwide.

In the spirit of Africa's historic 'hospitable reception' of new
people and ideas (Nsamenang 1992a: 105) and its inveitable
incorporation of elements of external cultures, I opt for the
third route. This option by no means represents a 'chickening
out' from difficulty. Rather, it is one way of excluding the celebration of provincialism implicated in the first option and the
avoidance of the reinvention of the wheel implied in the second.
Accordingly, I subscribe to 'one plain psychology that consists of
basic human principles and that recognizes the significance of
cultural factors and differences' (Kunkel 1989: 574).
    Of course, a project to evolve such a psychology does not yet
exist and necessarily is a cooperative venture. It requires the
involvement of psychologists the world over in genuine collaborative exchanges and respectful interstimulation in efforts to
generate theories, principles and methodologies that, in the true
sense of science, will apply to human psychological phenomena
throughout the world. This is a rather tall order, implicating not
merely dramatic shifts in mind-sets and current procedures, but
the acceptance and integration of psychologists in Africa and
other parts of the non-Western world, in spite of their poor
resource bases, as partners and collaborators with equal status
to that of their Western peers. The objective is to articulate
scientifically consistent theories of how mind and culture
shape each other in ways that do not presuppose the dominance of individualistic or collectivist values and norms.

Concluding statement

The culture of psychological science is shifting from a monocultural perspective towards a multicultural project. There is
need to give careful attention to both its content and process.

Gatekeepers of the discipline (editors, scientific committees, publishers and so on) would advance the discipline if they adjusted rapidly to it. Three major factors limit the contribution of African psychologists to this process. First, the discipline was imported as a ready-made intellectual package with its biases and limitations. Second, its roots are embedded in the racist colonial history of the continent and the historically oppressive use of the discipline. Third, it is practised in hybrid societies incidental to indigenous and imported psychologies living together in the same communities and individuals (Nsamenang and Dawes 1998).

Given this hybrid context, a liberatory project for psychology in Africa would more appropriately enter into critical discourse with external knowledge systems, to construct an understanding of patterns of psychological development in Africa (Nsamenang and Dawes 1998). This is crucial if African psychologists are to chart and inform the scientific community of how the African ecoculture imprints onto human psychological development and if they are to make a contribution to the evolution of a truly unified psychological science. This becomes even more critical if the discipline is to contribute to an improvement of life circumstances on the continent. In consideration thereof, my humble suggestion is not a wholesale rejection of scientific psychology as it is today, but its acceptance as a seedling that could be improved and nurtured into a mature psychological tree to bear fruits for the world's diverse peoples. Benefits will accrue if paradigms and methods (both qualitative and quantitative) are developed from the notion that psychological reality is subjective and diverse and that the 'nature' of the science might have been different had it been 'discovered' and cultivated within world views different from the Eurocentric – say, the African or the Chinese.

10

Connecting with Difference: Being Critical in a Postmodern World

John Morss

What is critical psychology?

Critical psychology is psychology with its eyes open. In a sense all it requires is a preparedness to recognize that psychology is never complete, never adequate – that the language and methods of psychology can never entirely represent any experience, event or phenomenon. As soon as this is accepted it is obvious that psychology is a human science and a human activity, constructed by human endeavour and subject to human frailty.

The analogy is clichéd, but the emperor's new clothes cannot but spring to mind; psychologists (although no more and no less than other professionals) maintain a collegial conspiracy of silence about the flimsy basis for their activities and claims, like a ring of free-fall sky-divers clutching each others' hands as they plummet. Critical psychology has the temerity to refuse to comply with this, to ask awkward questions and to direct people's attention (sometimes forcibly) to the bigger picture.

Yet it would be disingenuous, as well as disrespectful, to claim that opening the eyes or keeping them open is a simple matter. There are immense forces, most of them generated or at least maintained through interpersonal dynamics, that are dedicated (to pursue the analogy) to the closing of the eyes. The voice of the critical psychologist becomes the voice of the prophet if it is heard only in the form of heckling and hectoring – a voice from outside the arena, inveighing against the evils and the ignorance of the unenlightened. Psychology desperately needs *voices* for critical psychology, not a single voice (and many people may on occasion all speak with a single voice, always a potentially dangerous event).

There are many kinds of critical psychology, and any version that claims to be *the* critical psychology needs to be treated with suspicion. If critical psychology is totally coherent, systematic and systematized, if it has the kinds of 'developed' methods that can be transmitted in a routinized way, if it supports a career structure – and there are several versions of critical psychology that have had, or currently aspire to, these characteristics – then all that is happening may be the construction of yet another 'school' of psychology, sooner or later to be incorporated into the academy. In important respects, critical psychology must remain pluralist at all costs (or, in the sense of Deleuze and Guattari, a 'minor' language).

'Pluralist' does not mean 'eclectic'. Different versions of critical psychology are not in any sense 'equal'; they are perpetually warring with each other, and in any particular context some versions will be more effective and perhaps more valid than others. Hard-nosed Marxist kinds of critical psychology can be extremely effective, but they deteriorate into hollow rhetoric with great rapidity. (The same applies to feminist versions of critical psychology, which are sometimes recycled Marxism.) Soft-nosed hermeneutical or social-constructionist kinds of critical psychology can be surprisingly disarming of mainstream fortifications, but they relax into reassurance and self-congratulation rather too readily. And so on. The element of surprise must not be undervalued: apparently tired traditions can get suddenly reinvigorated, as with the younger, post-structuralized generation of Berlin's Marxist *Kritische Psychologie* (see Hildebrand-Nilshon *et al.*, 1999).

Critical psychology has its 'low' forms as well as its 'high' ones. Critical psychology of a significant kind arises whenever the activities of the psychologist are apprehended within a wider context – social, sociological, anthropological, economic, political or personal. Critical psychology in this sense is what every psychologist does when off-duty – chatting in the tearoom or locker room or in the bar at a conference; telling their partner what their day was like... Who has got what big grant from what funding agency? Who has had a publication accepted or turned down by what journal, and on what flimsy basis? What exciting new journal has been announced, and who has been included into/excluded from the editorial board? Which research topics are suddenly sexy, which ones are suddenly passé? Not one of such questions is about the science of psychology as a set of formal claims, methods, or 'findings'. They are about relationships, reputations, *realpolitik*. Like all other forms of human activity, psychology is concerned with persuasion. And psychology (like any professionalized human activity) insists that its 'real' activity takes place when it is on duty, busy and ready to be observed – on-stage. Critical psychology strolls backstage, and at times takes a bit part on stage as well. It always threatens to be subversive, but if it is always subversive it will lose its impact.

There are of course tendencies within critical psychology – perhaps inevitable tendencies – drawing it into the mainstream. To the extent that these tendencies win out, the practices that critical psychology despises are systematically reproduced. If critical psychology engages with the mainstream at any point – for example in seeking to publish its ideas in respectable locations, or seeking institutional advancement for its representatives – then some compromising contamination is probably inevitable. And for critical psychology to have any hope of political effectiveness, it has to move beyond the backstage and the fringes of decision-making. Yet even the adoption of similar formats and practices – the conference, the lecture, the edited book – gives rise to conformist pressures. Critical psychology generates its own stars, its own grand old men and women, its revered traditions and its revered forebears, its brash young upstarts, its embittered has-beens; critical psychology becomes lifestyle. (Is postmodernism in or out?) Critical psychology is in continuous need of its own attention. It needs to be its own permanent revolution.

What brought me to critical psychology?

There are several answers to this. The first, quite genuinely, was frustration with my progress in the mainstream. Building up a package of credible publications through experimental research was painfully slow. It involved compromises of a kind that became tedious. (I do however still harbour a feeling of superiority over those critical psychologists who have not proved themselves capable of the peculiar disciplines involved in publishing careful experimental work; while a prejudice against experimental work, if that is all it is, is inadequate as a justification for dismissing it.)

My own critical psychology work is a kind of sublimated marxism. I grew up with parents who were politically extremely active; both were members of the Communist Party in the UK, active in union affairs and in anti-military and latterly, anti-racist campaigns. My brother and I were carried, and later walked, in Ban-the-Bomb marches in the late 1950s, and Vietnam protests in the early 1960s; we threw darts at photographs of Jack Kennedy (giving rise to a hint of guilt after his assassination). I've never managed to get myself seriously committed to active political work, however. Studying psychology seemed a possible way into work that would be 'progressive' in a more general and perhaps safer sense.

Before that, while still at school, I'd read some Popper and was therefore cued into the wider context of discovery and hypothesis-testing in science, and had some awareness of the history of science (my father gently pointed me towards a Marxist response to Popper's attack on Hegel). I'd also taken my first psychology course, at an adult education class (Workers' Education Association) – an introduction to Kleinian child development theory as it happened – alongside a course in the history and philosophy of science.

(School experience never stays done. A former school colleague is currently (June 1999) the NATO spokesperson as Serbia is bombed to the conference table, generating a disturbingly ambivalent comfortableness and sense of trust to the apologetics. Surely this campaign, with its live TV broadcasts by bomber pilots, is much more the postmodern war than was Desert Storm with its fantasized rerun of Vietnam as the US would have liked it: lots of bombs and no cameras, a conveniently defoliated landscape on which to drop its flaming excrement. Yet every new war will be labelled 'the post-modern war', while refugees still look like refugees.)

I studied psychology in the UK in the post-1960s intellectual depression years (we turned to glam-rock), and became fairly successfully socialized into the quantitative experimental subculture, although I was always very doubtful about its relevance to social activity or experience. Most influential on me there (the

University of Sheffield) was the brilliant stoker-turned-psycho-logist-of-perception John Mayhew. I also maintained subsidiary interests in the history and philosophy of science (including evolutionary biology), and got sporadically enthusiastic about Wittgenstein and Feyerabend as well as the occasional psychologist (well, Chomsky). Wittgenstein I found intense and challenging, both in his austere early phase (of logical atomism) and in the more expansive later phase of the *Philosophical Investigations*. The continuities between these phases seem to me to be sometimes overlooked; it is in the *Tractatus* (that is, in his early writings) that Wittgenstein writes, 'The limits of my language mean the limits of my world.' At the same time I am not yet convinced by the fashionable Wittgenstein-as-postmodernist reading. (Here a personal definition of postmodernism might be called for. I would define postmodernism as a catch-all term for a collection of ideas critical of certainty, of foundations, of true methods and of traditional logic as these have previously defined intellectual activity).

The anarchic Feyerabend was attractive because of his iconoclastic approach to the more respectable philosophers of science such as Popper. My PhD (in Edinburgh) was supervised by the brilliant but wayward infant researcher Tom Bower, who immersed me in cognitive theory but also introduced me to the ideas of Gregory Bateson and various European psychologists. Scots psychology looks askance at English psychology (something to do with the 'Auld Alliance' with France) and I learned to be rude about some fairly respected figures within developmental psychology. Iconoclasm is an important ingredient of critical psychology.

I was subsequently encouraged by George Butterworth – one of many mainstream psychologists with intellectual interests vastly broader than those manifest in his publications – to write a book based on my PhD research. Instead I decided to pursue historical issues in developmental psychology, and after toying with a project called 'Piaget and his sources' (which I suspected might get catalogued as a cook-book) ended up writing a critique of the uses of evolutionary theory by the main figures in developmental psychology (*The Biologising of Childhood*). This wasn't yet critical psychology, although I included some praise for Marxist and for social constructionist approaches at the end, as antidotes to evolutionism. The most influential review of the book thought it was Marxist, however.

The historical and conceptual work on developmental theory got me more directly interested in contemporary alternatives to orthodox developmental psychology. I decided that developmental forms of explanation need to be treated with great suspicion, wherever they are found (the social sciences, history, biology, psychology, economics). Meanwhile, and as a result of writing a very short article about Piaget for the journal *New Ideas in Psychology*, I had met John Broughton who was playing an inspirational and organisational role in critical psychology around New York. Broughton allowed me to publish a rather mealy-mouthed review of that leviathan of a book, Henriques *et al.*'s *Changing the Subject* (still inexplicably unknown in the USA) and also an interview with Rom Harré, who generously encouraged my social-theoretic explorations.

Later, Broughton encouraged me to write a book about the critical psychology of human development, and also introduced me to critical psychologists like Erica Burman, Ian Parker and Barbara Esgalhado. By then I'd moved from Edinburgh to Northern Ireland and thence to New Zealand. A year at the University of Cambridge (England) gave me time to make progress on the book (*Growing Critical*, 1996) and to make contact with Rex and Wendy Stainton Rogers. (Martin Richards and King's College were very hospitable, and the University of Cambridge survived my intellectual onslaught unscathed. I'll be back.) Since then I've made a few false starts (on an introductory human development text for example), and a few (I hope) true starts (on the exciting and accessible *Don't Develop*, for example). When the going gets tough, the tough get writing.

The basic principles of critical psychology

I feel very diffident about basic principles, and I suspect that establishing basic principles may be a repressive act. More than one kind of critical psychology, past and present, has attempted to codify its practices in a scientific kind of way. I resist this, since my own brand of critical psychology is deconstructionist and tends to the anarchistic. I suspect that any principles one is likely to encounter would already have served as principles of earlier, failed programmes (transforming psychology, transforming society and so on and so forth – the modernist-humanist emancipatory tradition that has let down the citizens of the twentieth centrury on such a massive scale). Any basic principles that play a part in my thinking can probably be derived from what I've already said; the only principle I am conscious of is the only one that has ever been needed: 'know your enemy'.

The big debates and the unresolved issues

Critique versus deconstruction

There is in my view a major issue, which I define in terms of a distinction between critique and deconstruction. Critique – most clearly represented by Marxist or feminist critique – claims to reveal the truth about some effects of psychology, to uncover the processes by which ruling interests are served. It says to its (silent) audience, 'Look, this is what is going on.' In recent years, such claims have been increasingly expressed in the vocabulary of Foucault, which may or may not have helped. Critique is a militaristic and self-assured kind of activity; it sets up its battles, spears its enemies, and moves on to fresh conquests. It does not stay around to count the costs or to care for the orphans. I can't help thinking of it as a masculine style (partly because I've sometimes done it quite effectively myself).

Deconstruction, on the other hand, frequently raises questions to which it offers no answers, and perhaps has little to say about truth. It stubbornly limits itself to the surface of things. It stays around long after the party is over. It stirs and liquefies, and doubts itself and its methods. These styles of activity – critique and deconstruction – seem to me quite incompatible. 'Post-modernism' is sometimes supposed to have done away with critique as I have defined it here, but critique is reluctant to leave the academy. Instead, critique flirts with deconstruction, colonizing it to a large extent and perhaps even domesticating it (the ubiquity of 'Deconstructing the Next Bit of Psychology' as a book title threatens to give deconstruction a good name, if only through familiarity; but see Parker 1999). This issue is unresolved, as is the issue of the significance of 'postmodernism' itself.

Two cheers for postmodernism?

After some initially overenthusiastic celebrations of postmodernism in the very early 1990s (as far as psychology is concerned), evaluation has become somewhat more discerning. This does not mean that the rejection of postmodernism by conservative psychologists or by adherents of critique should be endorsed. Certainly, postmodernism has offered irresistible temptations for the less rigorous-minded of critical psychologists. Appealing to the advent of a postmodern era has allowed psychologists (and other social scientists) to package up all the nasties of the world into something labelled modernism and to cast it behind them. Pollution, statistics and ECT all become 'modernist'. There has been a very significant projective process at work here, I believe. Some of this has been harmless, but some of the proclaimed discontinuities are disturbing. Most strikingly perhaps, the Nazi era is defined as alien and unrecognizable, the terrible extremity of modernism. Without suggesting that anyone who grew up after the war should feel in any sense guilty, I do think it a dangerous mistake to erase the continuities between that time and this. (See the discussion in *Theory and Psychology*, Fall 1998.) Postmodernism still perhaps requires cutting down to size, but not in the interests of reaction, Marxist or other. Rigour is redefined by postmodernism (and too much of a certain kind of rigour is *rigor mortis*) but as redefined is as important as ever; the slogan of critical psychology should be 'vigour with rigour'.

Exemplification and personal practice

I find it a little odd to expect people to exemplify their conceptual work in their daily lives, as if that would somehow offer corroboration for it. This is in some ways a sentimental idea, akin to the expectation that soap-operatic actors will have personalities like those of the characters they portray. Any critical psychologist who is known internationally is likely to have a fairly comfortable lifestyle, to travel fairly often and to own property (with notable exceptions!), and so on. To expect a writer to live like he or she writes may simply be to encourage politically correct posturing.

Having said that, it has indeed sometimes been suggested in my present place of work that I offer critical and/or deconstructionist comments more frequently than many of my colleagues. I have certainly been accused (at an international conference) of being a dangerous person on account of my intellectual approach, and may have missed out on possibly worthwhile (from a career point of view) relationships as a consequence of speaking my mind rather bluntly on occasions. I dislike privilege, although I seem to detect it more readily in others' life circumstances than in my own. Overall, I write mainly out of melancholy, with little expectation of changing the world for the better.

What is to be done?

What indeed? When the world is striated by the tug-of-war between Jihad and McWorld, by the complicitous Punch and Judy contest of passionate localisms and impassive globalisms... The world inhabited by those who read this chapter is likely to be saturated with electronic transmission and electronic processing of information, running software that is North American in origin but global in distribution: software that controls our expression to such an extent that it will not allow a sentence to start with a lower-case letter, corrects our grammar as it is produced, and automatically converts a round-bracketed letter c into the copyright sign. Their world is also likely to be saturated with local identity, indigenous resurgence, family values. Word and wisdom, sign and soil. How can we fly past those nets?

Making sense comes at the cost of collaboration. We cannot escape the domain of capital by running from it (into activism or ecological nostalgia). Frontal assault on such a massively effective system also seems doomed to failure. Resistance will instead have to be dispersed, rhizomic, nomadic (the reference here is to Deleuze and Guattari), many-voiced... and the script is (regrettably) more likely to be *Starship Troopers* than *Independence Day*. Post-modern life is a B-movie and we're the good guys. Critical psychology may be impossible, but we need it. Saddle up!

11

Critical Psychology, Subjectivity and the Politics of a Lost Signifier

Kareen Ror Malone

Making of a critical psychologist

Critical psychology could be defined as the task of imagining the discipline of psychology in a way that properly considers its political and social context. As would follow, critical psychology must re-evaluate many of the values that psychology embraces as a result of its adherence to a natural science model of the human psyche. The social aims of critical psychology certainly are not compelling to all psychologists, and being a critical psychologist may simply be an accidental effect of a certain time, place, and thus socially sanctioned way of seeing the discipline. In my case, the ideals of social transformation originated in the 1960s and presupposed my apparently secure place in the socioeconomic hierarchy (as it did for so many of those revolutionary dropouts-turned-stockbrokers of recent decades). Captivated by the early Marx, appalled at race oppression and inspired by the utopias of Marcuse and Reich, I saw perhaps too clearly the shortcomings of my Skinnerian and cognitive professors and peers. Their vision was mechanistic, geared to social control, and alienating even to animals lower in the food-chain.

Equally galling, the reigning psychological approaches eliminated the question of subjectivity and, as far as I could tell, cognition did not bring it back. So in a certain sense I was a perfect candidate for the so-called 'third force' in psychology, a humanistic campaigner. Even if that branch was weak on theory, theoretical thinness was hardly a liability within empiricist psychology. The problem, for me, was rather that, within the humanistic paradigm, the social was secondary to the individual and, without a fuller articulation of the former, subjectivity would remain only partially illuminated.

Juliet Mitchell's *Psychoanalysis and Feminism* (1974) was the turning-point. With an eye to the most radical reach of feminist thinking, Mitchell thoroughly critiqued the politics of authenticity, the notion of a 'natural' human, and an ideal of desire that could conceivably be unmediated by social forces. With Mitchell, new readings of alienation, subjectivity and gender were in the making. This was the beginning, for me, of the linguistic turn with a political twist.

Still, it seemed that options to pursue a politicized psychology in the United States were few. In my undergraduate department, there was no crisis in social psychology. There was barely a social psychology. So, although piqued by Mitchell's work, I saw little opportunity to further explore the ideas her work had sparked. Instead, phenomenological psychology provided a vehicle for a continued critical perspective on, at least, the question of the subject. Here the phenomenological challenge over issues of embodiment, reflexivity, signification, negation and the perspectival nature of knowledge made possible significant conceptual advances over traditional accounts. Not that there are no problems. Accounts that depend on consciousness overlook aspects of subjectivity that escape self-report, that are so deeply inscribed by the social that the social origin is erased, and that only appear as they are dispersed through intersubjective relationships, history and in relationship to power. But at least in phenomenology, subjectivity is not presumed or avoided altogether.

In order to find a more complicated and social subjectivity, I turned to recent importations of psychoanalysis and post-structuralism, or rather I returned to the spirit of Juliet Mitchell's work. These approaches possessed a more politic notion of the subject that was indebted in its very being to the symbolic framework of meaning, desire and the body. Feminists in the humanities were often leaders in these importations. Feminists found post-structuralism and psychoanalysis appealing because gender is such a dense socially encoded embodiment – the body is the most ideologically weighted text – and is fraught with identity, desire and political ramifications (for example, Gallop

1982; Jardine 1985; Suleiman 1985). As with many of these feminists, I have never seen psychoanalysis as antithetical to Foucauldian critiques; I see both as focused on ways of situating modes of resistance to 'state-regulated' forms of individualism. (To treat Derrida and post-structuralism as merely a deconstructive tool of critical theory – a new way to undo bourgeois or patriarchal ideology – is to miss Derrida's ideas about the signifier and difference as supplement. It elides the 'bringing to bear' of subjectivity in Derrida, an elision that also misses the connection between post-structuralism and psychoanalysis. As Christopher Lane (1998) argues, setting up a false antagonism between psychoanalysis and Foucault is typical of American readers of Foucault. Psychologists have a number of separate historical reasons to eschew psychoanalysis that often influence the stances of more critical circles within the discipline.)

The issue that remains is this nagging question of the subject. Is there something that we can do that is truly critical and actually psychological? Is psychology just a chimera (less than even a text), or, worse, is it only an academic agenda? If just academic, we already forgo any claim to being critical. Put differently, we might look to this question of subjectivity rather than only to political conceptions of the subject for a 'place from which to emancipate' that would reflect most precisely our presumed vocation as psychologists.

The social dialectic of critical psychology: debates, principles and the nutshells around which critical psychology revolves

The complications of politics

Books, anthologies and articles suggest strong currents of controversy within critical psychology (for example, Ibáñez and Iñiguez 1997). The cause for so much discussion and so little unity is a consequence of the vast project that lies before us, one that must articulate the historically repressed dimensions of psychological inquiry, which are many indeed. As a result of the expansiveness of the critical project in psychology, one's work could in principle gravitate to a number of conceptual partners. Nonetheless, the path I suggest, generating a critical psychology that integrates ideas from social construction, post-modernism, science studies, psychoanalytic and non-psycho-analytic feminisms may appear, at first, as a wimpy eclectic option. After all, if we are attempting to create theory and research paradigms that interrogate the broader cultural and political horizons of 'psychological phenomena', there are cer-tainly more direct routes. Marxism fosters certain ways of understanding the class and economic investments that under-gird some of the tradition's research and theory. As the Marxist eye can see, the implicit endorsement of an ideal of a middle-class bourgeois consumer, producer or manager is unmistakable in traditional psychology (Pfister and Schnog 1997). So why not just use Marxist categories for one's critical leverage? The same claims can be made in behalf of certain more strictly political feminist approaches. It is clear that psychology is guilty of egregious sexism in theory and in practice. Using a feminist analysis would certainly orient critical paradigms to social hori-zons with direct and lasting impact on living human beings.

Even the 'subject' within traditional psychology can be said to possess definitions of the emancipatory possibilities that inhere to its discourse of rights and its understanding of law and subjectivity (Cornell 1993). Traditional social psychology in its problem definitions and ways of responding to those problems is clearly informed by the discourse of liberalism (for example, prejudice, conformity, rational individualism, and contractual relations). Indeed, were the liberal subject nearly as neutral as it aspires to be, or were such neutrality unproblematically desirable, then the way to a critical psychology might merely be a progressive step forward from its traditional liberal forebear (see Caudill 1997). The problem with the above more specifically political formulations of the subject is not that they don't pos-sess some salutary political aim. The problem is rather that these formulations, in so far as they presume a unified and perhaps rational subject, can be blind to those investments and over-determinations that darken their idealism or intersect their pro-grams for political action.

We see this in the case of traditional psychology with its liberal moorings: it is obvious, for example, that sexist science is somehow more than just 'bad' science (Fausto-Sterling 1985). There are social investments. But one is often hard pressed to characterize these political effects and cultural influences solely in terms of rational self-interest. Thus, one must complicate the relationship between so-called 'alienating' from the so-called 'emancipatory' and flesh out the intricate functioning of false consciousness (Dews 1987).

There is an unmarked subjective stake that participates in the formation of epistemological and political categories, one that I see as particularly germane to psychological research. This constitutive blindspot can not be theorized outside a more sophisticated notion of subjectivity. Thus one might see the reason for my mongrel collection of sources for critical psychology. We must keep the political horizon in mind, but also formulate a non-identical but collaborative dimension that marks how the political is subjectified (see also Walkerdine 1997). Oppression is sometimes quite simple to understand and the steps for its rectification obvious. But there are other occasions when the path is more entangled. It is this difficulty that forces critical psychology to turn to a spectrum of disciplinary approaches to conceive of a fully critical psychology.

Of all the disparate sources that contribute to my version of critical psychology, psychoanalysis probably seems like the interloper with its apparent emphasis on the intrapsychic. Admittedly, while many psychoanalysts are most concerned with maintaining their clinical practice, there are emergent cultural framings of psychoanalysis. Recent incarnations and revisions (for example Flax 1993; Merck 1993; Barratt 1993; Bracher 1993) would suggest a broader understanding of psychoanalysis as thinking through the moment of conjunction between the body in its particularity and broader social structures. When Félix Guattari and Gilles Deleuze (Rudinesco 1986/1990) reproached Lacanian psychoanalysis for reducing everything to mommy and daddy, they could as easily have said it reduced everything to law, the 'phenomenology of the body', authority, the signifier, the Other, and desire. These are neither intrapsychic nor reducible to a Victorian family romance. The archetypal figures, mom and dad, may be significant for your psychoanalytic hour or within certain cultural contexts and in relation to certain cultural functions (the family is not an indifferent structure), but mommy and daddy are not the concepts. So if psychoanalysis is allowed a furtive moment with more specifically cultural queries and relations of power, an unscripted alliance may be played out that would engender alternative paths for realizing the aims of critical psychology. I have argued that a turn toward the subjective deepens our political aims in critical psychology, but the question of the subject is not simply this.

The subject of subjectivity

In its current academic incarnations, critical psychology generates its own proud share of internecine disputes and sustains itself as a sort of psychology with certain methodological proclivities and a particular set of theoretical concerns. Still, as a discourse, critical psychology has derived a portion of its mandate from the failures of its parent discipline (Spears 1997). This initial inscription will without doubt mark what is 'critical' about critical psychology even if plans for disciplinary succession are realized or praxis and politics assume ascendance (see Ibáñez and Iñiguez 1997). If we begin with the tradition, one is clearly faced with sorely 'undertheorized' dimensions of the field. The omissions within psychology are uncanny in that many might appear to an untrained eye as essential to its very pursuit.

First, and this is no news, whatever subjectivity is, and we can take any of its commonplace incarnations – consciousness, will, feeling, continuity of identity, and so on – psychology seems loath to develop methods or concepts that do more than describe, police or reduce its effects. Decades of humanistically based critiques have drawn attention to the limitations of psychology's rationalistic and mechanistic models of psychological life, for example love as a cost–benefit analysis. This critical chorus has expanded to include those who enjoin conceptual frameworks provided by science studies, literary criticism, poststructuralist philosophy, feminism, post-modernism and cultural studies (see Bayer and Shotter 1998). Taken from these sources, such reformulations craft a more socially nuanced notion of the subject in which representation, history and the 'deployment' of power intervene on the yet-to-be-theorized psychological subject. The theoretic moves have opened up a few enticing paths.

Critical psychologists have undertaken a reconsideration of the body (Stam 1998), are reinventing traditional notions of reflexivity and are raising the question of human agency (Morawski 1994). Agency, once simply a matter of 'will' and desire, is considered a product of political, technological and linguistic effects. This reconceptualization of agency and subjectivity requires a robust yet mixed pool of ideas, metaphors and images. What is the subject now that she is more than experiential and expressive self-validation? What precisely constitutes the cusp/gap/structure that gives us the intimacy attributed to subjectivity – our own cosy relationship to the self – as well as its obvious complicity with current cultural forms and its apparent dispersal as the effects of these forms.

Critical psychology keeps adding pieces to this puzzle but we are not quite able to do more than champion a particular piece at one given time. This, I believe, is problematic. The body is opposed to discourse, experience to determinism, and more classical notions of politics to a focus on the post-modernized subject (Condor 1997; Burman 1997). The issue of the subjective requires an unusual degree of theoretical vigilance as we ascertain what various critical psychologists may mean by subjective function. Do we draw on Marx, humanism, psychoanalysis, feminism and what elements go into our theoretical concoction now that we have left the garden of explaining consciousness by our experience of it? Critical psychologists are also exiled, unlike the tradition, from any notion of a subject that uncritically imports culturally endorsed models of subjectivity, – that is, the subject as a less-informed scientist who both requires and reflects psychology, the subject as fundamentally masculine, or democratic, or, more generally, as a formation that is induced as a response to current social demands. Our parent discipline can both create and cure subjects who are unactualized, stressed, androgynous, neurophysiological, medicated or even post-modern. These formations define the discipline's social contribution. Psychology promises more actualized, productive, less-stressed citizens, but these promises are dogged by unexamined political effects and costs.

It is at this point where we must be ever so careful as to how we enter into dialogues about the meaning of critical psychology. Our sense of the subject is a bricolage and I am not proposing permanent 'deconstruction' of the subject or one singular definition of the subject. No one would want critical psychology to be a mass of similarly minded marginals. It is just we must remember that the question of the subject is rather complex.

Subjectivity and research

To begin mixing the various metaphors of subjectivity found in critical psychology, one can examine *some* of Jill Morawski's (1994) ideas on reflexivity. Her text, *Practicing Feminisms, Reconstructing Psychology*, works towards transcending notions of reflexivity founded on visual models (I see myself looking at me). Even if the reflexive turn is, in itself, somewhat subversive, these earlier models presuppose some a self-identical point, that is, self-consciousness. Morawski counters this more traditional take with conceptions that pose reflexivity within the terms of an unacknowledged history. This history is both individually and culturally inscribed. Class, gender, race are forms of representation that function as implicitly inscribed subject positions. Such positions support and condition the encounter between a psychologist and her or his data. In Morawski's version, 'the reverse camera angle' is an awareness of the unspoken press of a cultural context but also of *its particular emergence within a more dialectically conceived comprehension of psychological research*. The subjective dimension resides within a certain wave of effects, the ways in which the political and the particular reconfigure the research and the research data. Subjectivity is both in formation and ephemerally present in acts of resistance, subversion, discarded details, and as an enigmatic, paradoxical and unpredictable agency.

Morawski's work should be situated in light of the tradition's failure to really consider subjectivity at all. Subjectivity is the officially repressed dimension of objective methodologies. Once repressed, it typically reappears as an unreflective insinuation of psychology's ideological investments. Whether acknowledged or not, far from being the noisome distortion of an objective methodology, the subject is inevitably produced even within the most highly controlled experiment. Subjectivity cannot be evaded, because the experiment creates *meaning* for the experimenter as well as the research participants and confederates. We can softly push that which generates meaning and thus query subjectivity *per se* by thinking about signification.

Jacques-Alain Miller (1998), a Lacanian psychoanalyst, describes the 'signifier' as that which conditions one's asking, 'What does that mean?' (Signifiers are word images, the materiality of language. I more broadly use the notion of signifier as some symbolic inscription that must be defined in its relationship to other inscriptions, signifiers or words, much like in a dictionary.) We know that when we ask that question we are encountering a signifier and the possibility of a subject. So from the outset, the experimenter is a subject; he or she is overtly concerned with meaning. Adding another dimension, one can quote the usual Lacanian aphorism, 'A signifier is that which represents a subject for another signifier.' Research of all stripes thus leaves tracks when it comes to the question of the subject. All research in psychology 'puts out' this signifier, which is a matter of the experimenter's desire. The subject thus appears in a liminal space marked by the experimenter's desire and the response of the participants. Much of this 'interaction' is erased by objectivistic methodologies and only appears as a seeming accident, as with the 'laughter' that haunts the Milgram experiment (see Stam *et al.* 1998).

If one accepts provisionally these minimal definitions of the subject, it can be suggested that the question of subjectivity cannot be evaded in any research situation. The issue becomes how we can imagine alternatives to the merely symptomatic production of subjectivity within most of psychology, a production that implicates equally the researcher and the researched. The characterization 'symptomatic' simply means that subjectivity is ideologically foreclosed or *rather 'out of the dialectical loop' that would produce new research directions and interventions*. It is a symptomatic formation rather than outright and successful suppression, because the motivated rhetorical strategy of research psychologists cannot help but function in relation to some other X, for example the body, another subjectivity, or identity. Simply put, psychology asks humans for signifiers.

Unfortunately, signification and its dialectical movement are often perceived as a problem for objective methodologies to resolve. This so-called barrier to objectivity created by signification motivates stratagems, such as replacing bodies with machines, recruiting confederates and so forth. Ironically these decoys may replicate the subjectivity that was putatively excised – since subjectivity is not a matter of a biological body but of the structure of the signifier (see Bayer 1998; Morawski 1998). Reflexivity in research appears in that the signifier asks for a reply (the signifier is that which represents a subject for another signifier). Subjectivity and thus its political overdeterminations are in a sense dispersed throughout the experimental situation, located in neither one nor the Other.

As long as psychological theory operates from *visual metaphors*, it can pretend that it experiments and theorizes about something it sees and then records. It thus avoids an examination of what it must bring into the research situation. In reaction, one can trace the insinuation of such ulterior effects that chip away at any pretense of political or cultural neutrality. As well, one may take this unaccounted-for factor as the very basis from which to conduct research and consequently formulate methods that reflect such an understanding.

To garner maximum benefits from the critical paradigm, we must move beyond the assertion that representation and reality are incommensurate, that neither nominalism nor realism 'works' epistemologically (Hacking 1983). For it is quite simple, in order to circumvent the critique of psychological realism, to resort to instrumental or pragmatic forms of rationality. However, this very viable preservation of scientific canon leaves some of the more difficult issues of science untouched, namely the insulating function of rationality, the way in which the rational subjective supports a certain understanding of knowledge and any queries into the way in which particular methodologies of science guarantee that rationality (see Landan 1996). Within the paradigm I am formulating, science is an intersubjective, social and embodied enterprise that is in part defined by the logic of the signifier not by properties of consciousness. Unglueing representation from reality is just a meagre first step towards rectifying this underlying question of subjectivity and culture in science. Even without reality and a corresponding scientific description of it, seeing the meaning of knowledge as rational problem-solving absolves psychology of very significant tasks.

Another significant point, however, in the above reflections is the proposed interarticulation between two rather distinctive view points, one founded in psychoanalysis and the other starting from a more socially informed position. A fundamentally political deconstruction will reveal the social institutions and structures from which psychology purloins its forms of identity which then parade as the subject (see Harris 1997). This critique is not the sole dimension: there may be a specifically psychological angle on such fundamentally cultural and historical questions. What gives one the possibility of political resistance? What conditions self-destructive identifications with certain cultural formations? Such questions may reveal an autonomous realm of effects addressed by psychoanalysis that exists in tandem with social instantiations.

The disciplinary rearticulation of psychology is a politically pressing task and one demanded by a fully critical paradigm. What I have sketched in the previous paragraphs merely indicates some of the parameters of a social dialectic in psychology. One would be hopeless in the face of a formation of the psychological that renders the subject homogenous with language, on the same plane as narrative, so to speak (Morawski 1998; Bayer and Malone 1998; Copjec 1994; Bracher 1993). Nor can one, in good conscience, merely tinker with some humanistically formed model of the subject who surreptitiously binds the symbolic possibilities introduced by discourse or is self-transparently advancing political aims.

As for political power, critical psychology is still integrating certain repositionings of our notions of power that have been introduced from the tradition of political critique most trenchantly argued by Foucault. We have moved from a top-down notion of the imposition through economic and/or epistemological hegemony to a more nuanced notion of the imbrication of power effects in their immediate instantiation. These effects are not dictated through 'law'. They are composed of contradictory practices, appeals and complicities. For example, men don't simply obey the male sexual drive discourse as if to be male were a discursive after-effect. There must be enticements of power, and those enticements cross the issue of political institutions and formations of the subject. The latter is a matter of the interarticulation of the interdependence of subjectivity and subjection, an interdependence that is definitive for the body.

Power is *really* produced through practices that shuttle between discourses, practices, and the bodies so addressed, and operates through pleasure, complicity and desire. These aren't Foucauldian platitudes. This is significant for a psychology that by ample demonstration is clearly implicated in the propagation of societal ideals and normative formations. But shall a programme of social hygiene in any guise be the caption of psychology's political relevance? Is there anything psychological about the psyche and where is that found? Could deeper reflection on subjectivity give us a new conjunction with the political? These are the questions of critical psychology from my vantage-point.

The outside world?

The political clout of so-called family values never ceases to amaze me. Involved in campus outreach programmes concerned with rape, dating abuse, AIDS, homophobia and the like, I encounter the extraordinary pull of the religious right on the behaviour and imagination of students at the university in the Southern USA where I work. Through theatre and other formats, our programmes attempt to symbolize current sexual and gender possibilities and dysphorias, as well as initiating more 'self-protective' strategies with sex and dating. For me, it is an ambivalently embraced enterprise; such programmes typically if not always install certain forms of subjectivity based on very tried and true forms of psychological knowledge. And so the trick is to maintain the political gains (reporting and preventing rape, for example) while being equally vigilant towards what we are erecting in the place of earlier traditions and regimes. How do politics and our stupid bodies mesh? Is talking about fantasy and aggression, or working to prevent violence against women and gays while not preaching an authoritarian line, political? I don't know.

The problem is to integrate ideas about subjectivity forged in the frame of the particular (the singularity of the body's history as encountered in psychoanalysis) with larger programmatic goals with political ends – for example, the ideological traps of 'psycho-education'. These are issues that refer to subjectivity itself – that is, to how we understand the ways the body intersects with broader social demands, the fantasies that sustain these social ideals, and the way we can intervene at this interstice.

But the outside world for critical and noncritical psychology at the university level typically emerges in the form of a teaching and the commitments that follow therein. In a recent conference on psychoanalysis and culture, a number of academics and some clinicians tried to grapple with their own (lack of) social relevance and the anxieties generated by their respective positions. But it seems that a filtered form of cultural critique emerges from the university and that filtered form is a subtext in every moment that one teaches. As well, university discourse is a form of subjective seduction that can be undertaken in such a way that more is at stake than the production of knowledge. Were this seduction not a question of one's being and desire, our vocation would be a matter of indifference. Although I would happily imagine another more activist university and have participated in such alternative educational settings in the 1970s, I am not therefore utterly cynical about what it means to teach, write and think in the current climate.

12

A Central American Voice

Ignacio Dobles Oropeza

Critical psychology?

From my perspective and experience, critical psychology entails assuming a radical position toward the oppressive aspects of the social, political and economic order, and at the same time examining thoroughly the consequences of the practice of psychology as a discipline. I understand radicality in the sense of *'going to the roots'* of problems to identify and confront factors of power that underlie psychosocial issues and related sociopolitical concerns.

I understand perfectly that a general idea like the one I have just outlined can take very diverse forms, and that the pretence of 'criticality' can easily get lost in discourses or claims that are very distant from actual practices. The Marxist axiom that *'praxis is the best criterion for truth'* seems to be pertinent here. I also consider it important that reflexivity or self-critique plays a major role in this 'criticality'. By this I mean the possibility or at least the intention of identifying one's own inevitable limitations or contradictions while attempting to construct a psychological practice that differs from the hegemonic one. Spears (1997), while recognizing the great diversity existing in the realm of critical social psychology, proclaims that this reflexivity is a major characteristic common to the different critical stances in the discipline which distinguishes them from mainstream psychology. Let us assume and hope that he is right.

I also understand that the search for a critical position in psychology has been nourished from very diverse sources, and that this criticality must be understood in specific social, economic and political contexts. By no means can it be separated and isolated from what is occurring outside the discipline in social, political, cultural or artistic movements, for example. In this manner, I consider that the need to understand psychological practice in its historical and social context is paramount, as Martín-Baró duly pointed out when reflecting on the course of Latin American psychology as a whole (Dobles 1986). He insisted that psychological action engage the most important problems of the majority of the populace in our underdeveloped countries, including these sectors as valid and necessary interlocutors in actions that seek to widen spaces of liberation and autonomy, in individual but also in social terms. It is clear, however, that most of our psychologists, including some who label themselves 'critical', have a particular allergy for this perspective, because it is often more comfortable and safe to protect oneself behind the walls of college campuses, disconnecting theoretical elaboration from immersion in a reality that is, simply put, full of unpleasantries.

Maybe Roque Dalton, the revolutionary Salvadoran poet, put it in more poignant terms when he stated in the early 1970s:

> *Queridos psicólogos sociales,*
> *sociólogos progresistas*
> *no jodan tanto con eso de la enajenación*
> *aquí donde el problema es la nación ajena.*

> [Dear social psychologists,
> progressive sociologists
> don't bother us with that alienation stuff
> here is where the problem is, the alien nation.]

Critical psychology and the powers that be

In Latin America, a long and at the same time a very short road has been travelled in this search. So far, several attempts have made to articulate proposals and practices that question paradigms of social power: in political psychology (Montero 1987, 1991); in community psychology (Montero 1991); in the construction of psychological interventions in repressive contexts (ILAS 1994; Martín-Baró 1990); and in attempts to critically revise basic categories in the social psychology tradition (Martín-Baró 1983, 1989; Montero 1991). This is only a small sample, of course, of courageous efforts in difficult situations. But on the whole, I don't think that Latin American psychology is in a position very different from when Martín-Baró concluded with pessimism in 1989 that it had failed to deal with the realities and problems of our *people* (Martín-Baró 1990).

Old truths seem to survive, somehow, and the key issue is social power. I think that this 'critical' current in our psychology runs the risk, when it is not silenced or directly repressed, of being neutralized by power factors in our society. A lot can be said, from our experience working in marginalized communities, regarding the manner in which the concept of 'participation' has been adopted by government and sometimes non-governmental agencies to manipulate groups, or how the concept of autonomy or self-management (*autogestión*) has been used to reduce the responsibilities and social support functions of the state in the context of the neo-liberal transformation of our institutions. '*Hay que saber para quien se trabaja*' (You have to know who you work for) is something that a countryman (or woman) could say. In no way can we underestimate the capacity that established social powers have for reinventing themselves, and in this questionable role, psychology itself has proved useful, in both its practice and its discourse.

Finally, I have no doubt that this critical psychology, in our context, has not been able to articulate a clear and solid alternative that could successfully confront a hegemonic psychology that continuously reinforces its scientistic and technocratic foundations while it responds to a social demand that seeks from the psychologist the distribution of recipes for an 'easy' life, with no room for suffering or complications. This depends, of course, on the social sector involved. At the other extreme is a psychology so cryptic and abstract that, even with its most refined conceptual and linguistic games, it ends up being totally inoffensive and even blessed as a necessary luxury by the established social powers.

Background

I guess that this narration ends up being the tale of a search that has fortunately been shared by other colleagues. What has been my path in this slippery, complex and at times dangerous road? My professional training began in the field of engineering in the

University of Virginia. My immersion in an experimental educational alternative in Caracas, Venezuela, the Association for a New Education, quickly and inevitably led me to psychology. My training in Virginia was marked by a radicalized behaviourism and by Piagetian psychologists who were at the time the alternative 'others' to a firmly implanted traditional behaviourist orientation.

Later on, upon moving to Costa Rica, my place of birth, I quickly became involved with literacy programmes in communities in the northern part of the country using the methodology developed by the influential Brazilian educator Paolo Freire, and soon after that I also assumed responsibilities in the political and trade union movement, working as an organizer. At the same time, I formed part of a group of Costa Rican psychologists who were trying to develop and practise an alternative psychology in an academic context in which training began with psychology textbooks distributed by what was left of the USA-sponsored Alliance for Progress. Those texts, far from working on the universal problems as they claimed, tended to focus on the issues that preoccupied the same North American academic psychology, predominantly conservative and behaviourist, that I had seen questioned in Virginia by Piagetians and politicized behaviourists.

My introduction to Marxist contributions, and the influence of psychologists and social psychologists from the Southern Cone of the continent, were decisive for the development of a perspective that sought to engage the problems we identified in our society from critical positions. It is necessary to point out, at this junction, that unlike other countries in our continent, like Colombia or Brazil (Rodrigues 1975), Costa Rican social psychology (at the time the only one being developed in the region except for the initial efforts of Martín-Baró in El Salvador) never went through that peculiar phase of development that implied replicating laboratory experiments that had been carried out with undergraduate students in US universities. Instead, from the very beginning scientistic pretensions were abandoned and a very wide range of methodological alternatives were developed. Many research projects were developed with groups, communities, prison populations and so on. In hindsight, a major weakness was the abandonment of theoretical and conceptual elaboration in the midst of a pronounced activism. This was also true, I believe, of a great deal of psychological work carried out in the region in the 1980s, for instance, in Nicaragua. In the whirlwind of a process of deep social change, psychological work was not duly shared and processed, theoretically or methodologically.

It is not until the 1980s that a regional perspective with a critical outlook emerged in Central American psychology. We were also relatively isolated from what was occurring in other countries of Latin America, since eyes were usually set, following what seems to be a national and even continental tradition, on what was being done in the United States and in Europe.

In this context, my approach to a 'critical psychology' was heavily influenced by my life experiences as an organizer, trade union activist and political militant, strongly committed to the search for radical and profound political changes in the country and the region, and within a social order and system that I conceived as being basically unjust as well as economically dependent. While all this was happening, we found ourselves attempting to develop a Costa Rican social psychology that was basically born in a reactive manner, opposing itself to dominant parameters, and stressing the need to avoid dependence on hegemonic academic centres (Martín-Baró 1983; Dobles 1996).

Searches in Central American psychology in the midst of a regional crisis

Martín-Baró displayed a very shrewd perspective about all this, and there is nothing casual in his proposal for a 'social psychology for Central America' (Martín-Baró 1983, 1989). His work had a deep impact on many of us, because he was able to articulate the very poignant issue that the psychology in which we had been trained ignored the basic problems of the majority of the inhabitants of our beleaguered countries, and particularly those with whom we happened to work in politics, trade unions, communities and other groups. That psychology had very little to say about agrarian psychosocial problems, for instance, in countries that were predominantly agricultural. It had not trained us to contend with war and conflict situations (including psychological warfare) that we would soon be facing on a massive scale. Later on, in 1990, we attempted to develop a study programme in the School of Psychology of the University of Costa Rica 'De Cara a la Realidad' (Facing Reality) in which new fields were opened: psychology and religion, political processes, social discrimination, psychology and mass communication, and so on. Though we had some successes, it is also true that some professors and psychology students simply did not want to look at the reality they live in.

Something should be said about the national and regional context in which all this was occurring. The 1970s were years of 'social implosion' in the region. Transformative proposals of all sorts were unveiled. Revolutionary volcanoes erupted. Later, the reactions caused by the event of the Nicaraguan Revolution in 1979, and by the strength of guerrilla and revolutionary struggles in El Salvador and in Guatemala, along with a very pronounced US intervention, especially while Ronald Reagan was president, generated a strong war-mongering, militaristic and authoritarian wave that seemed to invade all social spaces. Revolution, we were suddenly reminded, breeds counter-revolution. It was no accident, then, that when we reactivated in 1987 the National Conference of Social Psychology in Costa Rica, after a decade of hibernation, and with the purpose of opening up possibilities in state agencies for social psychology work, the main thrust of that very successful event turned out to be the distinct dilemma of 'War or Peace?'

One of the first tasks of the Central American Public Opinion Program in 1987, an effort promoted and coordinated by Martín-Baró (Dobles 1990), was to use one of the most traditional instruments of social psychology – public opinion polls – to reveal the political misuse of this sort of survey to justify aid to the Nicaraguan Contras, which was then being ardently debated in the United States Congress. In general, previous official opinion surveys had been used to back militaristic solutions to the problems in the region, whereas, according to our studies, such solutions were clearly rejected by the population. The urgency of the problems facing the region, which also affected Costa Rica, conditioned much of our work. It should also be pointed out, however, that in the midst of that urgency, interesting reflections and discussions were also held concerning ethical aspects of public opinion work, or, to cite another example, about the use of national stereotypes in psychological warfare (McDonald et al. 1989). We did not assume, then, an

absolute rejection of quantitative methods employed by traditional social psychology, but rather attempted to re-elaborate
them as we developed an agenda that sought to engage problems that seriously affected the Central American population.
The idea was not that psychology could solve major social and
political problems by itself, but that it could not ignore them. In
the field of public opinion, in a very polarized and ideologized
regional context, psychology could contribute to a necessary
'de-ideologization' of the public debate, putting the people's
problems and concerns in the foreground.

Today, with a very evident fragmentation and dispersion in
efforts for developing a psychology that can respond critically to
our social problems, and with weakened regional coordination,
I believe it is more necessary than ever to make efforts that seek
to articulate critical perspectives in psychology, transcending
geographies. Efforts like the recent International Congress of
Social Psychology for Liberation, held in Mexico in November
1998, are good examples of what can be done. It is of the utmost
importance, I believe, to find links between those psychologists
developing critical stances in the developed countries and those
of us that work in undeveloped, poorer regions.

In the field of literature, critics like Ainsa have stressed the fact
that literary production in the last few years in Latin America
has helped to foster a dynamic in which the influence of different writers does not follow, necesarily, the unidirectional tradition of influences emanating from Europe or the United States,
but rather have created diverse mirrors in which different pro-
ductions are valued according to their styles and contributions,
not their geographical origins. I believe that this is an urgent
task for psychology, posing great challenges to Latin American
psychologists in particular, which could enrich different critical
efforts around the globe.

Challenges and tasks for critical psychology

In this terrain, those of us attempting to work from critical
perspectives in undeveloped societies face problems that differ
in some ways from those facing our colleagues in developed
capitalist countries, in that on the one hand we tend to face an
institutional apparatus linked to psychology that has less devel-

opment than the so-called psy-complex (Rose 1985) that has been confronted by critical psychologists in Europe and in the United States. For instance, criminal psychologists in our country, trained in a radical criminology tradition, have been suddenly faced with the challenge of directing prison reform systems. On the other hand, we face the immense power and prevalence that countries like the United States exert on psychology as a discipline (Moghaddam 1990). It is a challenge, indeed, that I barely gloss over, that the search for a 'critical psychology' should not reproduce the patterns of domination and dependence that have such a pronounced profile in dominant psychology.

In my opinion, and according to the previous considerations, critical psychology's basic tasks have to do with facing contradictions and power issues in everyday life and in the social order, with the purpose of widening personal and group autonomy and the possibilities for people to decide their own lives. This implies contributing to the development of true participation and democracy, and contributing to the creation of more just and equal social orders.

I am aware that this sounds quite utopian in an era of neoliberal globalization that widens the gap between the 'included' and the 'excluded' and that puts the possibilities for planetary survival in serious peril. But I think that a critical psychology, far from being dispersed in relativistic ethical parameters, must affirm basic ethical values, such as cooperation, solidarity, and justice, and confront a capitalist social order that creates increasing social differences and exclusions, and that seriously threatens ecological subsistence in our planet. In our Central American isthmus, poverty and other structural maladies are today even greater than when we began to search for alternatives in psychology. The fire from the volcanoes of the 1970s and 1980s may have ceased for the moment, but the earth is still quaking underneath. Democratic changes and living conditions are fragile, and many of the structures that fostered social inequality and repression in the past (including some armies with dismal records on human rights) are basically intact. Recent events in Guatemala, where a mobilized Right has defeated in the electoral booths constitutional changes that would have recognized the rights of the indigenous population, are a case in point.

Latin American community psychology, with its emphasis on participant research strategies, is still an important source of experience in the necessary construction of real domains of collaboration and democracy with authentic participation. The issue of power, however, including the researcher's institutional and personal power, is still a thorny one.

A critical psychology, paraphrasing the 'ethics of liberation' proposed by Dussel (1998), has to be a psychology for life, facing in a definite way the problem of its material and practical sustenance. In that sense, commitment becomes a fundamental aspect. That is, critical psychology needs to adopt, without romanticism or idealization, the perspective of those that suffer unjust systems of domination and inequality (Dussel 1998). Martín-Baró (in Dobles 1986) pointed out, on the basis of the teachings of liberation theology, that Latin American psychology has the urgent task both of identifying the 'popular virtues' that allow oppressed and discriminated sectors of the population to survive in even the most dire situations and also of adopting a 'critical commitment' that implies not only identification with those who suffer most, but also with the possibility of 'distancing oneself' to look with critical eyes at projects emanating from the oppressed. This is an extremely complex but necessary task.

I realize that such a proposal puts me near the camp of the defenders of 'empowerment', a concept that has been fundamental for feminist psychology and for some currents of community psychology. However, the critical discussion posed by Prilleltensky (1997) needs to be considered, because far from diluting efforts in the search for specific interests or anchoring them in the limited perspective of particular groups, it is necessary, in my opinion, to reinvigorate more general categories, such as the Marxist concepts of ideology and class consciousness, to place individual and specific issues in more global perspectives. Upon transcending these more specific domains, though, a critical psychology should not ignore the conflicts and contradictions that inevitably appear when it appeals to hypothetical 'common interests' that ignore class and ethnic factors and, in general, the people's real lack of power in concrete situations. After all, we are told day in and day out that globalization is a sort of 'land of opportunities', a global village where everybody gains something. However, as Orwell might have said, some groups (and countries) seem to be more equal than others. Once again, it seems to me that old truths die hard.

I have had the opportunity to work actively in projects with Costa Rican *campesinos* involved in land conflicts, working with pivotal issues such as identity, violence and its effects, historical memory and organization (Dobles 1995) and also in community and group efforts in organization. I believe that our experience in such projects shows the importance, in organizational and psychosocial work, of understanding the life experiences of specific groups in the major context of social contradictions existing in an underdeveloped capitalist country. Otherwise, it is likely that groups that lack social power will end up reproducing patterns of action that are fostered by hegemonic interests. Also, it is important to work on the power issues, including those that concern the psychologists themselves.

Another aspect, already mentioned, is the need for this 'critical psychology' to be necessarily self-critical, willing to examine its basic ideas, results and so on, and above all to nourish itself from what occurs outside psychology, in social movements that dynamize and invigorate the need for new approaches, for renewed consideration of old problems. The influence of the women's rights movement and of the gay or ethnic activists in European and US critical psychology has been duly pointed out by Sampson (1996). The critical psychologist must keep an alert eye and actively seek these developments. In our context, a particularly powerful and influential example is that of liberation theology, and the linkage of a historical and social theory of groups (Martín-Baró 1989) with the circumstances and actions of the popular and trade union movement in El Salvador.

I believe that the current stage of development of a critical psychology demands that particular attention be paid to the political effects of its actions, the interests to which it responds, the people it serves, the parameters that guide it, and its real effects. The reality in which we attempt to carry out our work, in which the problems of poverty, social inequality, ecological destruction, dependence and individualism have been aggravated in a world in which injustice gains ground every day, demands an enriching interchange in which we can learn from each other, examining the accomplishments and frustrations of our work, in conjunction with those who from disadvantaged positions still want to change the world to make it more human.

In short, psychologists must form part of that 'critical community' (Dussel 1998) that seeks equality and justice. I understand that, to contribute in the task of changing the world, psychology must also change itself, but it cannot fall prey to the narcissistic temptation of looking at itself most of the time. The water is not clear enough to provide a clear reflection anyway.

13

Critical Psychology as Critical Vision

Edmund O'Sullivan*

At a most fundamental level, a critical perspective on society involves an orientation that pays careful attention to systems of power and power inequities; the connection of the personal world to the systems of production within the society (that is, the economic base), and has a normative foundation that brings with it the passion for social justice. There is also a core intention of emancipation that is oriented toward the enhancement of human freedom. A critical orientation is that foundational concern that holds issues of power equity paramount and takes as one of its core tasks the examination of power within the economic, political and cultural forces of the society in which the psychological profession is embedded. Critical psychology is a more specific location for the foundational concerns for equity, where equity issues map into psychological theories and practices. A critical orientation to both psychological theory and practice makes the fundamental assumptions that power relations must be acknowledged and codified. These power relations are driven by the economic forces in the society (class), in the differentiation of culture that allows cultures to be in dominant and non-dominant relations (race) and in the differences between the sexes that also engender hierarchy (gender).

The unique standpoint of a critical perspective is seen when it is understood that the vast portion of the field of psychology masks and ignores these relations of power domination in both its theories and practices. In most conventional training for psychologists, in all their myriad forms, there is an absence of

---

*Note: All references after 1994 are O'Sullivan as pertains to my name. Sullivan and O'Sullivan are one and the same.

reflection on their own placement in the orders of power. As a professional field in this century, American psychology has not, in any of its major theorizing, taken serious the placement of its theories and practices in the social arrangements of the society in which it is embedded. When one looks at psychology's brief history in the twentieth century, it is clear in the case of IQ testing, as an example, that psychological testers have carried the imprint of the power dominance of the existing social relations of power in the areas of gender, race and class (Sullivan 1984, 1990). Having worked with very intelligent psychological professionals in the field of education for over thirty years, I have found them very hard cases when it came to reflective awareness on matters of power and equity. This is changing as critical orientations move into more prominent places in the profession.

As far as I know, my book *Critical Psychology*, published in 1984, was one of the first in North America to go under the title of critical psychology. Phil Wexler's *Critical Social Psychology* was the other (Wexler 1983). At the time of our writing, there was no such a thing as critical psychology in the field of psychology. Psychology as a profession was unique in its absence of a critical viewpoint, contrasting with other fields as sociology, theology, philosophy, anthropology, political science and so on, which had well-developed critical viewpoints (Sullivan 1984). When I started work in what is now a critical perspective, I was predominantly motivated by personal reasons and not professional ones. In fact, my attempt to develop a critical perspective was to keep myself from abandoning the profession of psychology, which seemed densely opaque on issues of social justice and power inequity.

What brought me to a critical perspective in psychology was a larger critical perspective that I had in my social and political life. I am a 1960s person and I was involved in and influenced by all of the major movements of that era. Bottom line, these include the civil rights movement, the peace movement and the women's movement of the late 1960s and 1970s. There was a chasm between my social and political beliefs and my professional endeavours that I found difficult to hold. When I started to try to remedy my situation, I found no path-breaking forerunners in the field of psychology at the time. I had psychologist friends who were politically aware, but this did not carry over into their psychological practices. By 1975 a number of psychologists formed a working group for radical psychology. We met once or twice a year over the next four years. We had meetings in Toronto, New York and Montreal. The following people were involved: Leon Rappaport, John Broughton, Joel Kovel, Adrienne Harris, Ricardo Zuniga, Howard Gruber, Harry Garginkle and Arnold Kaufman. All of us, at the time, were influenced by Marxist thinking and thought it could shed some new dimensions on our work. What we accomplished over several years was basically a support group that would help us develop a deeply radical orientation to our discipline. The distances that we had to travel made it difficult to continue meeting, and after several years we went our separate ways. It was a very productive experience for me to grope at with like-minded colleagues. I continued on my own to develop a critical orientation to psychology, and my first published articles were critiques of the developmental structural of Piaget and Kohlberg (Sullivan 1977a, 1977b) the formative influences on my developing critical perspective were from scholarship outside of the field of psychology. My major influences were Antonio Gramsci, the cultural Marxist, John Macmurray the Scottish philosopher, who helped me define the core features of a personal-relational psychology, Hans Georg Gadamer and Paul Ricoeur in the area of the hermeneutics of interpretation and Jürgen Habermas, the German philosopher of critical theory (see Sullivan 1984).

From my perspective, the *core elements of a critical psychology* had a number of distinguishing features (Sullivan 1984, 1990). The first feature deals with the tension of individual and society. A core assumption of a critical psychological perspective is that the individual and society must always be seen and interpreted within a dynamic interacting tension. This core working assumption is that personal development exists within a larger matrix of person and society and that these core dimensions are dialectically related to one another. The second feature follows from the prior assumption because it situates a critical psychology in a broader interdisciplinary inquiry whose effort has an emancipatory intent. I have identified this as 'critical interpretation' (Sullivan 1984, 1990). Critical interpretation attempts to understand the personal world within the context of wider social structures and their power dynamics (for example, gender, class and race and the wider economy where power dynamics are played out). A critical psychology rests on the assumption that the personal world exists, is influenced by and influences the wider social context and cannot be considered apart from it.

What is the meaning of interpretation and further what is a critical interpretation? Is it critical interpretation of a phenomenological psychology? Is it the task of psychological interpretation to simply understand the world from the phenomenological viewpoint of the conscious intentions of what I refer to as the personal world of agents? Without precluding a profound sensitivity to the personal world of actors, the answer to all of the above questions is in the negative. In my own formulation of critical psychology, critical interpretation of the personal world is grounded, at the outset, in the 'intentional projects' of the person: their strivings, desires,visions and so on. A critical interpretative psychology, if it stopped there, would only have a phenomenological or hermeneutic turn.

Therefore, the critical moment in the interpretative system takes cognizance of the fact that much of human action has elements that transcend the conscious control of personal agency and intention, and is embedded in the social conditions that surround personal human consciousness. I have called these the 'structural' as opposed to the 'intentional' conditions of human action. I have identified some of these structural conditions as class, race and gender, and have elaborated their dynamics in my initial treatment of critical psychology (Sullivan 1984). Notwithstanding intentional action, human action must also be understood as being influenced by conditions outside human intervention. A specific example will elucidate my point. We now know that fluctuations in the economy, specifically at the level of unemployment, are the single most important source of changing admissions to mental hospitals. This statistic is also related to class structural dynamics. For example, the lower one's economic standing, the greater the cumulative impact of economic dislocation and unemployment. A finding such as this raises a note of caution, which is one of the tasks of critical interpretation of human action.

The third feature identifies critical psychological interpretation with an extended mode of inquiry that goes beyond, but can include, conventional experimental and correlational modes. Here narrative forms of inquiry such as life history, as well as the various ethnographic modes of inquiry, are suggested. These narrative modes of inquiry are more readily seen in disciplines such as history, sociology and anthropology.

The fourth feature I have identified with a critical perspective is the assumption that critical psychological inquiry is normative in nature. In the tradition of Emile Durkheim, I have assumed that psychology as a discipline is a normative science. With that assumption in mind, the sense of a science of psychology as value-neutral is seen as impossible, unrealistic and undesirable. Thus, in pursuing the work of psychology in all of its many guises and varieties, the psychological practitioner understands that her work is seen in a moral context. In order to do this, there must be a radical shift in ground, from the traditional theory (*episteme*) to practice (normative) dichotomy to that of a praxis orientation. A praxis orientation starts from the point of view of human action and formulates reflection on that action (that is, theory). This point of view is not a reverse dichotomy (that is, between practice and theory). The notion of praxis assumes that human action is *intentional* in nature and that reflection is embedded in human action.

The final feature is the emancipatory nature of critical psychology. For the field of psychology, this emancipatory intent is radical in nature and departs in a fundamental way from traditional psychology. A critical psychology takes as its task the issues that are related to human freedom. In my own perspective, the emancipatory interest in human freedom rests on the assumption that human action is *creative* and motivated to enhance the projects of human freedom.

To me, the central debate in a critical orientation to psychology is the site or location of psychological praxis. Although I have written a text at the level of paradigm and consider it important, I believe that critical psychology must be embedded in progressive social movements in society such as the ecology movement, the feminist movement, movements dealing with anti-racism and equity, the gay–lesbian movement and the human rights movement (O'Sullivan 1999). Although I think it important to have a critical presence within the discipline of psychology (for example, a wing of the American Psychological Association for critical work), the larger vision must transcend any one vision in the society. Critical psychology must, of necessity, be a resistance movement within the profession, challenging the varieties of structures of domination in which the vast majority of the profession is embedded and implicated (Sullivan 1984; Sullivan 1990). Instead of having one's primary loyalty within the discipline (psychological professionalism), a critical psychology must be oriented towards and embedded within the varieties of progressive movements mentioned above. The visionary aspect of a critical psychology must carry an emancipatory intent. I would define emancipatory intent as that expressed interest, within both psychological theory and practice, in the possibilities and expansion of human freedom. Although this intent may seem strange to the ears of many psychological professionals, it is not without precedent in the social sciences outside of psychology. The emergent critical perspective that can be seen in this volume is antedated by earlier critical efforts in sociology, anthropology and theology.

My initial work in a critical psychology

This started in the 1970s, when, as touched on already, I did extensive critical analysis of the developmental theories of Piaget and Kohlberg (Sullivan 1977a, 1977b, 1979). After completing these critique, I embarked upon a major work that covered the field of psychology and ended in my *Critical Psychology: An Interpretation of the Personal World* (Sullivan 1984). Since 1984, the major concentration of my work has been in education. Specifically, I have attempted to be part of an effort to embed a critical perspective into educational theory and research. Since the discipline of education draws heavily from psychological theories and research, my paradigmatic efforts in critical psychology have informed my work in educational psychology, curriculum and adult education. In all of these areas, I am part of an effort in education that I initiated with Henry Giroux and Roger Simon, which we labelled 'critical pedagogy'. Critical pedagogy has now become a concern in education worldwide. Three of my critical studies in this area of concern are exemplary. The first example is a study that looked at computer use in schools along gender and social class lines. In the 1980s, computers were being touted as the new panacea for all educational ills (Sullivan 1983). What seemed to be lacking in all of the rhetoric around computer use was that technology was not neutral when it entered into the power dynamics of schooling

in society. We studied a number of schools that differed along
social class lines, and within those schools we observed and
interviewed students and school personnel. We found that
there were differences in computer usage along social class
lines. Our school studies found that middle-class children had
more frequent access than working-class children to advanced
software programs both in school and at home. Sex differences
were found along gender lines exclusive of class difference.
There is a much greater tendency to direct girls to those tasks
in the work force that veer toward secretarial use (Olson and
Sullivan 1987; Sullivan 1990).

The second study on critical education was in the popular
adult education in Santiago, Chile. With several Chilean colleagues who mutually shared a critical perspective on education,
we developed a critical orientation to understand and enable
popular resistance education to the military junta under
Augusto Pinochet (Sullivan 1990). In a resource-starved popular
sector in Santiago we studied the role of women in organizing
and sustaining food security in their community. Our investigation did an in-depth study of popular leaders and organizers
who mobilized the community around food production. Our
popular educational research demonstrated how women much
more than men were the mobilizing infrastructure for popular
movements in Chile. The third example was in the area of a
critical pedagogy of the mass media (Sullivan 1987; Sullivan
1990). This media analysis was designed to show the powerful
effects of the mass media on the consciousness of children and
adolescents. My work here was to develop a pedagogy that
formed a resistance to the deep structures of consumerism that
pervade our culture. These three examples are very briefly
summarized. They nevertheless reveal a type of critical research
that systematically builds into the inquiry the power dynamics
of the society and the emancipatory issues that ensue from
them.

My most recent work is in the development of a comprehensive vision for education in the twenty-first century. The book's
title is *Transformative Learning: Building Educational Vision in the
21st Century* (O'Sullivan 1999). At present, I believe that a critical
orientation must attempt to embed itself in a larger vision of
ecological understanding and it must continue to formulate a
deeper understanding of difference and diversity that is framed

in a non-hierarchical context (O'Sullivan 1999). As I have developed my perspective in a global context, I have come to the conclusion that critique must be one moment within a larger visionary context. Therefore, critical psychology must not only be counter-hegemonic to mainstream psychology. It must also be embedded in a wider vision of both the person and the planet. Critical psychology needs to expand itself to a global context. To end this treatment, I would like to focus on issues of diversity and difference in a critical global context.

The pretensions of progress, in the twentieth century, are belied when we look at the violence perpetrated against peoples all over this planet. We see the fear of difference in xenophobia, racism, sexism, homophobia and religious fundamentalism. Frequently these isms meld together, but their final outcome is treating another group harshly on the basis of one difference or another. What can be seen, by the politics of exclusion, is a sense that the world would be better in one way or another if there was a convergence towards monoculture. Hitler's idea of the master race and the idea of ethnic cleansing are expressions of this monocultural convergence. This desire for monocultural convergence has often resulted in genocide. We know from the best scientific evidence that differences between peoples are not based on any biological superiority of one group of peoples over another. One of the perennial problems of community life is the presence of differences in power that led to structures of oppression and domination. We can see oppression and domination both between and within human groupings. Structures of oppression and domination exist at all levels of human interaction and seem to be present in human history from its very beginning. What we should be striving for, at the planetary level of our species involvement, is a community that holds together without collapsing and obliterating human diversity. Thus our planetary community, within a human context, must hold simultaneously, and with creativity, the tensions of differentiation, subjectivity and communion. When these tensions are collapsed we have a drift toward monoculture and a loss of species creativity. We also have the ugly spectre of racism and cultural xenophobia. Under these conditions we are constantly plagued with the evil of genocide. At a less extreme level, we encounter the marginalization of peoples, which has resulted in an increase in human rights violations especially in those areas of the world that are subject to the economic exploitation of the West. For those people who are marginalized and subordinated, almost all basic human needs are lacking. For example, indigenous peoples all over this globe are the victims of human rights violations that leave their needs for subsistence, protection, affection, understanding, participation, idleness, creation, identity and freedom unmet at all of the existential category levels.

When we turn to intragroup relations within communities we see that women all over this earth suffer at the hands of men under the dominance and sub-ordinance structures of patriarchy. This type of dominance not only occurs in all cultures and races in the modern world, it is also operating over all classes and ages. The structure of patriarchy operates globally. A critical psychology with planetary vision must seek to resist and transform the institutions of patriarchy. Women all over the earth are subject to structures of patriarchal dominance and are the victims of pervasive male violence. At the same time, the structure of male violence operates differently in different cultures and also operate differently within the same societies. What we do know is that gender roles leave women in subordinate positions within the structural conditions of patriarchy and that these conditions of oppression operate globally. Patriarchal socialization shapes the consciousness of both men and women, not with uniform results among individuals, to be sure, but with an informing orientation. A pervasive message of subordinance goes out to women from a variety of sources, giving women the sense that they are not to be taken seriously. This happens in commerce, medicine, and government, to name a few institutions. The structures of dominance and subordinance that exist under patriarchy hold men at a level of emotional shallowness and leave the contribution of women ignored and marginalized. The critical path out of patriarchal dominance toward more equitable relationships between men and women will open up new areas of diversity both for women and men. This said, it must be understood that the issue of gender must be seen alongside other issues of discrimination, based on race, culture and sexual orientation. If this does not happen, these differences are put in competition with gender and each other. When we give attention to gender discrimination without calling attention to racism, we can expect that racism or racist dominance is likely to occur. The same applies to sexual orientation, an area of difference to which we now turn.

We know historically and into the present that some people have wanted and created relationships of intimacy, sexual or not, with persons of their own sex, and other people have done it with people of the opposite sex, or with both sexes, in every culture and time from which we have any historical or anthropological records (Wishik and Pierce 1995). We also know that categories describing sexual diversity are used to oppress and to create dominance and subordinance. We can say with certainty that in Western culture heterosexuality is the norm, with other forms of sexual orientation severely marginalized. Our own culture defines heterosexuality and homosexuality as polar opposites and there is a tendency to deny the existence of bisexuality or other sexual orientations or identities. Our own culture compels heterosexuality and stigmatizes homosexuality and bisexuality by attaching to them negative social, economic and religious consequences (Wishik and Pierce 1995). Compulsory heterosexuality forms the basic frame for our culture's sex/ gender system and it has caused incredible social and individual damage to people whose sexual orientation puts them in the non-dominant position (for example, gays, lesbians and people of bisexual orientations). Heterosexually dominant societies like our own make it very difficult for individuals to accept any orientation and identity other than heterosexuality. Compulsive heterosexuality ascribes dominance to heterosexual people and subordinance to lesbians, gay males and bisexual people. This situation is sustained by a rigid hierarchy between heterosexuality and homosexuality and a denial of the existence of bisexuality. Here again, the issue of diversity becomes paramount. We are beginning to see a transition away from a dominance mode of compulsory heterosexuality. Our recent past was characterized by an almost total denial of the existence of sexual diversity, or, when the existence was acknowledged, it was accompanied by negative judgments about non-heterosexual orientations. Today, we are beginning to accept that our world has within it different types of sexual orientation and a range of cultural lifestyles that allows the visible presence of gay men, lesbians and bisexual people to be part of a wider sense of community. To educationally challenge compulsory heterosexism is to open the community to a more inclusive sense of community where more diverse sexual orientations are accepted as part of a community's diversity.

To bring this issue of diversity to a close, I want to leave the reader with a final reflection. Globalization does not lead to a consciousness of a wider and diverse world. This is the incredible irony of the current globalization process. What appears to happen in the advance toward globalization is the simultaneous development of a monoculture. What is sorely needed, in our present historical moment, is critical psychology that counters the forces of monoculture and opens all of us to the richer planetary culture of diversity.

14

Critically Speaking: 'Is it Critical?'

Contributing Members of the Discourse Unit, Manchester Metropolitan University, UK[*]

(*Collective Voice*)   We welcome the publication of this volume as an opportunity to dispel some of the myths and anxieties, as well as political and professional guilt, surrounding what is now popularly referred to as 'critical psychology'. In this chapter we attempt to explore and address some of the questions proposed as the common theme for this volume of essays on critical psychology. The answers to these questions are presented as a series of dialogues because we feel this format most accurately reflects the multiple and diverse identities that constitute the membership of the Discourse Unit in Britain, as well as the manner of the chapter's production (that is, mainly through e-mail). For this reason the text below is fragmented into both collective and individual voices. This format effectively challenges the fiction of the Discourse Unit and critical psychology as a coherent body of voices, as well as the validity of promoting critical psychology as a homogenous enterprise.

---

* The co-authors of this chapter are: Hakan Durmaz, Dan Heggs, Brenda Goldberg, Angel Gordo-López, Rebecca Lawthom, Terence McLaughlin and Janet Smithson. *Editor's note: This chapter was constructed primarily from e-mail messages, with only minor subsequent editing. The result is a chapter that appears to be the record of a group discussion when it is not. Somehow the synergy of the chapter creates a tone that some readers may perceive as dogmatic or arrogant. My discussions with many of the co-authors assures me that this was not at all the intention. What is intended, however, is an expression of indignation about what dominant psychology continues to be and an articulation of alternative perspectives that have been developed through a lot of hard work by the members of the Discourse Unit.*

In a nutshell, what does critical psychology mean to you? What are the hallmarks of critical psychology?

(*Voice A*)   Critical psychology is a label often used to refer to a set of voices opposed to experimental and positivist psychology. The emergence of recent forms of Anglo-Saxon-based critical psychologies, in particular British critical psychology, comes hand in hand with the so-called 'crisis' of psychology. The crisis of psychology has been rooted in the fact that social representation and social cognition could no longer, of themselves, account for social reality. It is in this sense that critical psychologists appeal for further connections between sociopolitical issues, 'subjectivity' and psychological theories. The crisis of psychology and, therefore, the emergence of critical psychology in the Britain coexisted with the Thatcher years and the rise of the New Left in Europe. It is not surprising, therefore, that some of the hallmarks or politico-theoretical antecedents of critical psychology in terms of the Discourse Unit were anti-humanist versions of Marxism and feminism as a reaction against structuralist ideas in the social sciences – that is, anthropology, philosophy, sociology, linguistics and semiotics. It would be a mistake to underestimate the many tensions and different approaches prevailing in the various critical psychology groups, which in Britain are mostly located in discursive research centres. Here, some influential research groups have opted for more extreme forms of ethnomethodological research, which retain a psychological faith in transparent communication whether in the forms of shared meanings (symbolic interactionism) or structural frames (ethnomethodology or microsociology). Other groups, meanwhile, are more concerned with Foucauldian, Marxist and feminist analysis of power and discourse. Despite the differences, what seems to be a constant in British critical discursive psychology is the 'turn to language'. Within the Discourse Unit, this 'turn to language' has manifested itself as Marxist, feminist, post-structuralist and psychoanalytically informed types of discourse analysis.

(*Voice B*)   If the 1960s and 1970s were the decades in which sociopolitical movements (that is, student, feminist, peace, gay/lesbian, and environmentalist) shattered the foundations of modern capitalism, the 1980s and 1990s symbolized both the academization of those social movements and the maturation of hypercapitalism. If the 'turn to language' was the hallmark of critical psychology until the end of the 1980s, the turn to psychoanalysis and critical, but nevertheless therapeutic, discourses and interests seem to be saturating the 'self' of critical psychology at the dawn of the millennium.

(*Collective Voice*) How critical is critical psychology when it partakes of psychology's terminology and methodological practices? For instance, in this text our critical voices reproduce the interviewer–interviewee (questionnaire) format of psychological expertise, opaque language and amateur recipients (or readers). These structures are strongly invested with pedagogical, psychological, marketing and political discourses. Although we understand and support the motivation of this sort of material – we're inputting into it after all – we are wary of turning it into just another academic exercise. We are reminded that while capitalist relations in the West are moving into a post-modern phase, modernist (including mass production, low wages, child workers, poverty) modes of production are now being exported into Second and Third world countries. With the collapse of the Soviet block (and allied countries) an incredible amount of fresh resources (including, material resources and cheap labour/consumer markets, as well as psychological concepts) have been opened up for the exploitation of 'developing' countries. Already we find critical psychology in Third World countries being incorporated in a progressive form but with often 'unintended' oppressive effects. The psychological style of these questions, along with their expert-amateur investments, help to fuel doubts of the global/local repercussions of exporting Western-defined critical voices and theories to a worldwide audience. We could find critical psychology appropriating under one heading a diverse range of pre-existing radical groups and practices who have never even thought of themselves as associated with, never mind as, psychologists (whether critical or otherwise). Bearing this in mind, we believe that it is not possible to talk of an organized critical psychology that renders many different practices and purposes accountable under one label. Instead, as members of the Discourse Unit, we feel our specific role is to contribute to critiques of psychology both in academice and within the wider psychological culture, while at the same time respecting and supporting all other types of international action, irrespective of what the participants want to call themselves.

(*Voice C*) I see critical psychology as primarily critical action or intervention. However, as with all dependent action, when one is put on the spot, it can be very difficult to give a definitive description of what that content or action should be. By its nature, critique is defined by what it contests and, consequently, takes its shape and materiality in the act of contestation. Thus, critical analysts should watch for changes in the ideological landscape, especially those occurring in institutions like psychology. As with any critical activity, there is a problem of counteracting accusations of negativity. Thus both strategically and professionally there is a temptation to try to formalize critical action. On the plus side, giving form and coherence to critical perspectives means they will at last reach a wider audience among academics and students – a worthwhile endeavour. But on the other hand, we risk distorting the aims of critical projects by suggesting it is the methodology or structure that is critical, rather than the application that it is put to (a tendency that already afflicts some discursive methodologies). As we give rational shape to a new paradigm called 'critical psychology' we risk achieving credibility and empirical validity at the price of rejecting heterogeneity and, as the title to the book suggests, a plethora of voices. By trying to integrate these multiple voices of dissent, and diverse sites of critical action, we reject diversity in favour of the unified voice, which, although it might initially have some impact in getting critical perspectives noticed, will atrophy into collusion as all unified generalizing (psychological) models tend to. In doing so, we encourage the notion of criticality as a thing rather than as an ethical and political engagement. How do you put those things into a psychology book unless you obscure and encode the issues and agendas out of all recognition, so that it just becomes another psychology textbook?

(*Voice D*) I suspect that the questions we are being asked contain assumptions about critical psychology and so are limited in their scope. Critical psychology, in these questions, is something that can be done. I don't think that it is. As an empty concept it becomes open to reclamation and flexible enough to be used as justification for a number of differing practices. Does this make sense, or am I just ranting? Either way, I fear it offers an over-arching rubric that ties together very different practices and that it is not necessarily helpful to be identified as a critical psycho-logist

(*Voice B*)   I suspect 'critical psychology' is seen by some as a tactical move to disturb the hegemony of mainstream psycho-logy without necessarily challenging the concept of psychology itself and where any overt challenge might result in being marginalized in academia.

(*Voice D*)   I would like it to be an enquiring and interrogative attitude toward the practices and assumptions of mainstream psychology – not an alternative. I would also want critical psychology to be a set of practices (whether theoretical or not) that make interventions into psychological practices.

(*Voice E*)   Critical psychology or critical psychologies are diverse slants on mainstream psychology. They are necessarily 'other' to the dominant paradigm which has permeated aca-demic psychology. However, it is this very 'otherness' that cre-ates a space from which critical psychologists can theorize.

(*Voice F*)   Critical psychology is an approach to questions that psychology traditionally addresses, including the social and political aspects thrown up by psychology. But I think that really all psychology should be critical and that the term 'critical psychology' is a bit irritating, as surely all psychologists, just like people in all other academic disciplines, should be reflecting critically on their work. I would prefer to say that I am trying to 'do' psychology critically, rather than 'do critical psychology'.

What brought you to critical psychology?

(*Collective Voice*)   We were unaware of being located within this thing called 'critical psychology' until critical psychology started to manifest itself within the Discourse Unit via students, visitors, publications, conferences and so on. This is a paradoxical situation to come to terms with when being asked to contribute to a book on critical psychology. One way to clarify what we mean by being critical, rather than being critical psychologists, can be better understood by bearing in mind the shift of discourse analysis into discursive psychology. This move was one that split psychological trends. Within this context, appropriating the term 'critical' became a way of differentiating ourselves from more reductionist, empirical and even cognitive trends in psychology.

(*Voice D*)   I don't think anything brought me to critical psychology. There was no Damascene experience. One moment I was happily playing with discourse and cultural studies, the next there was a movement and a new legend to put on conference papers.

(*Voice E*)   Feminism and concerns with women's experience brought me into the fold.

(*Voice F*)   I was already using some of the approaches that are currently being collected under the 'critical psychology' heading, particularly feminist psychology, and discursive psychology, before the term 'critical psychology' was being widely applied. I came to these areas as a feminist who felt that traditional psychological methods ignored the social, political and environmental factors that I viewed as essential to an understanding of 'behaviour'.

(*Voice C*) How did I get into critical psychology? I was attracted there by a very unscientific gut reaction, which said there was something very wrong with a discipline that needed to construct and exploit pathology just to rationalize and justify its own existence. Having come from sociology I was also in search of 'the social' that seemed to be missing from social psychology, as well as any other type of psychology. I vaguely felt that language was the missing link I was looking for. There followed an interest in such writers as Bruner and Vygotsky, which eventually led to an interest in discourse analysis – not, I might say, as a methodology, but as a way of critiquing abusive ideologies where they primarily manifest themselves – in discourse.

(*Voice A*)   The tone of this question exemplifies the way North American ego psychology is accommodating new criticalities to its own interests and rendering visible the limits of critical psychology. The personal and confessional dimension of the question is symptomatic of a damaging and individualizing version of subjectivity that I thought critical psychology was supposed to contest. Consequently, the question is not what brought me or you or them to critical psychology, but what sort of institutional dynamics led us to perceive alliances and possibilities of cooperation against wider issues, whether psychological or not. Surely, the point is not about our individual critical choices but about the historical dynamics of institutional oppression and how we can best detect and counteract their self-perpetuating dynamics.

What do you see as the basic principles or concepts of critical psychology?

(*Voice D*)   An awareness of the importance of language, culture and ideology are, for me, all essential.

(*Voice E*)   What are the basic principles or concepts of critical psychology? If we accept that the aim of critical and political engagement is change then the agenda is set. It is to represent and advocate for individuals and communities who have been marginalized, excluded and oppressed. This representation should include critical thinking both within the discipline and outside it. Any theorizing we engage in should emerge from practice and the experiences of such people. If this is to happen, that is, without simply theorizing, then accessibility seems a key issue. This means engagement with oppressed and marginalized groups, and speaking and theorizing with them and from them. If our role as critical psychologists is to deconstruct and problematize psychology then science should no longer be powerful and/or opaque. We need to be open to all, recognizing academia as a privileged site that prioritizes accessibility to academic discourse over experiential accounts.

(*Voice F*)   Critical psychology should emphasize ethical issues in research and practice. This involves awareness of the oppressive uses and abuses of psychology and a desire to combat these.

(*Voice A*)   It is impossible to identify any key principles without first considering the context of articulation and the different international as well as disciplinary investments in each of those contexts. For instance, while mainstream psychological research has been used in critical ways in Central America (as, for example, by Martín-Baró), critical forms of developmental psychology have been incorporated and translated in rather reactionary ways in developmental programmes in other geographical contexts (for example, India), and with often devastating effects. We need to bear seriously in mind the ethics and possibly negative repercussions of unpacking and delivering critical psychology worldwide.

(*Voice F*)   Critical psychology should address the widening inequality and injustice between rich and poor nations, including the exploitation of poorer regions by the rich, powerful countries; injustices due to racism, sexism and ethnic differences. As we speak, overconsumption is progressing in the First World at a rate that is likely to destroy the environment. What should be done about these problems? Well, ideally everyone should live in a way that does not exploit other people and support an environment that is sustainable for all to live in that way. That's totally idealistic of course, but still in real life it would be nice if our research and activity (whether we call it psychology, critical psychology, or something else) had a net positive effect on these issues, so that the world was a bit more equal and just.

(*Voice G*)   Let's go back to the roots (Gk *krisis*, decision; *krites*, judge). In short, no crisis, no critical. Let's not forget that this crisis of representation is little different from the crisis in psychology in the 1920s in the USSR – set against the rise of Stalinism and the rising globalization of bureaucratic forms. The so-called 'critical' was always a science – or a literacy – in the name of the oppressed masses – was always a crisis of leadership. Remember the suppression of Lev Vygotsky and the assassination of Martín-Baró – and let's not pretend it won't happen again.

What have you done, or what do you do, that exemplifies these principles? In other words, how do you practise critical psychology?

(*Voice D*)   I don't practise critical psychology. I'm not even sure that critical psychology should be thought of in terms of practice.

(*Voice E*)   I teach critical perspectives even when teaching mainstream psychology courses, – that is, counselling, social psychology. I have also taught on women's studies courses, helped on a rape crisis line and done voluntary work with disabled people. Critical psychology doesn't have to be a mystical forum for academics and can be practised in small acts with individuals, for instance, reassuring a female student of her ability, or listening to difficult family experiences. Being a critical psychologist (whatever that means) is about challenge.

(*Voice F*)   Well, I try and approach issues from a critical position, questioning the methods, assumptions and uses of the research I'm involved in. But I would call this a feminist perspective rather than a critical psychology perspective. I don't feel I need the term 'critical psychology' to define my work.

(*Voice G*)   Some of us have helped to build the international hearing voices movement (Intervoice) which is directly concerned with the liberation of those pathologized by the psy-complex. As a researcher, my first position was as an open critic of psychology. The second was to establish that my involvement with deconstruction was not the deconstruction of voice hearers, which is how research and diagnoses is often felt, but deconstruction of the institutions of psychopathology. Deconstruction, by the way, is just about the worst thing that could happen to any person or institution. We have also established a publishing house, Handsell Publishing, which changes the face of power relations in print and in conferences – and a consultancy and training network (ACT), which has turned the knowledge base on its feet. Armed with this we march upon the academe demanding validation. Such a strategy, of course, deepens the 'critical' responsibility.

From your standpoint in critical psychology, what are the most pressing, general social/political problems?

(*Voice F*) These are my views of what the big debates are: (a) how to, or whether we should, move away from individualistic paradigms of psychology (as much of feminist psychology, and perhaps lesbian and gay psychology, have already done); (b) How to move away from a white Western perspective to include other approaches and perspectives in psychology (though it's much easier to acknowledge the importance of this than to do it); (c) How to make critical approaches accessible and meaningful to people who are not 'experts', such as those without an academic or professional background, given that much critical work is almost incomprehensible to most people and, as such, very exclusive and elitist.

(*Voice E*) This is a hard question – social injustice in any form seems pressing, so racism, prejudice of any kind and vast social inequalities are key issues for me.

(*Voice D*) The term 'critical psychology' implies expert knowledge, so reinforcing assumptions of psychology as an expert discipline where society and culture can once more be pathologized. It also seems to divorce politics from practice. I am not happy with this as a question that some might well take seriously.

(*Voice C*) I cannot remember ever self-consciously deciding to do critical psychology. I just felt that although psychology pretended to be a science it was in fact highly illogical and irrational. The experiments and theories it advocated for understanding human behaviour seemed at best spurious and at worst downright abusive. It is the fact that psychology is so theoretically bereft that allows it to propagate 'practice' so unproblematically. Consequently, 'theory', or rather theorizing practice, seemed the best way to contest some of the worst abuses. My interest in 'theory' led to an engagement with feminism and, in latter years, to theorizing or analysing the manifestation of psychological concepts in the wider culture. To return to a point I made above, I feel my role as a social analyst is one of vigilance: being aware of potentially abusive theories/

practices and challenging them when I think I see them. Because the social environment is ever changing, what constitutes 'the most pressing general social/political problems' is apt to reprioritization. Hence comes the importance, for me at least, of not appropriating one academic identity, of maintaining an interdisciplinary stance, and of keeping a critical distance from any theories and methodologies even as I use them, as in another context these themselves may need to be contested.

Design/answer another question

(*Voice B*)   Where does tactical positioning end and where does it become collusion? I believe a critical approach within any academic discipline must of necessity include self-reflection of that discipline's own discourses, and how these impact on the wider community. It is the act of self-reflection that enables us as critical academics to move beyond psychology to look at the power/knowledge relations existing in academic discourse. Without this, any claim to criticality is not only partial but risks being hypocritical. Following this, a critical attitude should work in bridging the gap between academics and everyday life in society. This involves intentionally undermining psychology's own mythical, rational, omnipotent place in society, challenging the *status quo*, and building genuine, mutual horizontal links with non-academic life. In this way genuine new modes of interaction will be created within and without.

(*Voice F*)   Is 'critical psychology' just a marketing tool for selling new textbooks by hailing it as the next new way of doing psychology? Is it a tactic to bring more people into this approach to psychology, which feminists, for instance, have been using already? And another thing, how come it's apparently dominated by white, educated, Western men, or is that just my impression?

Additional information about the Discourse Unit

Psychology Politics Resistance (PPR) is a network of people – both psychologists and non-psychologists – who are prepared to oppose the abusive uses of psychology. This means challenging the ideas within psychology that lead to oppressive practices, supporting those who are on the receiving end, and using psychological knowledge positively to help those engaged in struggles for social justice.

To subscribe to Psychology Politics Resistance, to write for the PPR newsletter or to organize something in your area, contact Ian Parker, PPR Psychology, Bolton Institute, Deane Road, Bolton, BL3 5AB UK; tel: 01204 528851 (ext. 3105); fax: 01204 399074; international fax: +44 1204 399074; e-mail: <I.A. Parker@Bolton.ac.uk>.

15

To overturn all circumstances in which the human is a degraded, a subjugated, a forsaken, a contemptible being

Thomas Teo

In a nutshell, what does critical psychology mean to you? What are the hallmarks of critical psychology?

The title of this chapter, a quotation from Marx, provides inspiration for my critical reflections and may represent the goal for critical practice. However, critical psychology in the Euro-American context does not necessarily always exhibit a connection between theory and practice. Of course, from an ideal point of view, critical psychology presents a unity of theory and practice, but what theory and practice means depends on the cultural-historical context. I believe that the role of critical psychology in the Euro-American world is different from that in Latin America, Asia or Africa. Indeed, critical psychology in Euro-America often assumes the role of a *status-quo*-challenging, reflective theory of the individual whose existence is mediated through the socioeconomic process. Often there are no immediate practical consequences of theoretical critical psychology, a fact that I do not consider a problem, given the many theoretical tasks of critical psychology. I suggest that critical psychology, as a theoretical endeavour, should be motivated by a practical utopia but not necessarily by immediate practice. Moreover, we should be reflective about critical practices, because these practices are prone to mistakes, compromises and justifications that themselves require critical evaluation.

Critical psychology as a theoretical endeavour should change our psychological knowledge about the individual in society, and in doing so may pave the way to overturn those circumstances in which the human is degraded, subjugated, forsaken and contemptible. An emphasis on theory constitutes my personal focus, as my main activities in critical psychology have been academic. In this vein, I have suggested (Teo, in press) that psychological knowledge in general serves different functions according to which subsystems of psychology and implicit utopias may be derived. Academics working within *scientific psychology* attempt to provide an analytic account of parts of psychological objects or events. They are motivated by the implicit utopia to produce better cumulative knowledge. From the perspective of critical psychology, this type of psychology can be labelled mainstream psychology or traditional psychology. In contrast, *cultural psychologists* attempt to produce meaning for individuals, communities and cultures. They are motivated by the implicit utopia to improve the human condition. Non-mainstream but traditional research programmes such as psychoanalysis, hermeneutics, humanistic and existential approaches may be subsumed under this category. Theoretical *critical psychologists* monitor and challenge traditional ideas and produce advanced critical theories, methods and concepts. Critical psychology may be based on a Marxist, feminist, post-structuralist, anti-racist, anti-heterosexist or critical-theoretical framework. Critical psychology has become an international network (see Teo 1997, 1998b).

In order to illuminate the activities of critical psychologists within academia I will differentiate between deconstruction, reconstruction and construction of psychological knowledge (see Teo 1999). I use the term *deconstruction* in the sense of a pure critique of psychological theories and practices. These critiques are based on philosophical or metatheoretical frameworks such as socialist feminism. Deconstructive critical psychology embodies a vast literature that explicitly criticizes bourgeois male psychology and areas of psychology such as clinical, personality or organizational psychology. Critical psychologists have challenged psychology's philosophy and ethics, its methodologies and methods, its assumptions about human nature and its numerous concepts and terms (see Fox and Prilleltensky 1997). As *reconstruction* I refer to the critical reconstruction of psychological theories, methods and concepts by theoretical, logical or historical means. Most significant for a critical reconstruction of contemporary psychology are historical works (see Danziger 1997). Topics such as how gender, class, race or power influences psychological research practices are included within the domain of critical reconstruction, as is the attempt to translate critical concepts for traditional psychologists (see Teo 1997).

As *construction* I denote the elaboration of specific critical categories such as emancipation, liberation, alienation, power and oppression within psychology. It refers to the development of psychological theories, concepts, methods and practices based on a critical framework (see Teo 1998b). Analyses that allow for an adequate understanding of racism, sexism and classism are also subsumed under this category. The critical construction of traditional concepts such as learning, perception, cognition and emotion are also included within this domain (compare Teo 1998a). Construction often goes hand in hand with deconstruction and reconstruction, and the division of theoretical critical psychology into deconstruction, reconstruction and construction is *ideal-typic*. Although critical psychologists have developed many skills in deconstructing and reconstructing psychology, it seems that the constructive part has been widely neglected. It is my hope that critical psychologists will contribute more profoundly to the constructive part of critical research than has previously been the case.

At this point I wish to emphasize that there exists no inherent connection between any particular methodology and critical psychology. Critical psychologists may use qualitative as well as quantitative methods in their work. For instance, qualitative methods are useful in *giving voice* to individual members of marginalized groups, whereas quantitative analyses are indispensable for determining pay inequities (see also Febbraro 1997).

What brought you to critical psychology?

This question requires some caution, as autobiographical information may suggest more coherence and continuity than actually exists. I think I have experienced a tremendous discrepancy between my expectations for the reflective power and problem-solution potential of psychology and the reality of how psychology was taught in university. I think I always had an intuition that mainstream psychology may be substantially limited. Especially frustrating and shortsighted were social psychology, personality psychology and intelligence theories based on a factor-analytic reification of statistics. I found the *methodologism* of psychology, which allowed for the study of a topic only when it could be pressed into the experimental-statistical corset, to be foolish. I achieved theoretical satisfaction with the study of philosophy, while developmental psychology seemed the only reasonable and interesting approach in psychology, as it appeared dialectical *per se*. Developmental psychology also allowed me to follow my interests in Habermas, who incorporated Piaget and Kohlberg into his theory (see Teo 1986).

Scientific psychology in Vienna (where I studied) meant general-experimental and method-dominated psychology while excluding all other approaches to the psyche. Intuitively I understood that a truly scientific psychology would be able to understand and grasp human subjectivity rather than exclude it. Only later could I label these intuitions and rephrase them in terms of the crisis phenomena within psychology (Teo 1993). Obvious to me were the lack of practice in mainstream psychology, the ideological biases, and the arbitrary inflation of concepts through operationism. Later, I became aware of the racism and sexism of psychology from a theoretical, a practical and also a historical point of view.

An important book in my development was Grubitzsch and Rexilius's (1981) *Psychological Concepts*. This book offered, in the form of a dictionary, alternative views on psychological topics. I still think that the Anglo-American context of critical psychology could benefit from such a project. The same authors edited a book on testing (Grubitzsch and Rexilius 1978) that showed blatantly the problems of power in psychological testing and offered a diametrically opposite view to university courses. If I think about which English books have influenced me, Chorover's (1979) impressive critical analysis of the power of behavioural control comes to mind. From a theoretical point of view the works of J. Habermas, K. Holzkamp and M. Foucault (in that order) became important. I read articles from the two German critical journals, *Forum kritische Psychologie* (Forum Critical Psychology) and *Psychologie und Gesellschaftskritik* (Psychology and Critique of Society). I also became active in a student group on critical psychology, which lead to the Austrian *Gesellschaft kritischer Psychologen und Psychologinnen* (Society of Critical Psychologists). I became engaged in the editorial board of the critical-psychological journal *Störfaktor* (Disturbance Factor) established by this society. These experiences, and the fact that students were able to organize, develop, and practice critical psychology, were significant to my development (as were of course interpersonal relationships). Very important to me were my readings of K. Marx and his analyses of capitalist society. Feminist and anti-racist writings became increasingly significant after I left Vienna (where I lived for seven years) and moved to Berlin (where I also lived for seven years). There, in this country of great economic, historical and political importance, I experienced in a profound way the significance of the analyses of racist and sexist politics. The fall of the Berlin wall and German unification, which took place while I was living in Berlin, will always be ingrained in my memory as a revival of German nationalism and racism.

Although I was interested in Freudo-Marxist, post-structuralist and critical theorists, Klaus Holzkamp, who identified the weaknesses of traditional psychology in a sophisticated way, attracted my most intense interest. For example, during his critical-emancipatory period (see Teo 1998a), Holzkamp (1972) challenged the relevance of psychology for practice. He argued that in real-world settings, all variables that had been controlled in the laboratory show relevance. He argued that experimental psychology cannot achieve technical relevance. Moreover, technical relevance alone would mean working for the powerful in society. Technical relevance must be tied to emancipatory relevance, which is accomplished when research helps individuals to obtain self-enlightenment about their societal dependencies. In addition, Holzkamp argued that there exists a basic difference between the subject-matter of physics and that of psychology. Research in physics can be characterized in terms of a subject–object relationship, whereas empirical research in psychology must be understood in terms of a subject–subject relationship. If the experiment depends on a cooperative subject, then the conceptualization of psychology as a natural science is misleading. Holzkamp argued from a Marxist perspective that the concept of the individual is not concrete but is extremely abstract, especially as long as traditional psychology abstracts the individual from her or his historical-societal context.

Finally, I would argue from a developmental point of view that deconstruction, reconstruction and construction not only reflect a general methodology of critical psychology, but may also represent a biographical trajectory of critical psychologists. I began critical endeavours with *deconstructive* arguments, identifying eagerly the many weaknesses of mainstream psychology and its role in serving the interests of the powerful. With the acquisition of more critical knowledge, *reconstructive* studies that allowed for a historically and theoretically sophisticated understanding of the problem became possible. Moreover, in my present work I am trying to contribute to the constructive side of psychology (see Teo 1998b).

What do you see as the basic principles or concepts of critical psychology?

I do not think that there exist time- and space-transcending principles or concepts of critical psychology. Concepts are cultural, historical and social events. Traditional critical discourses have maintained the idea of a grand theory, while being critical of reformist attempts at change. In traditional Marxism, social reality was viewed under the core concept of *capital*, while other issues of domination were interpreted as secondary contradictions of the class struggle. Psychologists who worked within the framework of traditional Marxism, such as the German Critical Psychologists (Holzkamp 1983a), proposed an inclusive and systematic-hierarchical critical psychology (see Teo 1998a).

It is obvious to me that a broad contemporary critical psychology may be realized only as a conceptual *network*, one that is able to incorporate different traditions of emancipatory psychology (see Teo 1998b). The best metaphor developed so far to represent this network is the concept of a *rhizome* as described by Deleuze and Guattari (1987). However, it makes sense to study those theoretical traditions that have taken issues of oppression, power, alienation, liberation, and emancipation as their theoretical focus. I am convinced that Marxism is a strong knot in this conceptual network, as is neo-Marxism which with its theoretical additions to traditional theory and post-Marxism went beyond Marxist ideas, but which nonetheless has roots in Marxism. Critical psychologists must accommodate and assimilate these knots according to their cultural-historical context. However, I do not believe that these three programmes are the only knots in a network of critical psychology.

Why do I think these are strong knots in a network? Let us take the example of power, which the reader may compare with power's inadequate portrayal in traditional psychology. In Marxism power is conceptualized as the material and intellectual domination of people over people. Material domination derives from a class society in which there exists unequal possession of the means of production. Thus, the vast majority of the world population is excluded from control over the societal process. In neo-Marxism (for example, Habermas 1984, 1987) power may refer to a disturbance in the sphere of interaction and communication. Power is a problem of interaction and refers to strategic social action coordinated through egocentric calculations of success and in which other people are used as means. Post-Marxist ideas have been provided by feminism, anti-racism, and the voices of marginalized groups in society. Foucault (1977) has shown how power targets the body and that it is worthwhile to study mechanisms of power in schools, prisons, hospitals, military and other institutions.

On a concrete level, I would suggest that class, gender, and 'race' are core categories for identifying oppression. For critical psychologists it is crucial to examine how classism, sexism and racism work, and how processes of action, cognition and emotion accompany them. Although classism, sexism and racism are central concepts for analysing and understanding psychology, I do not think that these issues determine the boundaries of critical psychology. Oppression is also related to sexual preference, physical and mental disability, age, body size, food preferences, attractiveness and so on. The question is where to draw the border of oppression. For example, I would consider claims of oppression relevant to critical psychology in terms of classism, sexism and racism, but not in terms of individuals who feel oppressed by having to pay too much income tax.

What are the big debates in critical psychology? What issues remain to be resolved?

Critical psychology features many big debates. At the moment, I suggest that it is theoretically important to rethink the *theory and practice relationship* and the notion of *universalism versus particularism*. Also of theoretical and practical significance – not discussed here – is the conceptualization of the relationship between the *individual and society*.

The demand for practice has been a core demand within critical philosophy and critical psychology. Marx's (Marx and Engels 1983: 7) thesis that the goal of philosophy is not to interpret the world but to change it still occupies huge parts of the critical conscience. However, in contrast to the idea that there should be an immediate connection between theory and practice, I am convinced that there is a place for theory in and of itself in critical psychology, and that interpreting a problem in a new way is a justifiable objective of critical-psychological work. A glance at the contemporary cultural-historical mainstream of Euro-American societies suggests that the theory–practice problem has in any case moved to the primacy of practice. It is considered self-evident that theory alone is of no benefit and that theories must have practical impact. The conservative *Zeitgeist* demands that research proposals have significant practical implications for society. Only practical (or practice-promising) research projects (or those with practical potential or implications) receive public acceptance, whereas theoretical endeavours, and among them critical analyses, are considered dubious and undeserving of funding. Critical social scientists, too, demand practice. Needless to say, critical psychologists understand practice as social change and not as system-maintaining action. However, critical psychologists, especially critical practitioners, seem to underestimate the significance of theory. Indeed, it is important to develop an adequate understanding of the functions of theory and of the dialectics of the problem. Given the theoretical weaknesses and ideological commitments of traditional psychology, it becomes particularly significant to emphasize that there is not only a place for theoretical critical psychology but also a necessity for it. Moreover, it should be evident that the theory–practice problem is not a fixed dilemma that can be discussed beyond specific cultural-historical contexts. The formulation of radical psychology as revolutionary practice cannot simply be translated into the late capitalist world at the turn of this century. However, in the context of Latin America I would agree with Martín-Baró's (1994) concept of liberation psychology, his criticism of the ivory tower and his demand for the primacy of practice. I agree with the idea that knowledge is not a form of doing, but I do think that producing and teaching critical knowledge *is* a form of doing, and that a critical social science should provide theories (and practices) for the oppressed (see Dussel 1985).

Some post-modern thinkers have challenged universalistic ideas, and it would be unwise to assume that post-modern critique is simply irrational. The difficulty for critical psychologists is embedded in the question of whether a concept such as liberation from oppression has a universal or a particular meaning. Are human rights universal or do they represent only the outburst of Western ideology, as some non-European regimes claim? Let's ask the victims of oppression in those countries! On the other hand, the Western world has had very peculiar interpretations of human rights, according to its needs, and has used these interpretations for oppressive practices. I suggest (see Teo 1996) that critical psychologists keep to a certain kind of emancipatory universalism, while at the same time recognize sociohistorical and cultural boundaries. Universals must be limited by contexts, and thus it makes sense to develop a *contextually limited universal critical psychology*. In any case, the victims of degradation, subjugation and contempt must decide whether critical psychology is useful to them or not. In this sense, critical practice will be the final criterion for critical psychology.

What have you done, or what do you do, that exemplifies these principles? In other words, how do you practise critical psychology?

Given the widespread primacy of practice in critical psychology, the question implies the need for statements of personal justification. I could mention my early involvement with psychiatric patients, my participation in an ecological organisation, my experience of living in a commune, or my involvement in Black History Month in Berlin. But there is no doubt that, as an academic, I had relatively little practical experience in the sense of revolutionary practice or in the sense of immediate clinical or applied practice. As an academic I suggest a different view on practice. Critical knowledge production is a kind of practice, and in this sense I contribute to the promotion of critical psychology mainly through my writing and my teaching. Critical writings allow subjects (including myself) to reflect upon self-practices. I have taught a course on utopia and liberation in psychology and I have co-edited two books in the domain of multiculturalism. The first (Mecheril and Teo 1994) tried to address the life conditions of immigrants to Germany, while the second (Mecheril and Teo 1997) attempted a systematic analysis of the interrelationship between psychology and racism. Both books were written for a wide audience and the latter won an award in Germany. Congratulatory words from the mayor of a mid-size German town may be interpreted either as a hint that we are not critical enough or as a sign that we should be glad about our mainstream impact.

From your standpoint in critical psychology, what are the most pressing general social/political problems? What should be done about them?

I consider racism, sexism and classism within a society and domination between nations as the major sociopolitical problems. Included are issues of poverty, injustice, economic exploitation, ecological irresponsibility, human alienation and denigration. From a critical-psychological point of view critical psychologists must be concerned, both theoretically and practically, with the suffering subject. Solutions may not be found within the individual but only within the structure of society. It may be that we will have to 'overturn all circumstances in which the human is a degraded, a subjugated, a forsaken, a contemptible being' (Marx and Engels 1956: 385). Psychologically interesting is the process of desensitization or *getting used to*. Which processes take place cognitively, emotionally, or behaviourally when we no longer exhibit reactions towards injustice? For example, how do we cope with the fact that, every day, many children, women and men are starving, although there is enough food for everybody?

Design a question of your own to help bring out something else you need to say

My momentary interest is the construction of a contemporary, critical-psychological theory of liberation (Teo 1998b). As the term *liberation* has been used in numerous ways, it seems necessary to rethink the concept of liberation. By liberation I mean the action options (possibilities) of the subject in contexts of power. I use Holzkamp's elaborations, prestructured through the concept of labour, to understand that subjects have the capacity to fight for the right to participate in determining their life conditions. I think that subjects have the option, in cooperation with others, to challenge and change a class-based society. Subjects have the capacity to recognize that personal arrangements with the powerful, a typical coping strategy within class societies, may perpetuate the *status quo*. Subjects may resist or work against their collaboration with power-laden contexts, for example, with regard to means of production, but also in the areas of employment, housing, and health care. I use Habermas's reflections, which are prestructured through the basic category of communication, to understand that subjects can participate in the formation of their lifeworlds and can fight against lifeworld deformations through stipulations of the system. I believe that subjects have the capacity to intervene in the public sphere, to take part in social movements, and to engage in activities directed against power. In all communicative situations, subjects have the ability to demand egalitarian processes of communication. Finally, I use Foucault in order to apprehend the notion that subjects have the capacity to install their life as a piece of art and to act against power. Subjects have the option to nurture their personal aesthetics of existence, to develop an individual lifestyle in the areas of sexuality and of bodily and other forms of self-expression, and to employ technologies of the self in order to resist power.

Author's note

I appreciate the helpful comments of Angela Febbraro. Correspondence concerning this chapter should be addressed to Thomas Teo, Department of Psychology, History and Theory of Psychology,

York University, 4700 Keele Street, Toronto, Ontario, M3J 1P3, Canada (e-mail: <tteo@yorku.ca>).

16

'Is Doing Good Just Enough?' Enabling Practice in a Disabling Discipline

Neil Drew, Christopher Sonn, Brian Bishop
and Natalie Contos

What is critical psychology?

Critical psychology is a pre-paradigmatic phase. It is the codi-fication of concerns about the lack of understanding of the con-text of peoples' lives. The ahistorical, asocial, apolitical nature of traditional psychology has been exposed by a number of dis-parate fringe groups, such as cultural, feminist and community psychology. Social psychology, too, has a long tradition of chal-lenging the perceived shortcomings of the dominant discourse in psychology. Faced with a discipline unwilling to believe it was wearing the emperor's new clothes, these groups have looked to other disciplines for guidance such as the fine arts (Gergen 1988), architecture and planning (Syme and Bishop 1993), anthropology, and so on. This has brought psychologists to a consideration of post-modernism as a rubric under which they can grapple with the malaise in psychology (Kvale 1992).

The post-modern perspective resonated with many psycho-logists and gave voice to the concerns that underpin critical psychology, yet is only half the battle. A truly robust identity for psychology is yet to emerge. In community psychology, for example, the rhetoric of a post-modern psychology has yet to be matched by methodological alternatives to traditional models of research and practice. We have still to shake off the shackles of the dominant discourse. This is not facilitated by publication practices which still favour the traditional over the innovative

(Trickett 1996). A perusal of the flagship journals in community psychology bears this out. Trickett observed that 'we are still working on the "community" of community psychology as it involves the intertwining of culture and social context' (1996: 211).

For us, critical psychology has two primary, though interlocking, dimensions. The first, as noted above, is the challenge to the dominant discourse in mainstream psychology. This has been particularly evident in Australia. While our message is as obvious as it is required, we have failed on the whole to convince mainstream psychology. Psychology in Australia exemplifies the adage that there is none so blind as those that will not see. Sheehan (1996), for example, commented that the peak body for research funding in Australia, the Australian Research Council (ARC), was highly critical of the contribution of psychology to research:

> Australian psychology is monocultural; its texts and outlook are very
>   North American/ Western European.
> It is not interested in the epistemological and ethical underpinnings
>   of the research enterprise and;
> It has not taken up the challenge of societal relevance, cross cultural
>   applicability, or appropriate subject matter posed by society itself.
>   (p. 184)

Australian psychologists have nevertheless been strangely silent, particularly given that Sheehan's paper was published in the journal of the Australian Psychological Society. In fact, Australian psychology has become increasingly insular, seeking to counter a perceived lack of influence in public affairs by taking refuge in a neoconservative return to psychology as science. Such a psychology has little of substance to offer a community experiencing significant social upheaval. Australian psychology has remained largely 'reproductive' of the *status quo*, rather than 'transformative', in Sampson's (1983) terms. There have been some small, but significant, social commentaries, such as the position papers on psychologists dealing with Indigenous people and on broader racism. These have been principally developed by critical psychologists (for example, Sanson *et al.* 1998).

So, in the first instance, critical psychology is an internal struggle to reshape the discipline because of the failure of psychology to make a meaningful contribution to the resolution of social problems and issues. The second dimension of critical psychology is that of striving to make a difference, to become an active participant in the hurly-burly of the construction of our social world (Gergen 1988). Critical psychologists eschew the cult of empiricism in favour of approaches to research and practice that not only recognize the 'valuational baggage' we carry, but value that baggage as part of the complex interplay among researchers and the communities of interest. For community psychologists the valuational baggage embodies values and principles that underpin the work they do. Central to these values is a commitment to social justice. In Australia there are critical issues that will shape the national identity and international reputation. These are, quintessentially, issues of social justice. Principal among them is the reconciliation process with the Indigenous community. Another is the challenge to locate ourselves as a multicultural nation within the Asian Pacific region. The commitment to justice is as much an ongoing process of being consciously reflective in our practice, in order to ensure that we do not perpetuate injustice, as it is about directly tackling injustice. There is a tension between the desire to do social good and the recognition that, by virtue of being part of the mainstream culture, we are inherently part of the problem. Failure to address these issues means that we become agents of social control without the awareness that we are so. We acknowledge that social justice both transcends and is located within the local context. By any yardstick, justice is socially constituted and can be understood only within the appropriate sociopolitical setting. This is a recurring theme.

Other elements of a critical psychology have emerged from the experiences of the authors. They include a process focus, a commitment to empowerment, collaboration and cultural pluralism. Critical psychologists also recognize the inextricable embeddedness of people (including themselves) in a complex sociopolitical, historical and cultural milieu.

What brought us to critical psychology?

For us, critical psychology is not so much a scholarly pursuit as a process of interrogating the literature in an iterative fashion to make sense of our experiences as practising community psychologists. In the following paragraphs each author, in turn, reflects briefly on their journey towards a critical psychological perspective in their research and practice. While their journeys are diverse, they arrived at a place where they felt a considerable kinship with each other within a dominant discourse that, they felt, marginalized and devalued their and their colleagues' contribution to the discipline. The role of personal experience coupled with our professional background has been instrumental in developing a critical perspective.

Neil Drew began professional life as an applied social psychologist working with young offenders and abused children. The principles of practice suggested by a background in experimental social psychology soon proved hopelessly inadequate. As a psychologist working primarily within an applied social or clinical framework in an institutional setting, he found the acontextual, individualistic interventions not only ineffective; in many cases they were harmful. Up to 80 per cent of the young offenders were from remote Aboriginal communities. It was very easy to subject them, as a captive audience removed from their environment, to standard individualistic interventions designed ostensibly to enhance their coping skills, improve their ability to respond assertively to peer pressure and improve their self-esteem. Programmes failed to take account of the fact that the young offenders were returning to an essentially unchanged environment, with a set of 'skills' often ill suited to the demands of their daily lives. In one notable, if somewhat apocryphal, case a young Aboriginal man was assaulted by police for responding in an assertive manner to their inquiries, as he had been trained to do during his period of incarceration. Finally, Neil realized the error of his ways and participated in the design and implementation of a very successful community-based programme for young offenders. Neil still considers this, some ten years on, as a highlight in his career and a turning-point in developing a critical perspective.

Christopher Sonn grew up in a 'Coloured' community in South Africa. He relocated to Australia with his parents after having started his tertiary education at the University of the Western Cape. At the time of migration there was considerable political protest against the apartheid system. The migration experience and settlement in a community that was predominantly

'Anglo' presented many challenges. Among other questions, there were identity issues such as what does it mean to be a 'Coloured' person and what are the implications of oppressive systems of human development? Mainstream psychology did not offer much insight, in that 'Coloured' people's experiences were not represented in the literature. Also, psychology seemed to be too individualistic, too pathology- and adjustment-focused, and to neglect to investigate collective and systems-level phenomena. He discovered that cultural psychology, social constructionism and other critical perspectives in other social sciences offered more to understanding how ethnicity, identity, culture, other social systems and people are jointly constituted through interaction. However, Chris did not give up on psychology and completed a formal programme in community psychology, which promoted multiple levels of inquiry, inter-disciplinary collaboration, and challenged taken-for-granted realities. It provided him with a context in which he could present the voice of his community of origin and similar groups. However, he is aware of the issue of representation and voice, that is, who can legitimately represent whom? Chris is currently drawing on a range of disciplines that focus on cultural and liberation psychology in order to understand how individuals and communities respond to adversity.

Brian Bishop first started to become dimly aware that not all was well in social psychology as an undergraduate student. He was exposed to the critical methodology papers of Ring (1967) and others. It was not until a subject in his experimental social psychology PhD research resented what he saw as social fabrication of the research context that the discrepancy between the critical methodologists' commentaries and his research became obvious. His initial defensive reaction to see research as being a compromise between science and reality was effective for most of the time, but dark thoughts emerged increasingly frequently. Having gone through an acrimonious divorce created a temporary social marginalization that allowed him to see social structures from the outside. Being in a vulnerable state, the dark thoughts about the nature of experimental social psychology, and psychology at large, could not be contained and a general cynicism emerged. This was only worked through by recognizing that other applied psychologists had seen the emperor naked, and had been able to continue functioning. From this, he was able to see that a critical stance need not be destructive, but could be constructive.

Natalie Contos spent part of her childhood in Western Australia's capital city, and part on a family farm in the wheatbelt. Her extended family, of English, Greek and Indian descent, provided a rich multicultural environment in which to grow up. Embarking on a 'traditional' degree in psychology, it was after completing her honours thesis in social psychology that she began to seriously question the underlying assumptions of mainstream psychology. Her research on the stigma surrounding people with disabilities was methodologically rigorous, but she was left feeling that she had created a perfect experiment to produce a perfect result, without making any contribution to the real-life issue. Returning to Australia after a period of overseas travel, she saw, for the first time, the oppression of Indigenous Australians. She was struck by the absence of a sense of spirituality and community in the dominant Australian society. Cynical as to what psychology could contribute to these issues, she nevertheless began conversations with Harry Pickett at the Centre for Aboriginal Studies, and Brian Bishop within the School of Psychology, at Curtin University. Community psychology, with its focus on social change and social justice, offered a framework from which to attempt to address the issue of oppression of Indigenous Australians. Accordingly, Natalie began a doctorate involving action research with a Southwest Indigenous community, focusing on social justice issues. Immersion in the research context resulted in an acute awareness of the vast differences between the worldviews of Indigenous and Western cultures. As a result of her increasing awareness of the role of the imposition of Western worldviews in the oppression of Indigenous people, her commitment to critical psychology became firmly established.

Rieff (1966) recognized the need for an alternative to clinical psychology, realizing that psychology, as constructed, could not explain the events occurring in his life. His theories were melded by his personal experience so that they became an expression of his life. Similarly, the experience of, for example, being a migrant, or the experience of divorce created opportunities for us to examine psychology critically. We all arrived at a point where it was clear to us that much of mainstream psychology was 'misdirected', asocial and ahistorical (Sarason 1981). We had tasted the 'sweet poison' (Gergen 1988) and could not maintain our commitment to mainstream psychology. Like Gergen and others before us, we found a literature we could agree with. It was not that this literature created an awareness, but that we found that their writings resonated with our beliefs. This was an important issue, which we only later understood.

In our practice and research we embarked on a course of social reform, to challenge Australian psychology, so that it could become the reformist vehicle in Australian society it had long promised, but failed, to be. Needless to say, we overestimated our impacts and had to satisfied with developing small cells of like-minded people.

What are the basic principles?

The principles of critical psychology emerge from the critique of mainstream (particularly social) psychology and the aspirations of community-minded psychologists. The principles are grounded in the by now familiar rejection of the 'cult of empiricism, which despite protestations to the contrary still dominates the dominant discourse in Australian psychology.

The basic principles of critical psychology revolve around locating research and practice within the appropriate sociopolitical-cultural milieu. We are actors in a socially constructed reality (Berger and Luckmann 1967). If we see ourselves as somehow abstracted from the context, we contribute to what Sampson (1983) called the reproduction of the status quo. *We seek transformative practice, which leads to meaningful social change (Prilleltensky and Nelson 1997).*

At a conceptual level, our work has been informed by that of Newbrough (1992, 1995) and Dokecki (1992, 1996) and the notions of reflective practice. Methodologically, Wicker's (1989) description of substantive theorizing was foundational. McGuire's (1983, 1985, 1994) perspectivism and Cook's critical multiplism (1985) provided stable and persuasive methodological frameworks for developing transparent and open practice. They were particularly useful as we began to explore the ephemeral and elusive nature of what we took to be 'knowledge'. If knowledge was not objective and knowable, what was it?

We pursued an alternative to the objective, universal knowledge of the positivist discourse. Schon's notion of technical, objective, scientific and professional knowledge gained by reflection and action was helpful. Similarly, Altman's (1996) concept of socially responsive knowledge brought us closer to understanding the nature of knowledge in context. As community psychologists, we sought to understand the construction of social problems from the perspective of communities of concern. This in turn demanded a willingness to relinquish the expert role in favour of an approach that recognizes and values the multiple realities and perspectives from which a social issue can be construed. The perspectival nature of knowledge brought us to a consideration of knowledge claims as contributions to the discourse about community concerns. This means that any knowledge claims, including our own, must be submitted to the community of concern. They must be asserted to the community for consideration. In doing so, knowledge claims are available for debate in a way not previously accepted in the positivist tradition. In the positivist worldview, knowledge is rendered indisputable by virtue of having been derived from an 'objective' and 'scientific' method. In this way positivists can colonize the truth, effectively marginalizing and disempowering those whose claims cannot be verified according to the same yardsticks. Assertoric knowledge (Polkinghorne 1983), on the other hand, is explicitly disputable. Such knowledge is conceived as a contribution to the discourse about the phenomena of interest, rather than an immutable truth.

Lately, we have begun to recognize the importance of developing an epistemology based on contextualism (compare Altman and Rogoff 1984; Pepper 1967; Payne 1982, 1996). Contextualism derives from Pepper's notion of world theories as contrasting grand narratives. The world theories of mechanism, formism, contextualism and organicism have often been contrasted in the debates for and against positivism and as perspectives for examining the shift from modern to post-modern. Pepper's concept of different but equally valid epistemologies deflects the debate away from the 'evils' of positivism and the 'goodness' of contextualism (for example), to one of recognizing that different epistemologies will apply in different contexts. For us, contextualism has been most suitable to the questions we most frequently address.

Consistent with the principles of a community-oriented psychology, we adopt a process focus that seeks to facilitate community voice and ownership of the issues and concerns. Most often this places us at the interface between decision-makers and the community. Throgmorton (1991) described the role at the interface as that of 'active mediator'. Different groups (decision-makers, community groups, scientists) represent different interpretive communities, each with its own norms, values, beliefs and language. When the different groups encounter each other, as they do in community life, this may lead to communication problems and the development of abnormal discourse (Throgmorton 1991). The role of active mediator is to seek a fusion of horizons to promote normal discourse between the parties. Working at the interface often provides genuine opportunities for incremental, often small, but nevertheless meaningful social change to occur. The role at this interface demands critical (community) psychology to become more transformative (Prilleltensky and Nelson 1997; Sampson 1983).

The overarching value of our critical psychology is social justice, exemplified through enabling practice. In community psychology, social justice has often been 'honoured more in the breach than the observance' (Prilleltensky and Nelson 1997). As one of the foundational values of the discipline, it has received little attention in the published literature. As described above, our practice places a high premium on collaboration and participation, and the mechanisms to achieve this are derived from a commitment to procedural and distributive justice. In this way, the realization of socially just outcomes can be achieved through empowering practice at the local level.

In essence, we seek to promote enabling, transformative practice that recognizes, and values, the multiple perspectives from which a social problem may be viewed. In this respect we locate practice as indivisible from a socially constructed reality in which we are active participants.

How do we practice critical psychology?

The big debates in Australia revolve around the search for a truly robust and durable national identity. To achieve such an identity, we must as a nation confront the largely hidden and whitewashed history of the colonization of Indigenous Australia, and seek to embrace the multicultural reality that now defines our nation. Focusing on the first of these issues, we may say that Indigenous Australians have, since the British

invasion of their land in the late 1700s, been systematically
deprived of their inherent dignity and rights as human beings.
Legislative changes since the 1960s represent gradual attempts
to restore the rights of Indigenous Australians; however, gross
inequities on almost all Western measures of well-being continue to persist (Riley 1997).

Racism against Indigenous Australians is still rife at all levels
of society. Nationally, when the Liberal–National Party coalition
won power from Labor in 1996, there was a perception that the
government had derided existing mechanisms aimed at addressing Indigenous disadvantage as the 'Aboriginal Industry', and
slashed more than $400 million from the Aboriginal affairs bud-
get (Pilger 1998). The Wik decision in the same year marked
formal recognition by the High Court of Australia that native
title rights could coexist with pastoral leases (as they have done
since the invasion). This was perceived as a threat to big busi-
ness, and many believe that the Howard government systematically undermined the decision, pushing through legislation
on the issue which, among other things, dramatically reduced
Indigenous rights to negotiate concerning their entitlements to
land. The social climate created by the new government paved
the way for the emergence of the Pauline Hanson phenomenon.
A representative of what she termed 'mainstream Australia', Ms
Hanson, elected a federal Member for Parliament in Queens-
land, established the infamous 'One Nation' party which gave
voice to those with racist views of Indigenous and migrant
Australians. Although she lost her seat in the Federal Election
of 1998, the party persists, and is still considered a political force
to be reckoned with.

At the local level, Indigenous Australians have been markedly
affected by this climate. In a small rural community in Western
Australia's Southwest, a community-based Indigenous association has worked since the 1970s in pursuit of social justice for
their people. The federal cuts to the Aboriginal affairs budget
resulted in the withdrawal of running costs to the association,
along with 67 other Indigenous organizations representing the
needs of people at the 'grass roots' level, throughout the Southwest. As a result, three of the four Indigenous people in employment at the time (out of a community of between one hundred
and two hundred Indigenous people) lost their jobs, although
they continued to work voluntarily, such was their commitment

to their people. Community members received several ano-
nymous letters proclaiming Pauline Hanson a heroine, expres-
sing racial hatred and threatening physical violence. Family pets
were poisoned, and racial tensions at local sporting events
reached an all-time high.

Within this climate, Natalie Contos engaged with the local
Indigenous association with the intention of conducting doctoral research on social justice issues. As a non-Indigenous person, she was faced with the reality of being a representative of
the dominant, oppressive group. A key challenge was to let go
of Western and positivistic ways of understanding and develop
an emic appreciation of the very different worldview of the
Indigenous community. This required tolerating considerable
uncertainty and ambiguity and surrendering the notion of a
psychologist as an objective expert. It required the negotiation
of a collaborative and meaningful role, which nevertheless
acknowledged the tension experienced as a member of the
dominant culture with a commitment to social justice.

As a result of this process, she developed a strong partnership
with the Indigenous community. At the same time, involvement
with the broader community led to the identification of key
people in the non-Indigenous community who were sympathetic to, but not in contact with, Indigenous counterparts.
Facilitating bridges between these groups provided a context in
which the she was able to actively address a critical community
issue. Of tremendous symbolic importance to the Indigenous
community was the need for broader community recognition of
a massacre of their ancestors in 1834. The massacre was led by
the first governor of Western Australia, in response to Indigenous resistance to the invasion of their land. Historic denial of the
incident by non-Indigenous locals manifested a more pervasive
sense of the invisibility and unimportance of Indigenous experience, ultimately resulting in a perpetuation of the *status quo* of
Indigenous disadvantage. Debate around the issue was exacer-
bating divisions between the Indigenous and non-Indigenous
communities.

Natalie worked at the interface between the two communities, local government, and a range of government bureau-
cracies to assist in identifying existing barriers, reframing the
issues, building bridges between the groups and, ultimately,
bringing representatives to the table to negotiate a positive

resolution. Engaging key non-Indigenous locals on reconcili-ation initiatives at a community level facilitated a simultaneous shift in attitudes among the broader non-Indigenous commun-ity. Although in the short term much has remained the same in terms of Indigenous disadvantage in the research community (and indeed, throughout Australia), the small gains that have been made constitute an important step in the direction toward our vision of social justice for Indigenous Australians. Ulti-mately, we take faith from the motto that has always guided the Indigenous struggle, captured in a song by the Australian folk songwriter Paul Kelly, 'From little things, big things grow.'

This example indicates the reflective process that is required when working with issues of social justice. The psychologist must maintain the pain of uncertainty and ambiguity to avoid being captured by the sense of 'doing good'. The ambiguity and uncertainty serves to remind us that we are, in a sense, inter-lopers with the opportunity to retreat to the comfort of the dominant society when things become difficult, in the smug belief that we have helped the Indigenous community.

What are the big debates for critical psychology?

From our perspective there are a number of crucial issues confronting psychologists who have adopted a critical perspective. Questions remain about the future of the critical perspective in the Australian psychological community. The Australian Psychological Society has responded to the challenge to become relevant by retreating to a neo-conservative view of psychology as science. Accreditation processes now require that all programmes, in order to maintain accreditation, teach only evidence-based methods such as the scientist practitioner model. This has been despite compelling evidence that so-called evid-ence-based approaches are not demonstrably better than other approaches (King 1998), particularly when judged against the empir-ical yardsticks they espouse. Many in the mainstream fail to appreciate the irony of this observation.

Many critical psychologists ask themselves, as Gergen (1978) did, why they should 'raise the tattered colours once again and lay siege to the bastion of tradition?' (p. 509). Some (for example, Drew and Bishop 1995) have suggested that it may be time to forgo the pursuit of recognition within the mainstream and seek alliances with like-minded colleagues in other disciplines. It is apparent that the values and principles of critical psychology are as much accepted by like-minded colleagues as they are vilified within the discipline. Whether we stay or go, there is a need to address (or perhaps redress), many of the problems of a mainstream, dominant discourse. We believe that many errors of omission, and indeed commission, are being perpetuated by psychologists in the name of psychology as science. It is important to find ways to ameliorate these without losing our professional identity or integrity.

17

My Postmodern Path to a Critical Psychology

Lois Shawver

In a nutshell, what does critical psychology mean to you?

I think of critical psychology as what psychologists do who are learning to speak with a voice that escapes the parroting of the *status quo*. For too long, psychologists have simply parroted the ideas and theories of influential thinkers of the past. If the fresh voice of critical psychology is silenced, then we are stuck in our traditions, or, as postmoderns might say, we are confined to a 'closure' where a closure is a kind of mental prison. Like children having been taught to answer questions in a particular way, when we are in a 'closure' we do not notice the possibility of seeing the world differently, or doing things differently, and so we are stuck in the *status quo*.

There are many forces that would confine us to such a closure, but two seem particularly important to me: education and scholarship.

First, consider the way education holds us in the closure of tradition. Our society privileges people who are educated, but to be educated we must commit to memory the ideas of authors whose writings most appealed to past cultures. In other words, in order to be privileged today as an educated person, one must become an expert in what people used to think. We need postmodern changes in our educational system if we are to break our children out of the closure of the past (cf. Wilson *et al.* 1994; Wilson 1997; Hlynka and Belland 1991). Can you imagine a system better designed to keep society circling around within old traditions? Even when they no longer serve us well?

Second, consider how standard scholarship holds people within the closure of history and tradition: until the internet, scholars depended almost exclusively on scholarly publications to learn what their colleagues thought about things. This made publication very important, so important that the phrase 'publish or perish' became popular. Without it, scholarship as we knew it would not have existed.

But in order to publish, scholars needed to practise a complicated system of cross-referencing the works of previous scholars, not just in a general sense, but in a detailed accounting of every major point (Lyotard 1984) – such as the reference I just gave you to Lyotard. Anything else has seemed less than scholarship because 'one of the main functions of scholarship is to preserve the *status quo*' (Said 1996: 27). What could hold a scholar more within the closure of history than a system like that – one designed to preserve the *status quo*?

In various ways, then, both education and scholarship perpetuate our dependence on the past. And because of these two forces it is difficult to find a forum to present radically new ideas. Students who do not learn the previous authors well, and iconoclast scholars who want to break with tradition, simply have had trouble publishing and being respected as scholars – and that means they have had trouble finding others who share their critical perspective on the way things are.

Still, various critical voices manage to wiggle free of our closure, wiggle out of the illusion that the past way of doing things is the correct and only way. The critical voice in psychology is one that wiggles free of unquestioned faith in the *status quo*. It is not that we critical psychologists want to forget the past, but that we want to avoid having our creativity trapped in past theories and paradigms. Just as Copernicus somehow found a way to break from the closure that had tradition imagining Earth to be the centre of the solar system, so we want to create a culture in which we, too, can escape our own closure within our own tradition.

So the question to my mind is: can we escape the closure enough to discover ways to improve our lives, in either small ways or large ones? If we can be critical of what we have worked so hard to learn – that is, if we can be critical psychologists – then perhaps some of us can begin to see a 'crevice through which a yet unnameable glimmer beyond the closure can be glimpsed' (Derrida 1976: 14).

What brought you to critical psychology?

I don't know what made me more critical of traditional psychology than some of my colleagues, but surely the seeds of my intellectual rebelliousness were planted in my childhood. I believe that too many parents focus their attention on inculcating children with the 'right' values, and the correct politics. Instead, I listened to numerous adult discussions in simple vocabularies in which people disagreed in a friendly but serious way. It provoked me to think and inspired me to want to speak in criticism of what I heard.

Perhaps the major conversation of my childhood was an ongoing debate between my grandmother and aunt, both of whom lived with us. My grandmother was an uneducated Christian Scientist. My aunt was a physician. The discussions took place over coffee and cookies in the late afternoon.

Over and over I heard them each make her pitch. My grandmother might say, 'I'm healthier than you are, Maryellen, and I never go to a doctor.'

And my aunt might say, 'You just haven't been sick yet'. 'I think you make yourself sick just by thinking about it. I'll never,' my grandmother would say, 'take medicine.'

Many a day I listened to this argument. Then, one day, I sat alone with my grandmother at the breakfast table and she complained that she was out of prune juice.

'Have apple juice,' I told her.

'It's not the same,' she responded. 'I need prune juice for my digestion.'

Suddenly, I realized, she used prune juice to regulate her bowels. 'Wow!' I responded. 'Prune juice is like a medicine for you, isn't it? I mean it's like a laxative.'

She looked surprised. I doubt if she understood my point. She certainly did not accept it. But I did. I had just deconstructed the word 'medicine'. I had come to see that things that were not called 'medicine' could be medicine, for all practical purposes. This meant, as I think about it now, that I was no longer confined to this particular conceptual closure. From this point on, medicine could be something that was not called medicine.

That is how I understand deconstruction (Shawver 1996, 1998a) today. Deconstruction is a window on conceptual closure. Our ordinary language defines things for us and unless we learn to question what we are taught we are caught in the box of our traditions. Today I can see that a book does not have to be something you hold in your hand. It can be something on the web. And a bed does not have to be something with a head-board. One can bed down on the floor. But back then, at the age of eleven, this insight, that the names of things could be decon-structed, was a heady insight indeed. In Foucault's (1972) lan-guage, I had reconfigured the 'unities of discourse'. That is the unity (which in this case was the collection of everything I had called 'medicine') now consisted of different items in my mind. I had 'questioned the divisions or groupings [of language] with which [I had] become so familiar' (Foucault 1972: 22).

Still, I had a long way to go to become a critical psychologist and my aunt and grandmother's conversation could not take me the whole way. Perhaps the next big step was my first encounter with the work of Ludwig Wittgenstein. Wittgenstein has shown many of us (compare Gergen and McNamee 1997) how tradi-tional ways of understanding things have us circling in a closure, or as he called it, 'the fly bottle'. His purpose, he told us, was to show us the way out of the fly bottle (Wittgenstein 1965: #309).

It happened one day in an undergraduate class. My professor, Fred Hagen, had given us the assignment of bringing a philo-sophy question to class. I did my assignment over coffee and donuts and so, when I was called on in in the class, I asked, 'What happens to the hole in the donut when we eat the donut?'

He raised his eyebrows, chuckled, and he said, 'Where was the hole before you ate the donut?' The class laughed.

'In the center of the donut,' I responded.

'Could you see it?'

'Not exactly, I mean, I could see that there was a hole there, but I couldn't exactly SEE the hole.'

'Suppose you were driving down the road and I was a pas-senger, and all of a sudden I shouted, "Can't you see that hole in the pavement!" Imagine this as a warning. Might you answer me, "No, I can't really see the hole, but I can see the sides of the hole?"'

'No,' I said, feeling the force of this confusion.

'Or,' he continued, 'if I said, "Lois, I see a hole in your purse and your money is falling out," would you correct me saying, "No, you only see the sides of the hole?"'

'No.'

'Well, then it seems to me that you do see holes, and not just the sides of holes.'

'Not really,' I said. 'That's just a way of talking.'

'Just a way of talking?' he said with feigned amazement.

'What other way do we have? Your culture has taught you to talk about seeing holes the same way it has taught the rest of us. Like the rest of us you have learned to talk about seeing holes. Still, you think you can't see something if nothing is there, don't you?'

'Yes,' I said.

'But look here,' he told me. 'Can you see this empty space between my two fingers? Answer in the way that comes most naturally to you.'

The answer came automatically. 'Yes,' I said.

'That is because, like the rest of us, you have been taught to speak with an inconsistent language. You are simply staring at one of the inconsistencies. If you think that it is odd that we say we can "see a hole" reflect on the fact that we also ordinarily say we can "see nothing" when there is "nothing to see".'

'What do you mean?' I asked.

'If you checked the mailbox and found nothing there, might you not say, "I see nothing" because there would be nothing to see?'

I nodded, seeing the paradox.

'Language is full of inconsistencies like this,' he said.

'Maybe we should change them,' I told him.

'Ah,' he said, 'if it were only so easy.'

Now I know that philosophers have known about these paradoxes since the ancient times. In the last century or so, many people have tried to improve language, but it is much more twisted and difficult to untangle than you might imagine. The way later Wittgenstein taught us to deal with these confusing areas is to give us a better picture of how these different regions of language work, and how they confuse us. If we can understand them as sources of confusion, then we can manage our confusion better.

And so it was. At ten I had deconstructed the concept of medicine, and at twenty-two I was shown that language was even more imperfect than I thought. In some places of language we said we could not see if there was nothing there to see, whereas in other regions of language one could see, even an empty space.

And so, a few years later when I entered graduate school in psychology, it was my destiny to become a critical psychologist. There, I often ran across psychologists who had not known about these paradoxes in language, people who took for granted their own traditions and continued to parrot them without noticing that we were confined to a conceptual closure, unable to envision better worlds and ways to reach them.

But in my graduate school at the University of Houston I also ran across professors such as Paul Dokecki and John Lubach, who encouraged me to work within my Wittgensteinian perspective. For example, Dokecki allowed me, a graduate student, to lead him in a reading of Wittgenstein and permitted me to be the senior author in our co-authored paper that followed from that reading (Shawver and Dokecki 1971), and Lubach allowed me do a dissertation that followed my own inclination which, at the time, was methodologically adventurous.

Were there also psychologists whose traditional thoughts deserved criticism in my graduate programme? Of course. All of us have thoughts deserving of criticism, and some traditional psychologists in my graduate programme I thought of even more critically.

However, the University of Houston at that time was highly influenced by community psychology and theorists such as Fritz Heider, who helped pave the way to a psychology more concerned with social interaction than individuality. I was particularly influenced by Fritz Heider's work, which deconstructed our cultural common-sense understanding of people's actions by investigating the 'common-sense' observer's way of thinking.

What do you see as the basic principles of critical psychology?

I do not think of critical psychology as a single school of psychology with its own set of basic principles. It is much too iconoclastic, too formless for that. All that unites critical psychologists, it seems to me, is our common incredulity in the face of the *status quo*.

But even so I have developed two principles that follow from my way of understanding. I believe we critical psychologists need to champion our values and not become mired in pure critique of other positions and that we need to champion these values with positive visions of how the world might be changed. Second, and even more important, I believe we need to support forums that facilitate and allow for the participation of diverse voices and diverse views.

The most important thing is to develop a culture that supports conversation among diverse views. Only if we can do that do the people who need their stories heard find a receptive audience. Moreover, I think this forum, whether at the dinner table, in our courtrooms, in the newspapers or in our classrooms, needs to hear the voices of critical psychologists do more than merely offer their critique. We need to create new visions, and these visions, I hope, emerge not just from the voices of a few but from a conversation of alternative views among a people collaborating by disagreeing with some things and agreeing with others, and by letting their opinions evolve and improve in the bath of all these alternative understandings. I call this new vision 'paralogy' – as it was named by the celebrated postmodern theorist Jean-François Lyotard (1984).

Think of paralogy as a stimulating conversation that leads the participants to better understand their own positions and to work them into more successful and well-thought-out positions. It does not necessarily lead to consensus, but, as the conversation continues, each position becomes more informed and the conversants feel increasingly satisfied with their personal progress in understanding. In paralogical conversations people learn from each other, and it is possible to improve one's own position without accepting someone else's position. With paralogy, the old way of thinking is shaken up and a new creative force for revision becomes possible. Paralogy, so Lyotard tells us, is the quest of the postmodern.

Therefore, the principles I will propose are ways of fostering our paralogy. What I am proposing are suggested rules of thumb. But if we follow these rules of thumb, I think this will help us avoid becoming mired in pure critique (Gergen 1994) while it allows us to champion our values in texts and public forums. And, since we critical psychologists are critics of the common wisdom, I think we should be patient with our own critics and address their issues as fairly and even-handedly as we can. Finally, I believe we need to be prepared to admit that our positive theories have their own flaws and to make space for better solutions than we have personally been able to devise.

I think we should do these things in order to cultivate an era of paralogy, an era in which we can learn to talk to each other and learn from each other. But, of course, once we have helped to create paralogy, we need to articulate and present our own views as well as criticism of other views. However, my belief is that the way we change the world needs to emerge from the vision that unfolds in community conversations, conversations constructed so as to foster new ideas rather than repeat old beliefs. When I champion my views I do not act to change the world but to invite others to join with me to create change that I cannot do alone. I realize and am pleased that the change I help to make will not be designed entirely by my individual vision, but I will, nevertheless, articulate my own individual vision as forcefully as I can.

What are the big debates in critical psychology? What issues remain to be resolved?

I think the most important debate in critical psychology is about what we should do to change the system we criticize. That is, when we psychologists become critical of the *status quo*, what do we do next? After all, the fact that we are critical does not imply that we have answers.

The dilemma is illustrated by a recent trialogue in which three prominent social constructionists discussed what professionals should do after they have thoroughly criticized the psychiatric categories (in the DSM-IV). This trialogue is recorded in the paper 'Is Diagnosis a Disaster?' by Kenneth Gergen, Harlene Anderson and Lynn Hoffman (1996). Here the discussants deliberated about the state of affairs for clinicians who diagnose their clients. All three participants agreed in their criticism of diagnostic practices. Diagnosis is a disaster, they told us, but, still, this agreement did not tell them what to do about it.

Kenneth Gergen put the dilemma this way: 'What do therapists do with their professional knowledge and past experience? How do we then communicate with professional colleagues, clients and insurance companies?' So, the question is: what do professionals, who have learned how to diagnose mental illness according to the established rule, yet dislike the illness categories, do? Do they just stand up at their job sites and say, 'Never again'? Do they roll their eyes when their colleagues discuss 'borderlines' or 'multiple personalities'? Do they shrug their shoulders when new private clients want diagnoses so they can use their insurance for payment? Do they just walk out on their jobs?

Or do they simply go through the exercise of diagnosing clients even though they feel that this is a destructive practice?

There are good reasons to continue to diagnose clients, at least some of the time. For example, Shields and his colleagues (1994) have argued that failing to render diagnoses will marginalize family therapists (or presumably any kind of therapist who does not diagnose). If clients need diagnoses in order to collect on their insurance, then they may turn away from the therapists who do not offer diagnoses.

And, if the whole profession refuses to diagnose, it may result in that profession being marginalized.

Gergen scoffed at this suggestion. He proposed – idealistically, I think – that insurance companies should offer the equivalent of non-fault insurance to therapy patients so that diagnoses would not be necessary to get insurance payments.

Of course, Gergen is looking for ways to improve the system. That's a worthy enough motivation. But refusing to diagnose can sometimes be contrary to that political aim. Consider the case of the institutional psychologist who refuses to render diagnoses and is therefore fired. Would this make the system better? Or would it just mean that a more willing professional, less enlightened about diagnosis, would be hired to take over the critical psychologist's job?

Of course, the basic unresolved issue here is not merely how to handle diagnoses once we are critical of them. It is how much to bow to a system once we are critical of the entire system, whatever the clinical technique that we criticize.

There is no simple answer here, but it is idealistic in the extreme to propose that critical psychologists, who are certainly in the minority right now, should never bow to the system that requires diagnoses or any other traditional procedure. Unless professionals have alternative ways of staying in the game, of being participants with influence on how things are done, we must, in my opinion, simply learn to balance our conscience with our authentic judgment about the practicalities that present themselves to us. Only if we can do that do we have a hope of having an effect on how things are done.

Critical psychologists shoot themselves in the foot if they become too idealistic, to the point where they are removed from the game, but this does not mean that we are without power. Much of that power resides in our learning to create paralogy in work places and other settings in which our ideas may eventually shake up the culture's habit of staying within the established system. In my opinion, it is not necessarily the case that any particular established system is bad in itself; rather, any system that is taken for granted and not seen as replaceable simply becomes vulnerable to abuse and loses the spark of life that allows it to adapt to changing cultures, needs and values.

What have you done, or what do you do, that exemplifies these principles? How do you practice critical psychology?

Although it seems to me that critical psychology does not have a consensually accepted set of principles, I have proposed two that inspire my work, and I have tried to shape my own actions to reflect these principles.

First, wanting to be a person who champions my values, who speaks up, and who makes their case forcefully, I have published and made presentations advocating my views (Shawver and Sanders 1977; Shawver 1980; Clanon *et al.* 1982; Shawver and Dickover 1986; Shawver 1987; Shawver and Kurdys 1987; Shawver 1993; Shawver 1994; Shawver 1995; Shawver 1996), and I have presented testimony in many court cases attempting to show that women and gays will be accepted by others so that job restrictions against them can be removed.

Second, in order to promote paralogy – this productive conversation among diverse views – I have created and am a listmaster for an internet list (a forum where people interact) and I have tried to present my voice by taking the opposing position at face value rather than attacking the character and hidden motives of my opponents. I think this invites the best presentation of the alternative position, which in turn stimulates me to develop a more adequate position. And, although, as Gergen says, challenging the opponent's character is an easy way to defeat one's opponent, it is not a good way to promote paralogy among diverse views. Therefore, in classes and public forums I have tried to learn how to give the floor to others, now and then, and to listen generously as well as to ask others to listen to me. Most importantly, I have tried to learn the difficult art of accepting criticism of my views. I still have much to learn.

From your standpoint in critical psychology, what are the most pressing problems?

I think the most pressing problem for critical psychology is: how do we learn to talk together? For a long time now, Western culture has been confined to the closure of thinking of discussion as war (Lakoff and Johnson 1980). I am inspired by the thought of finding new ways to promote paralogy (Shawver 1998a, 1998b), new ways of creating cultures in which we are all more able to think things through. Today, we often talk past each other, repeating ourselves to people who only want us to listen to them.

But we have all experienced paralogical conversation, conversation that stimulates us to think things through. So it is possible. I think it is most likely once we become thoroughly disillusioned with what Lyotard calls 'metanarratives', grand narratives that tell us they are the last word. People who are disillusioned with these metanarratives Lyotard calls 'postmodern'. Paralogy is an inventive way for coping with our postmodernism, that is, our scepticism in the face of each new theory. It is a kind of brainstorming (Lyotard 1984: 52) and an imaginative rearrangement of shared data (Lyotard 1984: 51), a way of collaborating with each other so that we can 'go on', not all in the same direction but still helping each other, not blocking each other's path, recognizing that any progress to a better world will negotiate a zigzag course with a changing destination. Our pressing problem is not merely our need to learn how to talk so others can hear us, but to learn how to listen so others can hear us – because listening is contagious, and we, too, want to be heard.

I believe it is because there are so few forums in which people can be heard that therapy has found a niche. Therapists are better able to listen than most, but it is not enough. If we can create paralogical forums in therapy and elsewhere, then we will enhance the spirit of our camaraderie, we will deconstruct the harmful illusion that things should always stay the same, and most importantly we will help each other find a voice that learns to speak, a voice that no longer merely echoes the voices of the past.

18

Thinking Critically About Psychology

John Kaye

'What these issues come down to is that there is no place in psycho-logy or even in discursive psychology, for critical work to start. A critical psychology has to be constructed from theoretical resources, life experiences and political identities outside *the discipline.'*

Ian Parker (Fox and Prilleltensky 1996: 298)

Prologue

If psychology has a dominant mission, it is to generate knowledge about human behaviour and for this knowledge to be applied to the promotion of human welfare. As readers of this book will be all too aware, this project has been conducted primarily within the frame of the natural sciences paradigm. Thus, academically, the mainstream has been committed to the 'scientific' study of behaviour, while humanistically it has been dedicated to the use of its knowledge together with the practices derived therefrom to benefit human well-being, primarily through enabling people's personal and interpersonal adjustment.

In this chapter, I argue that psychology, by virtue of the limits on knowledge generation imposed by its governing paradigm, is ill-equipped for its proclaimed welfare task at both the individual and the societal level. I argue that psychology, far from contributing to the sum of human well-being, is (albeit unwittingly) complicit in the maintenance of social arrangements and practices that act to the detriment of the already disadvantaged, thereby contributing to social injustice.

I question, too, whether psychology because of its positivist philosophy and associated methods is equipped to enable people to deal with change and whether it falls into the trap of helping people adjust to the unjust – thereby perpetuating inequity. This issue is particularly pertinent at a time of radical sociocultural transformation, with its attendant uncertainty, insecurity and increasing economic inequality.

In this context, I believe that if mainstream psychology is to contribute to people's welfare it needs to develop a metaposition from which to interrogate its paradigm and to increase its awareness of the interests served by its practices along with their political consequences. In order for this to occur and for its practices to evolve, the discipline needs to:

- view itself through the lens of disciplinary knowledges and investigative conventions other than the strictly experimental or scientistic;
- shape its practices in the light of critical perspectives extant in society together with considerations of social justice threatened by depersonalizing corporatism during this period of escalating change.

A psychology enriched by a critical perspective – that is, one taking into account developments in the philosophy and sociology of knowledge as well as ethical considerations – will, one hopes, prove to be of greater social value than sentimental appeals to doing good, utopian notions of bringing about a better world, or the grandiose aim of changing society. A critical psychology needs to be self-reflexively critical!

On becoming critical

Let me begin with the editor's request to address what brought me to critical psychology and what it means to me. I wish to state from the outset that I find myself unable to subscribe wholeheartedly to the idea of a domain labelled critical psychology. I find the connotations of entity thinking, homogeneity and imperialism implicit in the notion deeply problematic. Nor can I subscribe to the uncritically grandiose notion of a critical psychology dedicated to the ideals of bringing about a better world or of changing society. While I embrace the notion of a psychology open to radical theorizing and activism in local contexts, I do not see the grand, idealistic narrative of changing society as within psychology's brief – or capability! I certainly do advocate a perspective that

- offers an intellectual, theoretical and political critique of psychology and its practices;
- seeks to incorporate examination of how socially constructed ideologies, discursive formations and practices affect human behaviour, thought, experience and well-being;
- attempts to develop practices that act in the interests of the people it serves, rather than to their detriment.

How did I arrive at this position?

While it is difficult to divine all the influences (however self-reflexive I might wish to be!), I guess I, like many of us, entered psychology with the naïve expectation of coming to understand something of human experience, motivation and interpersonal interaction – expectations of which, still today, our mainstream academic colleagues think students need to be disabused. And I *was* disabused – but my disillusion was with the discipline itself, its atomism and reductionism. It was as if something was missing from all the findings masquerading as basic indisputable facts and I became critical of the limits placed on legitimate study – with intangibles such as experience, mind and what happens between people either barred from consideration or having their meaning so changed by operational definition as to become but an impoverished shadow of the phenomenon supposedly being studied.

I came to see that psychology's governing paradigm was drawn from an epistemology fitted for exploration of the world of the *non-living* rather than the world of the *living* – a distinction drawn by Gregory Bateson. In the world of the *non-living*, which Bateson called 'the Newtonian world of energy and objects', forces and impacts provide what is thought to be a sufficient explanation of events. It is a world of forces in which one part is thought to act on another part and is based on metaphors of matter, substance, energy and cause. The world of the *living*, which Bateson called 'the world of communication', is a world of form and order, of pattern and organization. In this world events are explained by responses to information.

Clearly then, I thought, there was a fundamental error built into psychology's paradigm when applied both to the living subject and people in interaction. Misconception and confusion in theoretical thinking, theory-building and theoretical explanation were bound to arise when we apply concepts appropriate for the world of the non-living to the world of the living.

My disenchantment found expression when critiques of the dominant paradigm emerged in the 1960s. Thus Jerome Bruner in his Wolfson Lectures raised the question of why experimental or academic psychology had not made more of an impact on the broad cultural conception of the nature of humankind. His answer, of course, was that psychology had initially defined its task in such a way that it could *never* have had much of a direct impact, given the nature of its concepts of explanation. Its initial concerns, he wrote, its theoretical orientation, its style of research were not fitted to the kinds of processes or patterns that shape human affairs as they occur in human societies: symbolic systems like language, conceptual structures in terms of which human beings carve up and interpret the world around them, and the cultural constraints imposed by human institutions were not within its frame of reference.

How anticlimactic this is, given psychology's original grand vision – knowledge and understanding of the human being, of human nature in the service of human welfare and betterment! Yet one can understand the seduction of the Enlightenment promise of steady progress via scientific study toward that beckoning light on the hill shining so brightly with its deceptive illusion of certainty. And it must have been so hopeful, the promise of enlightenment via the Enlightenment project that psychology had adopted as its vehicle toward a future predictable world based on reason and incontrovertible knowledge, of control over thought and action.

But the Enlightenment project was not only about the gaining of knowledge about the world and its governing principles. In its evolution to counter the forces of darkness, of barbarism, of superstition, it also had a moral–ethical dimension. However, in Western epistemology, the modernist conception that forms the cornerstone of the Enlightenment project – access to truth and reality objectively grounded in scientific study – has become so deeply embedded in our thinking, so entrenched in our knowledge generation, that it has come to define what it is to know and understand. Thus the moral–ethical dimension has become marginalized and the political effects of our practices have been omitted from consideration.

And while psychology, in its specification of the exemplary life, was saturated with a Judeo-Christian ethic, it proclaimed itself value-free! Entranced by the search for knowledge and a fascination with the human organism, it focused on intrapsychic processes atomistically considered and on the decontextualized study of the rational, unitary individual. The result, as Bruner pointed out, was that what needed to be studied was barred by the rules governing orthodox experimental method. And what a bizarre, fragmentary picture of the human being emerged: non-agentic, non-proactive, triggered into action solely by instinctual urges or environmental stimuli. An automation to be activated, a robot to be shaped, at the command of the external, a figure in a landscape considered largely independently of that landscape as if the two were separable, as if we do not co-constitute our world.

Enter the sociocultural

While my critical questioning of a paradigm assuming the possibility of presuppositionless, value-free, objectively-grounded knowledge became sharpened by acquaintance with post-foundationalism, it was further elucidated by my inevitable encounter with post-structuralist and social constructionist thought. While the impossibility of gaining unmediated access to some aboriginal reality is well captured by Peter Medawar's famous dictum that there is a mask of theory over the whole face of nature, essentialism was countermanded by the notion that our *known* reality is socially constructed and language-constituted. Along with this I experienced a sociopolitical concern, undoubtedly fomented originally by a South African upbringing. Perhaps I was not sufficiently indoctrinated by an ideology of black inferiority, nor by pseudoscientific images of black racial primitivity nor yet again by an essentialist psychology's cooption, into supporting a myth of genetic intellectual inferiority with culturally unfair IQ tests! Rather, I experienced increasing dis-ease at the damage inflicted by white imperialism, its devastation of functioning tribal cultures, the history of its undue assumption of superiority, its patronizing colonialist attempts to 'civilize' the 'savage'. And I was witness to the alienation and subjugation of a people, the social and spiritual damage, the devastation of servility, deprivation and poverty, the consequences of racial discrimination and marginalization.

At this time I abandoned a naïve but felt humanism for a critical social realism and became critical of the role I perceived psychology to play in the maintenance of discriminatory discourse and practices of power. Later acquaintance with post-structuralism (remember, we middle-class South Africans were inoculated against Marxism during our education!) brought me a clear understanding of psychology's broader role in the maintenance of the social order with all its structural inequities.

On critical psychology, psychological knowledge and practice

A critical perspective on psychology, then, goes beyond the constructionist recognition that in order to understand people and their interactions we need to understand their cultural embedding. While the critique offers a trenchant theoretical and ethical deconstruction of psychology's dominant paradigm, together with its scientific absolutism, it also highlights how:

- psychology, far from being neutral, serves social, ideological and political interests
- it privileges concepts and practices which benefit dominant groupings in society at the expense of the marginalized and less powerful.

Not the least reason for this is the societal institutionalization of what is taken to be factual psychological knowledge. In this sense, both traditional experimental and analytic psychology have been spectacularly successful in infiltrating human consciousness and practice. Society is permeated by psychological talk, psychological explanation, psychological practices. The arts provide plotlines suffused with psychological clues and the media speculate endlessly about the psychological bases or motivations for the bizarre, unusual or unexpected. Common parlance is suffused with IQs, learning disabilities, real selves and personality traits. From an early age we are measured, examined, tested and categorized and, according to standardized norms, fall on either side of a normalization divide. We are adjusted or maladjusted, normal or abnormal, sane or crazy, neurotic, psychotic, repressed or impulsive, extraverted or introverted, fitted for this or that career. We turn to the social sciences and its empirical finding to tell us how to live. And perhaps most tellingly, because of our learned intrapsychic focus, the psychological knowledges that have come to govern us wearing their seductively humane mask have led us to judge and discipline ourselves in their light. As Foucault would have it, becoming believers in the teachings by which we have been positioned we become self-governing, while at the same time internalizing many of society's ingrained inequities of class, race, gender and economic status. In this way in turn, psychology is, quite independently and however unwittingly, complicit in the maintenance of the social order, in the regulation of people and the reproduction of practices of power – often to the detriment of the disadvantaged.

The same problem potentially attaches to the process of psychotherapy. Psychotherapy, as with psychology, is a product of the ethos pervading at a given historical period and as such is part of and draws on the culture that developed it. It embodies a moral–ethical discursive formation, prescribing the normative and making the individual the locus of responsibility.

This justifies a critical troubling of the notion that therapy is socioculturally neutral and leads to a conceptualization of psychotherapy as a normalizing discipline implicitly caught up in maintaining a given social order, as Foucault would suggest, and therefore implicated in the regulation of people. Most psychotherapies are infused with ideologically saturated regimes of truth specifying particular power relations between consultant and consultee. Not only is the consultee initially placed in a subordinate position, but the process can entail particular techniques of discursive regulation or practices of power that in turn produce and reproduce those rules and practices implicated in the maintenance of specific technologies of the self. Further, the very practices prescribed by psychotherapy (self-examination, self-evaluation and self-regulation) precisely parallel the practices whereby people are recruited into limiting subject positions.

In this light, psychotherapy may be regarded as potentially if not necessarily regulative. It may position people to become complicit in their own subordination by implicitly inducing them to conform to specifications of personhood derived from dominant conceptions of normality or moral codes governing exemplary ways of being. From the perspective of a critical psychologist, psychotherapy may thus be plausibly construed as an ideologically driven practice, which supports and is supported by the institutions of our society, and which may serve as in instrument of social control, preserving the dominant culture and unknowingly maintaining inequitable, disempowering or subordinating social conditions and practices. Its individualizing of the problems people experience, together with the instantiation of self-scrutiny as a central therapeutic modality, draws attention to the personal and away from the problem's possible sociocultural source. And certainly, community problems are often transformed into or reframed as individual problems – at which juncture people become deemed to be suitable cases for treatment by socially sanctioned helpers whose intervention in turn serves to maintain the *status quo*.

On change

Having dwelt perhaps too long on the maintenance of the societal *status quo*, I would now like to turn to the question of sociocultural change and its challenge to psychology. If there is a constant in any society, it is the inevitability of change. Thus, as we move into the new millennium, we are inextricably caught up in the transformations wrought by changing ideas, mores, conventions and practices. We witness orthodoxy giving way to the simultaneous growth of new cultural norms, new guiding principles, new ways of thinking.

While globalism, corporatism, the market economy, consumerism, competitive individualism, and the information revolution prompt and are part of this change, the process is in no small part due to the readiness of the contemporary humanities and social sciences to question biologic, scientific and moral foundationalism and to explore the role language and culture play in forming our knowledge stores and systems of meaning.

More and more, our conceptual and moral frameworks, our grand narratives as well as the very rules governing our beliefs and practices – that whole panoply of culturally constructed values for so long accepted as given – have come under question. Their taken-for-granted status, their very givenness, is regularly challenged, their consequences for us examined and their regulatory effects on our behaviour – indeed our mode of being and relating – analysed.

Under such scrutiny (much of it prompted post-structuralist, critical and feminist theorists and activists) many of the foundational assumptions that once served to fashion our subjectivities and to regulate our behaviour have been unmasked as stories or shibboleths rather than as unquestionable truths. Of these, some, such as racial or gender stereotypes, have been revealed as oppressive or discriminatory rather than merely regulatory. A consequence of these realizations has in many cases led to legal as well as social reform – for example, in the area of women's liberation, abortion law reform, the decriminalization of homosexuality, the outlawing of racism.

Thus, while a great number of people remain threatened by the loss of their illusory certitudes and mourn the passing of what they see as a more disciplined age, and while yet others flail in rank fear of moral decay, a still greater number benefit from the recognition and removal of inequality, of discriminatory practices and from no longer being subject to institutionalized prejudice and victimization.

At the same time, change in the social ethos can be plausibly argued to have exercised deleterious effects on people's lives and relationships. The accelerating displacement of the Judeo-Christian and modernist codes of morality and practice that once provided community stability is associated with a loss of optimism, a loss of certainty, the erosion of many of the values and institutions around which people built their lives and relationships. The domination of market philosophy allied to competitive consumerism has witnessed the privileging of 'the economy' over considerations of a social and communitarian ethic. This has been accompanied by:

- job-shedding, with its corrosive effect on people's welfare, family relationships, morale and self-esteem;
- increasing homelessness, drug use and drug-related crime;

- social and economic inequity, with decline in real personal income for the majority, an ever-increasing gulf between haves and have-nots, and burgeoning poverty.

The above again raises the following questions:

- the role played by the human and social disciplines in either maintaining or challenging the *status quo*;
- their capacity to foster human well-being in a climate of deprivation, alienation and loss of morale;
- how to elucidate or make sense of the effects of post-modern society on human experience and relationships.

Where psychology is concerned, psychologists of a critical persuasion would assert that psychology's role in advancing human welfare is circumscribed; that, far from being neutral, the discipline privileges concepts and practices that serve the interests of dominant subgroups within society at the expense of the marginalized or less powerful. They question how a discipline which (a) seeks to hold the positivist line despite the evolutionary changes in scientific epistemology; (b) unwittingly serves the *status quo*, (c) is immured in scientific absolutism and dedicated to the 'discovery' of invariant laws, and (d) individualizes human problems at the expense of considering the sociocultural can elucidate the effects on people of the social transformations wrought by information technology, virtuality and a market economy that increasingly undermines human worth and emphasizes individual dispensability. They question also how it can act in the interests of the marginalized and adversely affected.

On being critical

Thus far I have written on changes in both the sociocultural and academic ethos and yet have treated psychology as unitary and unchanging. This of course is not the case. While the mainstream has maintained its positivist stress on the scientific study of behaviour and remains the dominant discourse, the discipline has undergone seemingly dramatic changes, influenced *inter alia* by Marxism, post-structuralism, deconstruction and the turn to language, which has allowed a critique to develop that challenges psychology's foundational assumptions, drawing on influences from outside its disciplinary borders.

This is perhaps the key to evolution in *all* disciplines – a criticality constituted by the ability to adopt a metaperspective on a given knowledge domain rather than attempting a critique from *within* the parameters of its governing paradigm. Without such challenge, disciplinary change would be difficult. That is, given that change to a paradigm cannot occur from within that paradigm, the discipline concerned would simply recreate itself in the same image *ad infinitum*! Criticality in our discipline, then, has enabled a challenge to the paradigm inhabited by mainstream psychology and in which it finds its warrant. It has triggered an interrogation of psychology's foundational assumptions, its research methods, its concepts and its practices. And more than that, it has alerted us to the role played by psychology in social regulation and to the discriminatory, inequitable and oppressive consequences of the distinctions it draws between normal and abnormal, male and female, intelligent and unintelligent...

Further, however, criticality for many also necessitates a moving beyond critique if we are to make a worthwhile contribution to society, its store of knowledge and social welfare. It requires

- action in the form of deconstruction or subversion of societal 'givens';
- the development of socially just, inclusive practices that enable people to question and challenge their positioning in a way that gives voice to the marginalized and does not reproduce inequitable power relations;
- activism in the sense of sociocultural intervention;
- research enquiry that gives rise to new knowledges, new ways of seeing.

With regard to this last point, perhaps we can legitimately claim that the methods of enquiry we have appropriated and developed (for example critical discourse analysis) throw light on the sociocultural determination of behaviour together with unjust, constraining social practices and in this sense justify criticality. Criticality too might add a creative dimension to psychological research. That is, it allows a generative enquiry that construes research as productive rather than reproductive, creative rather than representational. No longer constrained by the illusion of value-free objectivity, it might seek an alternative understanding of a given field of enquiry, to reframe it, or to provide creative answers and solutions to substantive, unclarified issues in that field. This can occur only on the basis of a reading that reaches for understanding by forging new connections between ideas and their referents in order to construct an illuminating account. Such a form of enquiry involves the reinterpretation or resymbolization of discourse via dialogic interchange in a novel context or from a novel perspective – one that

- differs from that which conventionally governs discourse in the area, and
- creates novel distinctions and thereby generates new meanings.

I am here arguing for an approach to enquiry that seeks both to illuminate the discursive formations that organize our knowing and to create meanings that might dissolve societal quandaries as well as give rise to novel solutions.

Here we might agree with John Shotter, that to the extent that new forms of talk tend to construct new forms of social relation, they begin to take on more of a 'real' existence as talk of them increases and gives rise to new social institutions.

There are of course ethical implications in the above conception of research as dialogic interchange. Given that we can never gain access to an uninterpreted reality, ethically we become responsible for how we frame our experiments or observations and how we interpret them. This is because, via our 'designs', we construct the realities we think we perceive and we create findings that might have consequences for people's lives. Psychological reproduction of gender stereotypes is one area that springs readily to mind. Criticality would also alert us to how, via mainstream construals of experimental procedure, we create a picture of humans (our subjects) of human relations (the right of the socially sanctioned expert to operate on the other), which in turn reproduce inequitable practices of power and maintain hierarchical sociocultural role demarcations. Criticality would promote a form of collaborative research as an alternate procedure in which all participants have or gain equal 'voice'. That is, research can take the form of a collaborative dialogue aimed at the exploration of social and policy issues as they affect human experience and behaviour, the dissolution of dilemmas in living and the generation of useful knowledges about these concerns. This collaborative search for meaning not merely fosters a participatory ethic, but is capable of generating revealing readings of social process that might trigger socially just outcomes.

Critical approaches, then, in the form of collaborative discursive inquiry, can make a contribution to social evolution and justice at a community level. This is evidenced at a local level in many centres around the world, the Dulwich Centre in Adelaide, South Australia, the Family Centre Group at Lower Hutt, New Zealand, and the East Side Institute in New York being but some examples.

A further question relates to how else we might foster a critical sensibility and practice. In my own work, I have developed a discursive approach to therapy that avoids an intrapsychic focus by situating the problem not within people, nor yet within their personal narratives but rather within the socially constructed discursive formations, practices and conditions by which they are positioned. That is, I seek to open up choices by having the person interrogate the discourse and their life situation (for example, unemployment) rather than him or herself.

In my university work, similarly, I seek to inculcate a critical consciousness and to have students trouble the given, question the dominant paradigm and interrogate the effects of social constructions on individual thought, feeling and action. I hope to have students attend *to* constructs they have taken for granted rather than *from* them. In class, indeed in lectures, I use a variety of methods to trigger this and to promote conjoint learning (experiential exercises, media examples, video, narrative, discussion, enactment). I do all this with the aim of raising awareness and opening up new, possible ways of construing relationships between people and the world we co-constitute. These considerations will often find their way into the conversations I have with friends and colleagues – hopefully making a difference at a local level.

Yet I must still pose the question of whether a psychology infused with criticality can exercise influence at a broader societal level. Certainly there is a desire on the part of psychologists who work under a critical banner to bring about social and political change. And clearly, psychologists have worked for gay rights, black rights, the rights of the psychiatrically labelled and other stigmatized groups. But these changes did not come about by virtue of psychology; they did not issue from psychology but from perspectives, philosophic and political sensibilities in the wider general and academic communities. We are psychologists working for change, psychologists who hold values congruent with and now incorporated into the critical agenda – but the values were not developed *by* critical psychology.

Infused with critical values, we might perhaps jettison our utopian dreams of changing society toward some impossible ideal state and content ourselves with working at a local level, not being unwittingly complicit with oppressive practices of power and not reproducing them via our texts, talk, research and practice.

Alternatively, if we want a broader influence, we will need to ask ourselves, 'In partnership with whom?', 'In alliance with whom?', viewing ourselves in an interdisciplinary way as an integral part of a larger discipline rather than anchored within uniquely psychological boundaries. I think it is time to strategically suspend disciplinary boundaries and think of psychology both as a discipline with legitimate concerns with the subject and as part of a broader and continuing social project. In this way we might develop that critical mass of voices sufficiently to be heard, sufficiently for our ideas and practices to gain public acceptance, sufficiently for our ideas to inform community practice.

To achieve this, inhabiting as it might a space at the intersection of the personal, interpersonal and social, a new discipline of social criticality will need to develop a popular language just as mainstream psychology has. Its concepts need to become part of public consciousness. Perhaps that might herald a discontinuous change, enabling societal evolution towards the critically impossible dream! Such a change, one might hope, would keep us in a dialogical world rather than forging a new oppositional dualism, a new oppressive hegemony.

Concluding remarks

In this chapter I have sought to illustrate a critical position by offering a critical deconstruction of mainstream psychology while offering alternatives from a position of criticality. In the process I have attempted to outline some features of a critical perspective while trying to avoid implying the existence of a unitary critical psychology. Having, examined the implications of criticality for research and ethical practice, I see criticality predominantly as a metaperspective allowing a critique, questioning and at times a subversion of dominant disciplinary paradigms and practices, one that also moves beyond critique to action. I suggest, finally, that to exercise influence beyond the local level we will need to develop a critical mass of voices and a popular language and see ourselves as partners in an interdisciplinary project at the interface of the individual, the community and the sociopolitical worlds. This is crucial at a time of profound and in many ways profoundly troubling social transformation.

Acknowledgments

I thank all whose writings have informed this chapter. Among contemporary thinkers and authors, I owe a particular debt to Gregory Bateson, Jerome Bruner, Ken Gergen, Ian Parker, Nik Rose, John Shotter and Wendy and Rex Stainton-Rogers. I also acknowledge the profound influence of Michel Foucault.

19

Critical Psychology or Critique of Psychology?

Colectivo Contrapsicológico Esquicie

When English and American *compañeros* invited us to contribute a chapter for a book on critical psychology, besides being pleased to hear that such a publication was being prepared, we had to figure out how we, as a collective, could prepare our contribution. We decided finally to record the conversation among us in which we responded to the questions posed to us, then to summarize and extract from the transcript in a manner that would convert our eight voices, and the innumerable other 'voices' that accompanied us, into one lively but contradictory voice.

Our collective* defines itself as counter-psychological [*contrapsicológico*, hereafter 'contra-psychology', to retain the flavour in Spanish – T.S.]. We hope that in these few thousand words we can convey an inkling of our critique of psychology, both in word and action.

What does critical psychology mean to you?

Silence. The question, kindly translated for us from English by a *compañera*, has left us with perplexed faces. We recognize that the interviewer has shot right at the heart of the matter with this

---

* Those who participated concretely in the writing of this essay are: Conchi San Martín (clinical psychologist/contra-psychologist), Jesus (ex-psychiatric patient in permanent struggle against psychiatry), Josep Alfons Arnau (social educator/contra-psychologist), Pep Requejo (clinical psychologist/contra-psychologist), Victor Jorquera (psychology student/contra-psychologist) and Yolanda Nievas (psychologist/contra-psychologist). Others helped us through their spirit and desire. We send cordial greetings to the readers of this book and to the *compañeros* who took the initiative to make it possible.

first question. After collecting ourselves and commenting timidly that we wish others would answer the question for us, the following reflections emerged.

Our general sense is that we should probably emphasize the *critique of psychology* rather than develop a *critical psychology*, in the sense that we would not want to stay trapped in the illusion of a possible partial reform of a discipline that appears to be situated as an apparatus for control and social normalization, as Michel Foucault and others have already explained. Let us explain.

At this moment, in the Spanish state from which we write, the majority of the psychologists and the discipline they develop in the universities defend and sustain the following situation. There are more than 50 000 people interned in psychiatric institutions, the majority of them against their will, suffering aggression against their persons, and living in conditions that usurp all sorts of civil and political rights. For example, they lose their rights to move freely, to use their own money, to communicate freely with the exterior, to relate sexually according to their desire, to organize their time and activities. They are subjected to obligatory medication, often without their awareness and without being informed about their secondary effects. Electroshock and lobotomies are used with increasing frequency these days. Sterilizations are also done. Their belongings are registered and controlled. They are used as cheap labour, under the guise of work therapy. Furthermore, being labelled as mentally ill implies incapacitation at the legal level, that is, loss of the rights of a 'normal' citizen, perhaps for the rest of one's life, as well as the impossibility of access to certain work positions.

In Barcelona alone, the city in which our collective was born, in one year (1995), more than 3400 persons were admitted involuntarily by judicial decision. The majority of these had not committed any criminal acts as defined by penal legislation. Hundreds of psychologists work for temporary labour companies, where they administer tests and indoctrinate workers in order to send them to jobs with precarious contracts and starvation wages (up to 50 per cent of their earnings is creamed off to cover administrative costs). The Universidad de Psicologia de Barcelona sends hundreds of students to gain the required practical experience with these companies.

In the public health services, psychotherapy either simply does not exist, since treatment is reduced to medication, or it is performed with long waiting-lists and monthly visits of fifteen minutes, always with a quick diagnosis. Private psychologists take advantage of this situation and charge an average of 7000 pesetas (approx. $39) per hour, in a country where welfare pensions are less than 35 000 pesetas (approx. $193) per month and the minimum professional salary is approximately 65 000 pesetas (approx. $360) monthly. In schools, psychologists and social workers diagnose children as 'antisocial,' 'problem children,' 'learning-disabled', and so on, and perform individual treatments that in the majority of the cases lead the children into schools or routes that are traditionally designed for those of whom one expects nothing, the 'failures'.

In homes and shelters for abused and poor children, psychiatric drugs such as Haloperidol, Modecate and Tranxilium are routinely administered to children who cause problems in discipline. In prisons, 'professionals' develop so-called rehabilitation programmes on the basis of the most primitive and radical-behaviourist principles, using inmates more than therapists to form treatment teams that decide who may or may not receive leave permits and so forth. They are also silently complicit in the tortures and assaults that occur in prisons, leading annually to sixty deaths in suspicious conditions.

As you can see, this situation is what makes critical psychology, that is, the critique of psychology, an urgent necessity.

What brought you to contra-psychology as your form of critical psychology? What do you see as the basic principles and what have been your major influences?

Pensive faces. A few ask for another glass of wine, others ask for tea. Cups and glasses are filled, then: Our collective emerged from the need to import the lessons of anti-psychiatry into psychology. Anti-psychiatry has been the major influence on how we understand our practice: contra-psychology is political and subversive.

It is political in the way that it contests the positivist illusion of the neutrality of psychological practice. Positivist psychology, that is, the hegemony that believes itself to be scientific, becomes ideology precisely at the instant in which it denies that it assumes any particular value positions, because it then works in accord with and in favour of the dominant values. The positivism that sets up the axes that direct official psychology leads to a view of problems as technical matters rather than as conflicts that are ethical at heart. Thus, contra-psychology is not only inevitably political, but it must be political, inasmuch as once the inescapability of values is assumed then an ethical decision is made in favour of excluded values.

Contra-psychology is subversive because it denounces the false neutrality of official psychology and joins with the oppressed in practices that transform reality and challenge the *status quo*.

At the level of theory, it thus becomes our social responsibility to denounce the situations where psychology gives an individualistic or psychologistic explanation of problems that are social or political in origin.

At the level of practice, anti-psychiatry (especially the existential phenomenology of Cooper, Laing, Esterson, Shatzman, and Mary Barnes, but also of Bassaglia, Antonucci, and a bit of Thomas Szasz) offers us a new way of conceiving of therapy. In particular, it denies the medical-biological etiology of mental illness. This is not to deny the existence of emotional suffering, nor the fact that people 'go crazy'. Rather, it implies attention to the importance of social and cultural factors in people's existential projects and the breakdowns that their projects can suffer. The task is therefore to offer an alternative to the medical model of mental illness, one that neither rejects difference, nor confuses statistical norms with 'health'. The medical model inherently makes value judgments about how one should view one's life and, with its reductionist explanations, it obscures and denies widespread social and cultural factors such as marginalization, poverty and exploitation, blames the person who suffers the emotional consequences of such factors, and excuses the welfare state policies that perpetuate these conditions.

We believe that no help can be therapeutic is if is imposed against the will of the person who receives it. Part of our commitment to social justice is to refuse to collaborate with violent therapeutic practices imposed 'for your own good' – as Alice Miller says.

We see contra-psychology as an alliance with the excluded in order to break the power structure set up by professionalism and the asymmetric and unequal relation between the roles of patient and therapist. Hegemonic psychology situates itself in a position of power in which the persons who receive help are treated as patients and not as active persons who are subjects of their own knowledge and decisions. They are separated from their symptoms, which lowers the communicative value of their hallucinations and deliria. In sum, their symptoms are interpreted, not listened to, transmitting a sense that they do not have the best knowledge of themselves. The possibility that people who have experienced similar things might be in the best position to help them is never considered. The experiences of therapeutic anti-psychiatric communities like Kingsley Hall in the 1970s shows that such fellow sufferers can offer very important help (see *Two Accounts of a Journey Through Madness* by Mary Barnes and Joseph Berke).

Finally, we agree with anti-psychiatry in its opposition to diagnosis. Diagnosis involves an epistemological prejudgement, based in previously developed categories that impede an open, unprejudiced approach to the person who asks for therapy. Politically, diagnosis functions as labelling with the aim of classifying, segregating and marginalizing. Anti-psychiatry sees diagnosis as a social function and not as the scientific function it pretends to be. The point is to intervene in the system of macro- and micro-relations that envelop the person.

Our influences come from sources other than anti-psychiatry. We are also indebted to Sartrean existentialism, Goffman, Camus, Foucault, Marx, de Beauvoir, Dostoyevsky, Reich, Lerena, Rodoreda, A. Miller, Cortazar, Fromm, K. Mitchell, Illich... and especially to all the popular resistance movements and social rebellions that existed or were carried out before us.

It is worth pointing out that in Spain institutional policies have perverted some of the key anti-psychiatric concepts. Public administration has promulgated supposedly progressive laws that have led to the closing of certain mental hospitals. Actually, it was not the adoption of progressive ideas, but real estate interests that motivated these closures – they closed asylums in cities where the properties had great value. Of course, it was irresponsible to close them without creating alternatives, and thousands have become homeless and indigent or returned to families that could not offer adequate attention or – worse – were the origin of the person's problems. Anti-psychiatry never wanted all this, but the failure of deinstitutionalization has been blamed on it.

What are the principal debates in critical psychology or contra-psychology?

Silence. Rapid glances. Serious faces. A smile. Someone prepares a cigarette of diverse natural substances, another makes coffee. One of us begins:

Cooper's final reflections come to mind. He thought that maybe the only way to end psychiatric violence would be through the total negation of psychiatry and related know-ledges/practices such as psychology. That is, at this point, no reform is possible. We can only advocate the disappearance of these psychiatric specialists along with their farcical theory and practice.

Current forms of therapy aim for a normalization of malad-justed organisms, to put them back in the places that made them sick, but with more resistance against future maladjustment. They are programmes for rehabilitation, reintegration, and re-ideologization...the delusion of the 'therapeutic welfare state'.

In part, our collective grew out of our therapeutic activity, and we still do that sort of work, but we do not want to hide from the contradiction: to what extent does therapy – even its ethical and humane form – simply perpetuate the system that makes therapy necessary? To what extent is it just a bandage, a way of patching things up? Will therapy always inevitably reproduce the unequal power relation between the expert and the person needing help?

A Spanish poet, a member of the *Colectivo de Psiquiatrizados en Lucha* (Collective of Psychiatric Patients in Struggle), Leopoldo María Panero, writes: 'In the current system, some fall and others don't, and those that fall are called crazy – and no one really knows why.' So, is it possible to help those of us who fall? Is it possible to develop a sort of revolutionary therapy that does not betray or silence the oppressed? How can we stand up when they knock us down?

Another voice offers these reflections: The therapeutic-technocratic state presents itself as the fruit of liberal democratic progress in the so-called developed countries. The bourgeois-scientific democratic technocracy dictates which relations are sane and punishes (pardons, helps) those who deviate from them. The imposition of bourgeois liberal-democratic discourse has achieved a thorough destruction of social support networks, generating a continuous delegation of responsibilities to its official representatives: if there is an act of violence, as in a case of a battered women, for example, the police or the experts are called, but passers-by or neighbours do not intervene.

Another voice adds that the problem is to create spaces in which we can demonstrate that it is possible to live in a different way…

What does it mean to help? Who helps? What is the difference between those who help and those who are helped? In friendship, one is accompanied, listened to, witnessed. But Alice Miller warns us against the professional social experts who are trained in blindness in order to maintain emotional neutrality and to help objectively. These are lies that must be scrutinized.

In a society that was not based on the survival values of exploitation and competition, therapy might not be necessary. This is the desire that inspires us: to determine our own lives collectively and freely.

Someone mischievously asks… What about the danger of creating little islands of happiness? And what happened in the therapeutic communities of the 1970s? Wasn't there repression, fear, exhaustion, impotence…? What can we learn from what they tried to accomplish? This is the core of the debate. It is not a matter of finding the perfect solution, but of going a little bit further than we have gone before. When Allende was already surrounded in the Palacio de la Moneda in Santiago and about to be assassinated by Pinochet's forces, he said: The people must not let themselves be harassed or murdered. Others will come; this is but one more page in the history of the people.

An ironic smile and we hear a voice:

This sounds like a messianic discourse or a political pamphlet!

Silence and then another voice in response:
No, it sounds like the struggle, an attempt neither to save oneself nor to sell oneself.

Another voice:
From the yard of the T. Borda asylum in Argentina a radio broadcast done by the people interned there, one hears: 'They put me in here and I have lost my freedom. They tell me I am crazy. Does anyone know what that means? I can't leave when I want. I am no longer a person.' That is the question: does anyone know what that means?

At the end of the 1970s, Cooper thought that anti-psychiatry ran the risk of being reduced to small communal experiments for six or seven people. It might become elitist and marginal, or simply devoured and assimilated by the institutions as part of the supposed reform. It seems that he was right. There was also repression. Anti-psychiatric workers' names were on blacklists and some of them were imprisoned, like the SPK (Socialist Patients Collective) workers in Germany. The illusion that public mental health could be reformed or socialized has been part of the decline of anti-psychiatric practice. This is an issue we need to reflect on further.

By way of synthesis we offer a multi-faceted strategy: to be inside the official institutions to alleviate what suffering we can – and given that we are talking about people who are suffering psychiatric and psychological violence, it is crucial that we be inside to denounce the barbarities that occur there, but without the illusion of enduring reform. And from outside the institutions, we try to construct experiments in self-determination, created from below, from the grassroots. And to continue with therapeutic work in a manner that is conscious of its contradiction and works across them.

What do you do to put these principles in practice?

More voices in the room: 'Whatever we can.' 'We should neither exhaust ourselves nor give up, and that is an art.'

Then we continue reflecting: We formed this collective in April 1995 and in these few years our main activities as a group for therapeutic support, study and protest has been the following: the organization of a place where we can meet and talk among ourselves and meet others. The organization of an open contra-psychological and anti-psychiatric seminar. It meets bimonthly for study, debate, and decision making among forty professionals and other interested persons. The publication of the first issue of a bulletin of contra-psychology and anti-psychiatry (*El Rayo que no Cesa*) and collaboration in several other publications. Networking – public talks or meetings – with other groups that share our interests, ranging from professors and students in related disciplines to popular resistance movements. Therapy with over fifty persons who have freely asked for therapeutic help and who collaborate with our collective by making donations of money, food or things they have made.

From your contra-psychological perspective, what are the most pressing sociopolitical problems? What should be done about them?

Someone sighs deeply and this produces an explosion of laughter that leads to a series of shouted slogans: 'Freedom for Euskadi, Galicia, Catalunya and all the people of the Iberian peninsula!' 'Down with monarchy!' 'Federal Republic of the armed and self-organized people!' 'Global revolution and long live Zapata and forward with Chiapas!' 'Black and Indian power!' 'Free orgasms for the oppressed, now!'

The compañera who is translating the questions from English calls us back to order and we manage to get a bit more serious.

We have been saying that psychology has increasingly become an apparatus of social control, but hasn't it always been one? A brief look at the history of this 'discipline' shows us a sinister tradition over a century old, from Wundt and his experimentation, trying to trap human thought and feeling in his laboratories and laws of reaction; through the Yerkes, Binets and Cattells and their tests applied to detect and segregate immigrants, women, child, the elderly, workers, blacks... as 'inferior' for being below the mean in 'intelligence', or 'social skills', and other denigrating constructs; continuing with the behaviourists with their reward–punishment focus; up to the current bio-social-cognitive theories in the Kraepelin clinical diagnostic tradition, which label an unusual or painful experience as mental illness or pathological social deviance. Just try to read, if you can bear the healthy repugnance that they provoke, the DSM or the ICE, or the MMPI.

It seems that we are straying (or are we?) a bit from the question.

Then there is the case of psychoanalysis. With a few honourable exceptions, such as the Wilhelm Reich of *Sex-Pol* and *Listen, Little Man!*, it has gone completely off course, with its language of power and florid over-interpretations, its mystification of the experience of the other, in the Laingian or Marxian sense of negating the other's psychic experience. This is done in the name of the concept of the unconscious, which is promoted to the level of God, and which only the psychoanalyst or the psychiatrist on duty can understand, thus defining patients as people who cannot know what they desire or say.

The anti-psychiatry from which we have learned and continue to learn has also committed errors, despite its honest struggle, because of unfavourable social forces at the beginning of the 1980s. These led radical psychiatrists like Claude Steiner to criticize anti-psychiatry's therapeutic methods as conservative for being too individualistic and for not taking into account the need to form groups for political struggle in the phase immediately after recognizing alienation. Also, David Cooper denied psychiatric practices in the name of no-psychiatry. We also see the decision of some of our comrades in anti-psychiatry to support the socialization of psychiatry in the form of community psychiatry as an error. The new tendencies such as family systems and community psychology attempt to reformulate previous positions that clearly perceived the social order as the cause of the pathological. These reformulations strip away the original revolutionary content (and the need for revolutionary change) from their basic assumptions about the need for reform of pathological structures such as families, schools, hospitals and prisons.

Again, what are the most urgent sociopolitical problems? What can be done? We do believe that something can be done. We need to leave pessimism for better times. So, since we are inside the psychology that we criticize, we need to bring this critique to its logical end, in the style of Foucault or the Zapatistas, or simply in a style that is human.

At the beginning of the twenty-first century, we think that psychology expresses its character as an apparatus of social control in five fundamental aspects, which we can synthesize as follows:

- The negation by clinical psychologists of the experience of those who break because their sensibility cannot stand the reigning social dementia (wars, ecological disasters, the massacre of desire, competition...), labelling such persons as mentally ill, segregating them, and locking them up.
- Collaboration with prisons, our structures for social punishment, where forensic psychologists decide who will have certain levels of freedom.
- Collaboration with schools and institutions where children who do not accept social pre-formation are subjected forcefully to special psychopedagogic plans.
- The assistance offered to capitalist production by industrial psychologists. Capitalist production is based on the exploitation of many by some, in compulsive consumerism, in the production of unneeded products, and the destruction of nature (weapons, cars, freeways, uninhabitable cities, televisions, computers and their virtual social networks, nuclear energy...)
- Collaboration in the alienation of the public through advertising and consultations with the electoral campaigns of corrupt bourgeois politicians and/or the creation of public opinion through the mass media.

And the question still remains, what can we do about all this?

Among other things, we can denounce these four aspects and say, *Basta!* (Enough!) There must be something that can be salvaged from psychology, the study of human experience, to develop an applied psychology that includes ways of helping with emotional suffering when help is freely requested.

We think that since we have passed through the universities and have been trained as technical professionals, we must work to create structures in which those who have no voice are able to make their own decisions.

Therapy only makes sense as a hand held out to those who fall if it is accompanied by an open position and a struggle for decision-making by so-called 'mentally ill' in psychiatric centres, by inmates in prisons, by the marginalized in their barrios, by children in their schools.

This can be done by creating networks of self-critical revolutionary therapists. We need to continue studying those who have preceded us in putting therapy at the service of human beings as well as the ways of life and thought of peoples that were probably more humane than we are, but which the West has massacred.

Translated by Tod Sloan

20

The Critical Psychology of Everyday Life

Barbara Duarte Esgalhado

To the teachers who have taught me and to the students from whom I learn

Critical psychology means to question – to question the underlying assumptions of theory and practice and the way in which they may maintain and perpetuate ignorance, inequality, oppression – in short, – the stuff of human suffering. The way I understand this questioning to be elaborated is through a commitment to exploring the processes – conscious, unconscious, social, historical and ideological – that come to constitute subjectivity.

One way this exploration takes place is through a continuous critique of assumptions that underlie our understanding of who we are and how we become. And while this critique can function on a metalevel of understanding, accompanying it is a commitment to grounding it in the force and circumstance of the world today by examining the consequences of the lived-out lives of those persons we have become. For fundamentally, I believe, the impetus for understanding psychology in this way is to be able to respond to the face of the world as it presents itself and, as a result, to help reformulate the ways we understand ourselves and others and live out that understanding (or lack thereof!) in our everyday lives.

For example, when looking at something like oppression, critical psychology calls us to examine the personal and social circumstances that create, maintain and perpetuate it. In the case of women's oppression, for example, both personal and social factors have contributed to the still precarious relationship we have to the patriarchal world in which we live our lives.

Another example is the case of United States citizens who have become increasingly disengaged from our political process as we consciously and unconsciously collude in the machinations of powerlessness perpetuated by social (including technological, specifically 'the media') and institutional practices that distance citizens from a true democratic practice. Circumstances such as these call for an approach that examines the processes – unconscious, conscious, social, historical and ideological – that constitute who we are, how we become and how, ultimately, we live the everyday of our lives.

My major influence in leading me to this way of thinking about the world was John M. Broughton – professor, mentor, dissertation sponsor and friend. I had the pleasure of sharing Professor Broughton's engaging mind, sense of social commitment, day-to-day activism and creativity as I pursued my doctoral training at Columbia University. John is particularly gifted at conveying the importance of a critical stance to all that is naturally assumed. In this way, I learned that much of everything rests upon assumptions offered by a particular historical period, social and economic circumstances, and political and ideological agendas. His expertise in the history of ideas, particularly critical theory, psychodynamic theory and semiotics helped further my understanding in the subtle ways human behaviour is formulated.

Professor Howard Gruber, who I had the pleasure of studying with during my undergraduate and graduate careers was also a strong influence on me. Howie's approach to studying creativity through the case-study method necessarily included an examination of the social and historical influences in the creative life of the case in point. Also, Howie was a politically engaged individual – a quality nearly lost in today's academic climate – and fought against injustice and oppression on and off the college campus.

Finally, Professor Dorothy Dinnerstein, whose mind and spirit I had the pleasure of experiencing both as an undergraduate and graduate student, made a great contribution to my life. Sure-footed, radical, brilliant, sensual and womanly, Dorothy, for all four feet ten inches and ninety-five pounds, conveyed, in her work (the feminist and psychological classic *The Mermaid and the Minotaur* bears her name) and in the gestures of the everyday, the incredible power and dignity of what it means to be woman.

In all three cases, my mentors went beyond the task at hand. Clearly, John, Howie and Dorothy knew the field of psychology exceptionally well, but their approaches to exploring deeply psychological issues reflected sophistication in a multitude of disciplines and ways of thinking and in the world at large. This sophistication of thought, word and deed made each of them a mentor in the full meaning of the word – one who shows a student a way of being in the world that includes but extends beyond precious ideas.

On a more personal level, my family life influenced me in ways that are still unfolding as I write. I am the daughter of Portuguese immigrants who made their way to these United States for – quite simply – a better life. However, alongside pursuing that increasingly elusive 'American dream', they maintained their sense of identity despite their involvement with the non-Portuguese world. One such way of maintaining their identity was through their language, which became my own. In fact, English was rarely spoken at home – Portuguese prevailed. I lived in two worlds, further enhanced by our travels to and from Portugal to visit family and the country of my parents' origin. As a consequence, I developed a sort of 'split consciousness' – totally in keeping with the post-structuralism and post-modernism of today. Perhaps this sort of consciousness helped me to be simultaneously engaged in and critical of the circumstances around me – including the bourgeois sensibilities that my hard-working, immigrant parents tried to perpetuate through their daughter.

My political consciousness began when I was about thirteen years old. I recall sitting alone on one side of my eighth-grade classroom with the rest of the class on the other side, arguing for women's rights to equal pay for equal work. I was delighted when, soon after, another girl, Debbie Parente, joined me. By that time, I had written several essays on racial equality, women's liberation and peace as a much-needed resource in the world. Although I was too young to participate in the tumultuous political climate of the 1960s, I had watched it on one of the most magnificent inventions of modern times – the television. Alongside the cartoons and sitcoms of the day were the continuous newscasts of racial riots, protests against women's oppression and racial inequality, and the ongoing depiction of the transport home of body bags containing the remains of soldiers who had lost their lives in the – eventually – much-challenged Vietnam War.

Despite early stirrings, my political consciousness and sense of social commitment did not come all at once, but rather emerged over time. In fact, it is still emerging as I find new possibilities for social activism, particularly through the understanding derived from the day-to-day of my life with others. Based on the daily opportunities life presents, I try as best I can to formulate, reformulate and actualize this consciousness and commitment through action in the areas of this life I call my own: theory, research, community involvement, spiritual life and artistic practice.

I suppose that, in this way, I attend to the everyday of critical psychology rather than the big debates that exist in our field. However, some concerns that manifest themselves in this everyday are in keeping with the theoretical trajectories with which we occupy ourselves in the field of critical psychology, such as the delicate balance between what can be considered to be polarities or tensions that often emerge within a socially committed group of intellectual persons: critique vs. creativity, recommendation vs. participation, prescription vs. collaboration, intellectualization vs. complete and total engagement or action.

While many of us share similar 'intellectual roots' so to speak, critical psychology goes well beyond intellectual work to the practice, particularly as much of our theory emerges in and through the many sites of inequality and oppression. This is not a 'natural' progression – quite the contrary. I think that, more often than not, intellectuals are particularly vulnerable to getting caught up with the elaboration of their ideas in such a way that they lose sight of the realities of lived life. Therefore, the theory and practice of critical psychology is a constant reminder of a perpetual tension and, like most tensions, needs to be understood as such rather than resolved – precariously or otherwise.

Many of these tensions are maintained in the types of I work I am engaged in at present – specifically, teaching, theory, research methodology, artistic practice and community work. In my work sites, alongside critical psychology precepts, I cleave to the idea of the imagination as a venue to 'imagine' other than what is, or, as Jean-Paul Sartre (1963) wrote, 'a flight and a long leap ahead, at once a refusal and a realization' (p. 92), referring to the realization of the unendurable and the glimmer of the possibility of something better. Without imagination, we would not be able to envision other than what is, what we know to be the *status quo*. That would mean the painful demise of humanity.

In teaching, I try my best to engage students in the imaginative process of making knowledge. I integrate exercises that call upon their imagination to create a space from which to learn, to interpret and to come to understand. In this kind of classroom setting, little is assumed; much is questioned, explored, critiqued – and created. The production of knowledge, in this way, comes to be a dialogically constructed process between student and teacher.

One exercise I use continuously in my classes in developmental psychology is 'the body print'. I begin with a lecture and class discussion on the literal and symbolic meanings of the body and our specific body parts. I encourage them to make these connections to their own system of meaning – for example, what do their hands, heart, feet and so on mean to them? I ask them to set aside a box in their rooms and to drop in items that they may want to use to represent different aspects of themselves and their lives in relation to their body print. After a week or two, the students are asked to bring a sheet of paper, long enough and wide enough to cover the dimensions of their bodies, along with a box of crayons and the materials they have collected thus far. We meet in the gym for a class period, where they pair off and help each other outline their bodies. In this initial session, they just begin to dialogue with this 'outline' of themselves. However, over the course of the semester, they engage in the continuous process of 'filling in' the body print by adding something each week, inspired, directly or indirectly, by a specific topic we have covered in class. For instance, as a response to a class on parenting, specifically mothering, one student painted her torso in white acrylic paint, symbolic of a white blouse her mother has always wanted her to wear but which, as she chronicled in her written account of the process, 'has become a bit too tight as I grow older and assert my own code of values.' Another student, in response to the same material, wrote that she had added six seeds that 'lay dormant until that "ring" of my life comes along, if I am meant to be married and a mother.' All the students struggle throughout the semester with making meaning of the class material, themselves and the world. While initially doubting the merit of the project, as well as my sanity, their written reactions at the end of semester speak to the meaningfulness of the assignment for them. Most, in fact, have felt that the experience has transformed them in some way, particularly in calling upon them to imagine and to use that imagining to create new ways of accessing creative aspects of themselves in the service of their educational process.

My work in theory and methodology has been motivated by the desire to explore the changing face of the world and the psychological consequences of such changes. I have been particularly curious about the state of Europe as it has been faced with changes as a result of the collapse of the Berlin Wall, the fall of the Soviet Union and the growth of the European community. I wanted to begin this exploration in a country I knew well, whose language I could speak and where memory flowed alongside social, historical and political events – Portugal. I, like many others of my intellectual generation, felt that the time for making theory based on generalizations had passed. Instead, by focusing on a particular case and by describing the social, historical and ideological processes by which that the particulars of that case have come to be, I felt I could better make a contribution to the theoretical and empirical domains in the human sciences that would be in keeping with the needs and workings of our times.

A research project emerged from these concerns and from my background in critical psychology. In addition, my interests in post-structuralist and post-modern theory prevailed in a work in progress on Portugal's post-modern psychology, funded by my home institution, Duquesne University. In this work, I have been examining contemporary Portuguese society using social, historical, political and literary texts, interviews with persons from various social and economic strata, and photographs taken during my research sojourns in Portugal. My interest in semiotics has led me to forge a description of the processes by which subjectivity is constituted in and through the metaphors that reveal themselves in lived life, recollection, memory, time, space and fantasy. I have my colleagues Valerie Walkerdine and Frigga Haug to thank for their work on the ways images can house a great deal of psychological significance. In turn, I am in the process of making meaning of the metaphors revealed in the

written, oral and visual texts in order to understand the processes
by which subjectivity is constituted. In addition, my new-found
academic home, Duquesne University, houses a well-established
psychology department with a focus on existential-phenomenological psychology. Through conversations with students and
colleagues, I have been exposed to the significance of lived
experience in the formulation of subjectivity. This exposure has
resulted in an additional dimension to my work that is reflected
in my emphasis on space, time and being as a way of understanding the multi-layeredness of significance represented by
these metaphors. In a number of the photographs, for instance,
a number of 'sites of subjectivity' or loci of time, place, space and
instance, have emerged – all understood as socially, historically
and ideologically constituted – and yet lived as well.

Furthermore, by examining contemporary Portuguese society
using written, oral and visual texts, I have begun to develop a
new methodology with which to understand the processes that
constitute subjectivity. Also, I have begun to articulate the theoretical underpinnings of such a methodology using semiotics,
post-structuralism and phenomenology. Using these theoretical
frameworks, several aspects of what constitutes who we are and
how we become can be explored: the signs and symbols in the
world in which we live; the significance or meaning of those
signs and symbols both personally and socially; and the way in
which those signs, symbols and 'other aspects of being and
becoming' constitute real and fantastical aspects of life. (These
'other aspects' are in the process of formulation. One that
emerged from last summer's research and is currently under
study for its significance in people's lives is the notion of 'juxtaposition' – a characteristic that has nearly come to define modernism and post-modernism.)

One example among the significant events and circumstances
that emerged from my research last summer as constituting the
fabric of Portuguese post-modern sensibility was the ways Portugal's imperial past is still very much alive in the present-day
lives of the Portuguese. From the traditional imperial colours
that are still chosen to be painted on the many time-worn
edifices, to the contemporary architecture emerging today
replete with the sails of yesteryear, the Portuguese still maintain
their tie to their imperial past. This past functions to root the
Portuguese in a sense of history despite their ever-changing

world of dual-working couples, an increasingly heterogeneous population, technological advances and participation in the European Union.

By the same token, despite modern-day changes and shifting market demands, the phenomenon of things seeming to have changed a great deal and, simultaneously, to have not changed at all, is ever-present in a certain sort of way. For example, one photograph I took last summer illustrates two women seating in an outdoor café with a television set up for viewing the World Cup. A closer look reveals that this timeless European scene (albeit altered slightly with the presence of the television!) has been layered with an additional level of significance – McDonald's infamous golden arches are emblazoned on the café's umbrella. This is only one demonstration of the way in which old and new seem to coexist side by side, or layer upon layer – the 'multi-layeredness' that has been articulated as constituting post-modern sensibility.

Another observation made during last summer's research was the contribution women made to maintaining, perpetuating and revising Portuguese post-modern sensibility. Women of all generations maintain and perpetuate the fabric of social life in and through social and familial relations. However, there seems to be a generational difference between the women of the '*terceira idade*' or 'third age' and their modern-day daughters – namely, education, work sites, and economic freedom. The ways in which these two generations work together – yet, in very different ways – to maintain family life and cultural identity is one part of my current research agenda.

In addition, I have decided to experiment with this method of image-making and meaning-making of images with another critical issue – violence. I am going to examine violence as manifested through the ideology of landscapes. I plan on photographing violence in landscapes, both literally and metaphorically, as in levelling and penetration, as well as alternatives such as multi-layering, juxtaposition and reformulation. My background in critical psychology re-emerges as I question the ways in which we create and recreate our landscape(s) – including the natural, constructed, and 'architecturalized' aspects – and how these (re)creations serve to maintain and perpetuate violent ideologies, particularly in relation to ourselves, others and the world in which we live.

Finally, my artistic work often extends from and is often synonymous with my theoretical and methodological explorations. I refuse to accept that academic discourse must be purely intellectual in the most limited sense. We do neither ourselves nor our readers and students any good writing, teaching and living from such an ossified existence. Rather, I continuously include the most divergent, aesthetic, obtuse and playful aspects of my being (which necessary includes my thinking!) into the work I do. In addition, there are artistic sites for me where 'spoken words' are not predominant, but where, rather, images solely prevail. I am currently working through the interstices of memory and subjectivity and the continuous redefinition of being that emerges as one engages oneself in the imaginative interaction between self and the material world through a combination of photography, video, object assemblage and sound.

Critical psychology has contributed a great deal to my way of understanding the stuff of life. Its influence maintains in me a critical stance that includes the questioning and exploration of the underlying assumptions that operate to maintain and perpetuate – as I said in the beginning – the stuff of human suffering. This stance has become interwoven into the fabric of everyday life, using teaching, theory, research methodology, and artistic practice as the multicoloured and multi-textured threads of possibility. It is my hope that this woven tapestry-in-process will make use of the theory's possibilities for a better understanding of the impediments to human emancipation that persist in the world today.

Epilogue

I have been struggling to collect my thoughts about this volume for a few months. What can be said after hearing a couple of dozen articulate voices for critical psychology? One could shout 'Bravo!' One could point out differences of opinion or attempt to articulate common ground. The task of summing up has become even more complex because I have recently had the opportunity to hear dozens of other voices for critical psychology at international conferences focusing specifically on critical psychology. In May 1999, the Millennium World Conference in Critical Psychology, hosted by Valerie Walkerdine and the Centre for Critical Psychology at the University of Western Sydney, highlighted the links between critical psychology and cultural studies. In particular, the conference presentations featured feminist and discourse-analytic research methods and issues in post-modern psychoanalysis, gender studies, queer theory, and postcolonial studies. Then, in July 1999, Ian Parker and Erica Burman in the UK hosted the conference on Critical Psychology and Action Research. There, the discussion gravitated toward strategic issues facing scholars and activists hoping to challenge and change everyday psychological practices and other institutions that sustain oppression. Neo-marxist and post-structuralist frameworks predominated. Both conferences highlighted the need for a double critical reflexivity among critical psychologists, both toward dominant practices and toward the alternatives we propose. The utopian in me had hoped semi-consciously that some sort of global, *fin-de-siècle* convergence around critical psychology would emerge from these conferences, but, of course, there is no single, unified critical psychology, just as there is no psychology. Instead, we have psychologies, critiques of psychologies, critical psychologies and critiques of critical psychologies.

As I write, I find myself sitting on a grassy bank atop the Great Orme at Llandudno on the coast of north Wales. The Great Orme is a massive limestone dome rising up from the Irish Sea. It is so named because Viking sailors thought it resembled an immense sea monster. The image of the sea monster is apt, for I am certain that some readers, especially those less familiar with critical psychologies, will have decided by now that critical psychology is some kind of monster. This monster – a multi-headed one, to be sure – rises up amid the currents of dominant psychology, tearing with its claws and teeth at the sides of the psy-Titanic, ripping at its theories, its practices, its impact on common sense, it failure to address social problems in a significant way, and so on. The critical psychology monster's claws and teeth also tear at itself, for it senses that it cannot be sufficient. It is grotesque, a dream, a symptom. It is doomed to be exterminated, veiled in fog, forgotten.

So, in the interest of contributing to the long-range mythical-legendary status of critical psychology, I offer the following reflections on the struggle that lies ahead for our multi–headed monster.

First, we have the question raised by the diversity of theory, method, practice, aims and impulse among critical psychologies. Diversity can be seen either as fragmentation that leads to reduced impact or as a font of creativity and strength. I tend to prefer the latter view, but achieving strength through diversity will depend on greatly improved capacity for dialogue and debate between people representing diverse theoretical orientation and practical settings. The present volume fails in this regard, since there is no mechanism for direct dialogue between the voices published here. We need to make extraordinary efforts in our journals, conferences, and collaborative efforts to transcend individualistic, academic modes that provide space only for monologues. If critical psychologists continue to operate in this mode, caving in to pressures from academic centres to present and publish monologues to build individual reputations, the entire effort will be in vain. We need to learn to listen, really listen, in order to understand. A related issue that needs attention is the use of technical jargon. There is certainly space for specialization, and that peculiar enjoyment of elaborate theoretical systems, but we need to be able to communicate with diverse academic and non-academic audiences in understandable ways. In short, we cannot assume that listeners share even a basic knowledge of Freud, Foucault or Derrida, and we need to put as much effort into speaking clearly as we put into listening better.

A second issue relates to strategy. Should we work to transform psychology and society from within psychology or without? Should we abandon psychology altogether? These questions arose frequently at the recent critical psychology conferences. Ian Parker, in his lead article in volume 1 of the *Annual Review of Critical Psychology*, offers some productive ways of thinking this through. My take on this issue is that the first step is clearly to avoid either – or thinking on the matter. As Parker suggests, we can work creatively and critically on the inside in the light of an external assessment of psychology's situation and work from the outside against oppressive psychological practices. A second consideration is that each of us will be inclined for reasons of temperament, ethics, politics and even aesthetics to position ourselves differently. Some will continue to work as professors or therapists, others will move toward more direct political action. Some will write while others will build coalitions or do street theatre and media actions. Yet, wherever we choose to situate ourselves, it will be essential to network effectively with people who have chosen other strategies if we hope to build momentum and maximize impact.

The strategy issue leads us to an issue that is equally fundamental. What exactly are we trying to change? This volume is replete with calls to work to end oppression and social injustice, but short on clear specifications of the social mechanisms through which oppression is reproduced and even shorter on concrete proposals for actions that might lead to social transformation. This shortfall is understandable. Our problem as people who care about psychology is still psychology. In our efforts to move beyond mainstream psychology through internal critiques, we have slighted the task of analysing the specific structures of power, ideology and institutional practice that sustain relations of domination in particular zones. My sense is that by now the critique of psychology has been sufficiently developed and, while it may have to be repeated from time to time, most of those who will hear have already heard. We need to focus now on constructing the institutions that will eventually supplant the practices associated with dominant psychology. Doing this will require collaboration with scholars in other disciplines such as sociology and political economy and with activists in political movements. Examples of this sort of collaboration are the Psychology Politics Resistance group in England and the recently formed Chiapas Praxis Project, in which alternatives to traditional mental health interventions are being developed in collaboration with indigenous community leaders.

Many of the voices in this volume have articulated the stresses and personal struggles associated with adopting a critical position within and against psychology. I personally appreciate these accounts, not only because they reveal the amount of courage that must be mustered to stand up and challenge dominant ideas and practices, but also because they prove that these debates are not simply arbitrary arguments in the academic sideshow of psychology. Major resources are at stake, including the power to define what people are and what they need. People get nasty when their access to resources and power to define reality are threatened. The critical psychologies, energized by feminist and post-modernist critiques of psychology's scientism, have clearly shaken the foundations of the dominant psychology, prompting a rush to carve out a middle ground so as not to lose all. Fishman's (1999) highly acclaimed *The Case for Pragmatic Psychology* is certainly but the first of many such efforts.

To conclude, rather than go on saying things that feel obvious, I simply want to commend those who took on the challenge of contributing to this book. Their work certainly shows us that the monster of critical psychology is colourful and powerful. Its claws and teeth are sharp. Its heads speak in many tongues and its eyes glare at oppression even where it disguises itself as a benign practice. It is my hope, and the contributors' as well, I am sure, that this work will spawn new monsters in forms adequate to the situations they will face in the future, monsters beyond psychology and critical psychology.

Bibliography

Adorno, T. (1973) *The jargon of authenticity.* Evanston, IL: Northwestern University Press.

Ainsa, F. (1995) *La reescritura de la historia en la nueva narrativa latinoamericana.* Serie Conferencias no. 8. Centro de Investigación en Identidad y Cultura Latinoamericanas: University of Costa Rica.

Althusser, L. (1984) Freud and Lacan. In *Essays on ideology.* London: Verso. (Original work published 1964.)

Altman, I. (1996) Higher education and psychology in the millennium. *American Psychologist, 51,* 371–8.

Altman, I. and Rogoff, B. (1984) World views in psychology: Trait, interactional, organismic, and transactional perspective. In D. Stokols and I. Altman (eds), *Handbook of environmental psychology, 14,* 1–40. New York: Wiley.

Anders, G. (1987) *Die Antiquiertheit des Menschen. Band 2. Über die Zerstörung des Lebens im Zeitalter der dritten industriellen Revolution.* München: Beck.

Anders, G. (1992) Die Antiquiertheit des Proletariats. *Forum, 39* (462–4), 7–11.

Banton, R., Clifford, P., Frosh, S., Lousada, J. and Rosenthall, J. (1985) *The politics of mental health.* London: Macmillan.

Barber B. (1995) *Jihad vs McWorld: How globalism and tribalism are reshaping the world.* New York: Ballantine Books.

Barglow, R. (1994) *The crisis of the self in the age of information: Computers, dolphins, and dreams.* London: Routledge.

Barratt, B. (1984) *Psychoanalytic knowing and psychic reality.* Hillsdale, NJ: Analytic Press.

Barratt, B. (1993) *Psychoanalysis and the postmodern impulse.* Baltimore, MD: Johns Hopkins University Press.

Bayer, B. M. (1998) Between apparatuses and apparitions: Phantoms of the laboratory. In B. M. Bayer and J. Shotter (eds), *Reconstructing the psychological subject: Bodies, practices, and technologies* (pp. 187–213). Thousand Oaks, CA: Sage.

Bayer, B. and Malone, K. (1998) Feminism, psychology, and matters of the body. In H. Stam (ed.), *The body and psychology* (pp. 94–119). Thousand Oaks, CA: Sage.

Bayer, B. M. and Shotter, J. (eds) (1998) *Reconstructing the psychological subject: Bodies, practices, and technologies*. Thousand Oaks, CA: Sage.

Beattie, J. (n.d.). Supplements to philosophy. In S. C. Brown (ed.), *Royal Institute of Philosophy lectures: vol. 17. Objectivity and cultural divergence*. London: CambridgeUniversity Press.

Benjamin, J. (1998) *Shadow of the other: Intersubjectivity and gender in psychoanalysis*. New York: Routledge.

Berger, P. and Luckmann, T. (1967) *The social construction of reality*. New York: Anchor.

Bracher, M. (1993) *Lacan, discourse, and social change*. Ithaca, NY: Cornell University Press.

Brown, N. (1959) *Life against death*. Middletown, CT: Wesleyan University Press.

Bruner, J. (1990) *Acts of meaning*. Cambridge, MA: Harvard University Press.

Bulhan, H. A. (1985) *Franz Fanon and the psychology of oppression*. New York: Plenum Press.

Bulhan, H. A. (1990) Imperialism in the studies of the psyche: A critique of African psychological research. In L. J. Nicholas (ed.), *Psychology and oppression: Critiques and proposals* (pp. 1–34). Skotaville, South Africa: Braamfontein.

Burman, E. (1997) Differentiating and developing critical social psychology. In T. Ibáñez and L. Iñiguez (eds), *Critical social psychology* (pp. 229–40). Thousand Oaks, CA: Sage.

Burman, E. (ed.) (1990) *Feminists and psychological practice*. London: Sage.

Burman, E., Aitken, G., Alldred, P., Allwood, R., Billington, T., Goldenberg, B., Gordo López, A., Heenan, C., Marks, D. and Warner, S. (1996) *Psychology discourse practice: From regulation to resistance*. Bristol, PA: Taylor and Francis.

Butler, J. (1995) Melancholy gender: Refused identification. In M. Berger, B. Wallis and S. Watson (eds), *Constructing masculinity* (p. 31). London: Routledge.

Castells, M. (1997) *The power of identity*. Malden, MA: Blackwell.

Caudill, D. (1997) *Lacan and the subject of the law: Toward a psychoanalytic critical legal theory*. Atlantic Highlands, NJ: Humanities Press.

Chesler, P. (1973) *Women and madness*. New York: Doubleday.

Chorover, S. L. (1979) *From genesis to genocide: The meaning of human nature and the power of behavior control*. Cambridge, MA: MIT Press.

Cixous, H. (1981) The laugh of the Medusa. In E. Marks and I. de Courtivon (eds), *New French feminisms*. Sussex: Harvester. (Original work published 1976.)

Clanon, T. L., Shawver, L. and Kurdys, D. (1982) Less insanity in the courts. *American Bar Association Journal, 68*, 824–827.

Cole, M. (1996) *Cultural psychology: A once and future discipline.* Cambridge, MA: Belknap Press.

Condor, S. (1997) And so say all of us: Some thoughts on 'Experiential democratization as an aim for critical social psychologists.' In T. Ibáñez and L. Iñiguez (eds), *Critical social psychology* (pp. 111–46). Thousand Oaks, CA: Sage.

Cook, T. (1985) Postpositivist critical multiplism. In R. Shotland and M. Mark (eds), *Social science and social policy.* Beverly Hills: Sage.

Copjec, J. (1994) *Read my desire: Lacan against the historicists.* Cambridge, MA: MIT Press.

Cornell, D. (1993) *Transformations: Recollective imagination and sexual difference.* New York: Routledge.

Danziger, K. (1997) *Naming the mind: How psychology found its language.* London: Sage.

Dasen, P. R. (1984) The cross-cultural study of intelligence: Piaget and the Baoule. *International Journal of Psychology, 19,* 407–34.

Deleuze G. and Guattari F. (1986) *Kafka: Toward a minor literature.* Minneapolis: University of Minnesota Press.

Deleuze, G. and Guattari, F. (1987) *A thousand plateaus: Capitalism and schizophrenia* (B. Massumi, trans.). Minneapolis: University of Minnesota Press.

Derrida, J. (1976) *Of grammatology* (G. C. Spivak, trans.). Baltimore MD: Johns Hopkins University Press.

Dews, P. (1987) *Logics of disintegration.* London: Verso.

Dobles, I. (1986) Psicología social desde Centroamérica. Entrevista con el Dr Ignacio Martín-Baró. *Revista Costarricense de Psicología, 10–11.*

Dobles, I. (1990) Guerra psicológica y opinión pública: Costa Rica y El Salvador en el contexto de Esquipulas. In M. Montero (ed.), *Acción y discurso: Psicología política en América Latina.* Caracas: Eduven.

Dobles, I. (1995) Psicología y lucha campesina:Una experiencia costarricense. *Revista Costarricense de Psicología, 22,* 21–34.

Dobles, I. (1996) Retos teóricos y práxicos de la psicología social costarricense. In T. Cordero, I. Dobles and R. Pérez (eds), *Dominación social y subjetividad.* San José, Costa Rica: Editorial de la Universidad de Costa Rica.

Dokecki, P. R. (1992) On knowing the community of caring persons: A methodological basis for the reflective generative practice of community psychology. *Journal of Community Psychology, 20,* 26–35.

Dokecki, P. R. (1996) *The tragi-comic professional: Basic considerations for ethical reflective-generative practice.* Pittsburgh, PA: Duquesne University Press.

Drew, N. and Bishop, B. J. (1995) Social impact assessment: Wherefore art thou psychology. In W. Vialle (ed.), *Why psychology?* Wollongong: Australian Psychological Society.

Dussel, E. (1998) *Etica de la liberación en la edad de la globalización y de la exclusión.* Mexico City: Universidad Nacional Autónoma de México.

Dussel, E. D. (1985) *Philosophy of liberation* (A. Martinez and C. Morkovsky, Trans.). Maryknoll, NY: Orbis Books.

Earnest, W. R. (1992) Ideology criticism and life history research. In G. Rosenwald and R. Ochberg (eds), *Storied lives* (pp. 250–64). New Haven, CT Yale University Press.

Eliot, T. S. (1920) Whispers of immortality. In T. S. Eliot, *Collected poems.* (p.55). London: Faber, 1963

Eweka, C. (1985) Psychological apartheid: A case study for Nigeria. In E. Okpara (ed.), *Psychological strategies for national development.* Benin: Nigerian Psychological Association.

Eze, N. (1991) The progress and status of psychology in Africa. *Journal of Psychology in Africa, 1,* 27–37.

Fausto-Sterling, A. (1985) *Myths of gender: Biological theories of women and men.* New York: Basic Books.

Febbraro, A. R. (1997) *Gender, mentoring, and research practices: Social psychologists trained at the University of Michigan, 1949–1974.* Unpublished doctoral dissertation, University of Guelph, Ont.

Fellman, G. (1991) The truth of Frankenstein: Technologism and images of destruction. *Psychohistory Review, 19* (2), 177–231.

Flax, J. (1993) *Disputed subjects: Essays on psychoanalysis, politics and philosophy.* New York: Routledge.

Foucault, M. (1972) *The archeology of knowledge* (A. Sheridan Smith, trans.). New York: Pantheon Books.

Foucault, M. (1977) *Discipline and punish: The birth of the prison* (A. Sheridan, trans.). London: Allen Lane.

Foucault, M. (1979) *The history of sexuality.* Harmondsworth: Penguin.

Fowers, B. J. and Richardson, F. C. (1996) Why is multiculturalism good? *American Psychologist, 51,* 609–21.

Fox, D. R. (1983) The pressure to publish: A graduate student's personal plea. *Teaching of Psychology, 10,* 177–8.

Fox, D. R. (1985) Psychology, ideology, utopia, and the commons. *American Psychologist, 40,* 48–58.

Fox, D. R. (1993) Psychological jurisprudence and radical social change. *American Psychologist, 48,* 234–41.

Fox, D. R. (1994) Observations on disability evaluation in the social security administration. *Journal of Social Behavior and Personality, 9,* 237–46.

Fox, D. R. (1996) The law says corporations are persons, but psychology knows better. *Behavioral Sciences and the Law, 14,* 339–59.

Fox, D. R. (1999) Psycholegal scholarship's contribution to false consciousness about injustice. *Law and Human Behavior, 23,* 9–30.

Fox, D. and Prilleltensky, I. (eds) (1997) *Critical psychology: An introduction.* London: Sage.

Fox, D. and Sakolsky, R. (1998) From 'radical university' to agent of the state. *Radical Teacher, 53,* 13–18.

Freire, P. (1973) *Pedagogía del Oprimido.* Buenos Aires: Siglo XXI.

Freire, P. (1975) Cultural action for freedom. *Harvard Educational Review Monograph, 1.*

Freire, P. (1994) *Pedagogy of the oppressed* (rev. edn). New York: Continuum.

Freire, P. (1997) *Pedagogy of hope.* New York: Continuum.

Freud, S. (1976) Das Unbehagen in der Kultur [Civilization and its Discontents]. *Gesammelte Werke.* vol. xiv. Frankfurt: Fischer.

Frosh, S. (1987) *The politics of psychoanalysis.* London: Macmillan.

Frosh, S. (1991) *Identity crisis: Modernity, psychoanalysis and the self.* London: Macmillan.

Frosh, S. (1994) *Sexual difference: Masculinity and psychoanalysis.* London: Routledge.

Frosh, S. (1997a) Postmodern narratives. In R. Papadopoulos and J. Byng Hall (eds), *Multiple voices: Narrative in systemic family therapy.* London: Duckworths.

Frosh, S. (1997b) Fundamentalism, gender and family therapy. *Journal of Family Therapy, 19,* 417–30.

Frosh, S. (1997c) *For and against pychoanalysis.* London: Routledge.

Gallop, J. (1982) *Feminism and psychoanalysis.* London: Macmillan.

Gallop, J. (1997) *Feminist accused of sexual harassment.* Durham: Duke University Press.

Game, A. and Metcalf, A. (1996) *Passionate sociology.* London: Open University Press.

Gergen, K. J. (1978) Experimentation in social psychology: A reappraisal. *European Journal of Social Psychology, 8,* 507–27.

Gergen, K. J. (1988) *Towards a postmodern psychology.* Paper presented at the 23rd International Congress of Psychology, Sydney.

Gergen, K. J. (1991) *The saturated self: Dilemmas of identity in contemporary life.* New York: Basic Books.

Gergen, K. J. (1994) The limits of pure critique. In M. Billig and H. W. Simons (eds), *After postmodernism: Reconstructing ideology critique.* London: Sage.

Gergen, K. J. (1996) Is diagnosis a disaster? In F. W. Kaslow (ed.), *Handbook of relational diagnosis and dysfunctional family patterns.* New York: Wiley.

Gergen, K. J. and McNamee, S. (1997) Foreword. In E. Riikonen, *Reimagining therapy: Living conversations and relational knowing.* London: Sage.

Gioseffi, D. (ed.) (1993) *On prejudice: A global perspective.* New York: Anchor Books.

Gordo López, A. J. and Linaza, J. L. (eds) (1996) *Psicologías, discursos y poder.* Madrid: Visor.

Graumann, C. F. and Sommer, M. (1984) Schema and inference: Models in cognitive social psychology. In J. R. Royce and L. P. Mos (eds), *Annals of Theoretical Psychology, vol. 1* (pp. 31–76). New York: Plenum Press.

Greenfield, P. M. (1966) On culture and conservation. In J. S. Bruner, R. R. Olver, P. M. Greenfield *et al.* (eds), *Studies in cognitive growth* (pp. 225–56). New York: Wiley.

Greenfield, P. M. (1997a) Culture as process: Empirical methods for cultural psychology. In J. W. Berry, Y. Poortinga and J. Pandey (eds), *Handbook of cross-cultural psychology: vol. 1. Theory and method.* Boston: Allyn and Bacon.

Greenfield, P. M. (1997b) *Culture and universals integrating social and cognitive development.* Paper presented at the Annual Symposium of the Jean Piaget Society, Santa Monica, CA, June.

Greenfield, P. M. and Suzuki, L. K. (1998) Culture and human development: Implications for parenting, education, pediatrics, and mental health. In I. E. Sigel and K. A. Renninger (eds), *Handbook of child psychology: vol. 4* (5th edn). New York: Wiley.

Greeno, J. G. and the Middle School Mathematics Through Applications Group (1998) The situativity of knowing, learning and research. *American Psychologist, 57*(1), 5–26.

Gregg, G. (1991) *Self-representation: Life narrative studies in identity and ideology.* New York: Greenwood.

Grubitzsch, S. and Rexilius, G. (eds). (1978) *Testtheorie, testpraxis* [Test theory, test practice]. Reinbek: Rowohlt.

Grubitzsch, S. and Rexilius, G. (eds). (1981) *Psychologische Grundbegriffe* [Psychological concepts]. Reinbek: Rowohlt.

Habermas, J. (1984) *The theory of communicative action: vol. 1. Reason and the rationalization of society* (T. McCarthy, trans.). Boston, MA: Beacon.

Habermas, J. (1987) *The theory of communicative action: vol. 2. Lifeworld and system: A critique of functionalist reason* (T. McCarthy, trans.). Boston, MA: Beacon.

Habermas, J. (1990) *Moral consciousness and communicative action.* Cambridge, MA: MIT Press.

Hacking, I. (1983) *Representing and intervening.* Cambridge, MA: Cambridge University Press.

Haraway, D. J. (1991) Modest_Witness@Second_Millennium. FemaleMan©_Meets_OncoMouse™. In *Feminism and Technoscience.* New York: Routledge.

Harris, B. (1997) Repoliticizing the history of psychology. In D. Fox and I. Prilleltensky (eds), *Critical psychology: An introduction* (pp. 21–33). Thousand Oaks, CA: Sage.

Henriques, J., Hollway, W., Urwin, C., Venn, C. and Walkerdine, V. (1984) *Changing the subject: Psychology, social regulation and subjectivity.* London: Methuen.

Hildebrand-Nilshon M., Motzkau J. and Papadopoulos D. (1999) *Reintegrating sense into subjectification.* Paper presented at Conference of International Society for Theoretical Psychology, Sydney, April.

Hlynka, D., and Belland, J. C. (eds). (1991) *Paradigms regained: The uses of illuminative, semiotic, and post-modern criticism as modes of inquiry in educational technology: A book of readings.* Englewood Cliffs NJ: Educational Technology Publications.

Hollway, W. (1989) *Subjectivity and method in psychology: Gender, meaning, and science.* London: Sage.

Holzkamp, K. (1972) *Kritische Psychologie: Vorbereitende Arbeiten* [Critical psychology: Preparatory works]. Frankfurt: Fischer.

Holzkamp, K. (1983a) *Grundlegung der Psychologie* [Foundation of psychology]. Frankfurt am Main: Campus.

Holzkamp, K. (1983b) Theorie und Praxis im Psychologiestudium. *Forum Kritische Psychologie, 12,* 159–83.

Holzkamp, K. (1991) Was heißt 'Psychologie vom Subjektstandpunkt?' Überlegungen zu subjektwissenschaftlicher Theorienbildung. *Forum Kritische Psychologie, 28,* 5–19.

Holzkamp, K. (1992) On doing psychology critically. *Theory and Psychology, 2* (2), 193–204.

Holzkamp, K. (1993) Lernen. Subjektwissenschaftliche Grundlegung. Frankfurt: Campus.

Holzkamp, K. (1996) Psychologie: Verständigung über Handlungsbegründungen alltäglicher Lebensführung. *Forum Kritische Psychologie, 36,* 7–112.

Hopkins, G. M. (1876–89.) Pied Beauty. In *The poems of Gerard Manley Hopkins* (p. 69). Oxford University Press, 1970.

Huygens, I. (1997) *Towards social change partnerships: Responding to empowerment of oppressed groups with voluntary depowerment of dominant groups.* Paper presented at the Biennial Conference of the Society for Community Research and Action, Columbia, SC, May.

Ibáñez, T. and Iñiguez, L. (eds) (1997) *Critical social psychology.* London: Sage.

ILAS (Instituto Latinoamericano de Salud Mental y Derechos Humanos). (1994) *Psicología y Violencia política en América Latina.* Santiago, Chile: CESOC.

Ingelby, D. (1995) Problems in the interplay between science and culture. In N. R. Goldberger and J. B. Verhoff (eds), *The culture and psychology reader.* New York: University Press.

Jardine, A. A. (1985) *Gynesis: Configurations of woman and modernity.* Ithaca, NY: Cornell University Press.

Kagitcibasi, C. (1996) *Human development across cultures: A view from the other side.* Hillsdale, NJ: Lawrence Erlbaum.

Kim, U. and Berry, J. W. (1993) *Indigenous psychologies: Research and experience in cultural context.* Newbury Park, CA: Sage.

King, R. (1998) Evidence-based practice: Where is the evidence? The case of cognitive behaviour therapy and depression. *Australian Psychologist, 33,* 83–8.

Kovel, J. (1995) On racism and psychoanalysis. In A. Elliott and S. Frosh (eds), *Psychoanalysis in contexts.* London: Routledge.

Kristeva, J. (1991) *Strangers to ourselves.* London: Harvester Wheatsheaf.

Kunkel, J. H. (1989) How many psychologies are there? *American Psychologist, 44*(3), 573–4.

Kvale, S. (ed.). (1992) *Psychology and postmodernism.* London: Sage.

Lacan, J. (1982) God and the *jouissance* of woman. In J. Mitchell and J. Rose (eds), *Feminine sexuality* (p. 144). London: Macmillan. (Original work published in 1972–3.)

Lakoff, G. and Johnson, M. (1980) *Metaphors we live by.* University of Chicago Press.

Lamb, M. E., Sternberg, K. J., Hwang, C. P. and Broberg, A. G. (1992) *Child care in context: Cross-cultural perspectives.* Hillsdale, NJ: Lawrence Erlbaum.

Lane, C. (1998) *The experience of the outside: Lacan against Foucault.* Paper presented at Turn of the Century: End of Analysis? Jacques Lacan's Legacy and the Twentieth First Century, Philadelphia, PA, April.

Laosebikan, S. (1982) *A constituency for clinical psychology in Nigeria: Implications for training.* Paper presented at the second Annual Convention of the Nigerian Association of Clinical Psychologists, Benin City, Nigeria.

Laosebikan, S. (1986) Why we must develop our African perspective. In E. B. Wilson (ed.), *Psychology and society.* Ile-Ife, Nigeria: University of Ife Press.

Laudan, L. (1996) *Beyond positivism and relativism: Theory, method, and evidence.* Boulder, CO: Westview Press.

Lira, E. and Castillo, M. I. (1991) *Psicología de la amenaza política y del miedo,* Santiago: Instituto Latinoamericano de Salud Mental y Derechos Humanos, ILAS.

Lira, E. and Loveman, B. (1998) Authoritarian legacies from which past? Chile 1998. Paper presented at the Conference of the Working Group on Authoritarian Legacies, Buenos Aires, August.

Lyotard, J- F. (1984) *The postmodern condition: A report on knowledge.* Minneapolis: University of Minnesota Press.

Lyotard, J- F. (1988) *The differend.* Minneapolis: University of Minnesota Press.

Lyotard, J- F. (1989) Defining the postmodern. In L. Appignanesi (ed.), *Postmodernism: ICA documents* (p.186). London: Free Association Books.

Lyotard, J- F. (1994) *Just gaming.* Minneapolis: University of Minnesota Press.

McDonald, J., Poveda, A. and Serrano, E. (1989*) Relaciones internacionales conflictivas e identidad nacional.* Thesis. University of Costa Rica: School of Psychology.

McGuire, W. (1983) A contextualist theory of knowledge: Its implications for innovation and reform in psychology research. In L. Berkowitz (ed.), *Advances in experimental social psychology: vol. 16.* New York: Academic Press.

McGuire, W. (1985) Towards social psychology's second century. In S. Koch and D. Leary (eds), *A century of psychology as science* (pp. 558–90). New York: McGraw-Hill.

McGuire, W. (1994) Uses of historical data in psychology: Comments on Munsterberg (1989) *Psychological Review, 101,* 243–7.

Maiers, W. (1991) Critical psychology: Historical background and task. In C. W. Tolman and W. Maiers (eds), *Critical psychology. Contributions to an historical science of the subject.* New York: Cambridge University Press.

Mama, A. (1995) *Beyond the masks: Race, gender and subjectivity.* New York: Routledge.

Maquet, J. (1972) *Africanity.* New York: Oxford University Press.

Marcuse, H. (1966) *Eros and civilisation.* Boston: Beacon Press. (Original work published 1955.)

Marcuse, H. (1972) *Negations.* Harmondsworth: Penguin. (Original work published 1968)

Marras, S. (1998) *Carta apócrifa de Pinochet a un siquiatra Chileno* (Aprocryphal letter from Pinochet to a Chilean psychiatrist). Santiago: Demens Sapiens.

Martín-Baró, I. (1983) *Acción e ideología:Psicología social desde Centroamérica.* San Salvador: UCA.

Martín-Baró, I. (1989) *Sistema, grupo y poder. Psicología social desde Centroamérica II.* San Salvador: UCA.

Martín-Baró, I. (1990) Guerra y salud mental, in I. Martín-Baró (ed.) *Psicología social de la guerra* (pp. 24–37). San Salvador: UCA.

Martín-Baró, I. (1994) *Writings for a liberation psychology.* Cambridge, MA: Harvard University Press.

Marx, K. and Engels, F. (1956) *Karl Marx – Friedrich Engels Werke: Band 1* [Karl Marx – Friedrich Engels works: vol. 1]. Berlin: Dietz.

Marx, K. and Engels, F. (1983) *Karl Marx – Friedrich Engels Werke: Band 3* [Karl Marx – Friedrich Engels works: Vol. 3]. Berlin: Dietz.

Mattes, P. (1988) Das PI in Berlin – Wissenschaftskritik und Institution. Zur Geschichte eines psychologischen Instituts. In G. Rexilius (ed.),

Psychologie als Gesellschaftswissenschaft. Geschichte, Theorie und Praxis kritischer Psychologie (pp. 28–61). Opladen: Westdeutscher Verlag.

Mecheril, P. and Teo, T. (eds) (1994) *Andere Deutsche. Zur Lebenssituation von Menschen multiethnischer und multikultureller Herkunft* [Other Germans: The life-situation of people of multiethnic and multicultural origin]. Berlin: Dietz.

Mecheril, P. and Teo, T. (eds) (1997) *Psychologie und Rassismus* [Psychology and racism]. Reinbek: Rowohlt.

Merck, M. (1993) *Perversions.* New York: Routledge.

Miller, J. A. (1998) The desire of Lacan. *Lacanian Ink, 13,* 38–59.

Mitchell, J. (1974) *Psychoanalysis and feminism: Freud, Reich, Laing, and women.* New York: Vintage Books.

Moffitt, D. and Owusu-Bempah, J. (1994) *The racism of psychology.* London: Harvester Wheatsheaf.

Moghaddam, F. M. (1987) psychology in the three worlds. *American Psychologist, 42*(10), 919–20.

Mogghaddam, F. (1990) Modulative and generative orientations in psychology: Implications for psychology in the three worlds. *Journal of Social Issues, 46*(3), 21–41.

Moghaddam, F. M. and Taylor, D. M. (1985) Psychology in the developing world: An evaluation through the concepts of 'dual perception' and 'parallel growth', *American Psychologist, 40,* 1144–6.

Montero, M. (ed.) (1987) *Psicología política Latinoamericana.* Caracas: PANAPO.

Montero, M. (ed.) (1991) *Acción y discurso: Problemas de psicología política en America Latina.* Caracas: Eduven.

Montero, M. (ed.) (1994) *Construcción y crítica de la psicología social.* Barcelona: Antropos.

Morawski, J. (1994) *Practicing feminisms, reconstructing psychology: Notes on a liminal science.* Ann Arbor, MI: University of Michigan Press.

Morawski, J. (1998) The return of phantom subjects. In B. M. Bayer and J. Shotter (eds), *Reconstructing the psychological subject: Bodies, practices, and technologies* (pp. 214–28). Thousand Oaks, CA: Sage.

Morss, J. R. (1990) *The biologising of childhood: Developmental psychology and the Darwinian myth.* Hillsdale NJ: Lawrence Erlbaum Associates.

Morss, J. R. (1996) *Growing critical: Alternatives to developmental psychology.* New York: Routledge.

Morss, J. R. Don't develop: A guide for change. Manuscript in preparation.

Mundy-Castle, A. C. (1974) Social and technological intelligence in Western and non-Western cultures. *Universitas, 4,* 46–52.

Newbrough, J. R. (1992) Community psychology in the postmodern world. *Journal of Community Psychology, 20,* 10–25.

Newbrough, J. R. (1995) Toward community: A third position. *American Journal of Community Psychology, 23,* 9–38.

Nicolson, P. (1996) *Gender, work and organisations.* London: Routledge.

Nicolson, P., and Ussher, J. M. (ed.) (1992) *The psychology of women's health and health care.* London, Macmillan.

Nsamenang, A. B. (1992a) *Human development in cultural context: A third world perspective.* Newbury Park, CA: Sage.

Nsamenang, A. B. (1992b) Perceptions of parenting among the Nso of Cameroon. In B. S. Hewlett (ed.), *Father–child relations.* New York: Gruyter.

Nsamenang, A. B. (1995) Factors influencing the development of psychology in sub-Saharan Africa. *International Journal of Psychology, 30*(6), 729–39.

Nsamenang, A. B. and Dawes, A. (1998) Developmental psychology as political psychology in sub-Saharan Africa: The challenge of Africanisation. *International Journal of Psychology, 47*(1), 73–87.

Olson, P. and Sullivan (1987) Beyond the mania: A critical appraisal of computers in education. In L. M. Steven (ed.), *Foundations of Canadian Educational Psychology.* Toronto: Copp, Clark and Pitman.

Orbach, S. and Eichenbaum, E. (1988) *Bittersweet: Envy and competitiveness in relationships between women.* London: Women's Press.

Osterkamp, U. (1999) Subjectivity and the other. In W. Maiers, B. Bayer, B. Esgalhado, R. Jorna and E. Schraube (eds), *Challenges of theoretical psychology.* New York: Captus Press.

O'Sullivan, E. (1999) (ed) *Transformative learning: Building educational vision in the 21st century.* London: Zed Books.

Papadopoulos, R. and Byng Hall, J. (eds), (1997), *Multiple voices: Narrative in systemic family therapy.* London: Duckworths.

Paranjpe, A. (1997) Piles of data that contribute little to the *mutual* understanding of cultures. *Cross-Cultural Psychology Bulletin, 31*(2), 11–17.

Parker, I. (1999) Deconstruction and psychotherapy. In I. Parker (ed.), *Deconstructing psychotherapy* (pp. 1–18). London: Sage.

Parker, I. and Spears, R. (eds) (1996) *Psychology and society.* Chicago: Pluto Press.

Pattman, R., Frosh, S. and Phoenix, A. (1998) Lads, machos and others: Developing 'boy-centred' research. *Journal of Youth Studies, 1,* 125–42.

Payne, R. L. (1982) The nature of knowledge and organisational psychology. In N. Nicholson and T. D. Wall (eds), *Theory and method in organisational psychology* (pp. 37–67). London: Academic Press.

Payne, R. L. (1996) Contextualism in context. *International Review of Industrial and Organisational Psychology, 11,* 179–217.

Peirson, L., Prilleltensky, I., Nelson, G. and Gould, J. (1997) Planning mental health services for children and youth: Part II – Results of a value-based community consultation project. *Evaluation and Program Planning,* 20(2), 173–83.

Pepper, S. C. (1967) *Concept and quality.* La Salle, IL: Open Court.

Pfister, J. and Schnog, N. (1997) Inventing the psychological: Toward a cultural history of emotional life in America. *The American Historical Review,* 102(4), p. 1286–1308.

Pilger, J. (1998) *Hidden agendas.* London: Vintage Books.

Plath, S. (1963) The munich mannequins. In Sylvia Plath, *Collected poems* (p. 262). London: Faber, 1981.

Polkinghorne, D. (1983) *Methodology for the human sciences: Systems of inquiry.* Albany: State University of New York Press.

Poortinga, Y. S. and Malpass, R. S. (1986) Making inferences from cross-cultural data. In W. J. Lonner and J. W. Berry (eds), *Field methods in cross-cultural psychology* (pp. 17–46). Newbury Park, CA: Sage.

Prilleltensky, I. (1989) Psychology and the status quo. *American Psychologist,* 44, 795–802.

Prilleltensky, I. (1994) *The morals and politics of psychology: Psychological discourse and the status quo.* Albany, NY: State University of New York Press.

Prilleltensky, I. (1997) Values, assumptions, and practices: Assessing the moral implications of psychological discourse and action. *American Psychologist,* 47, 517–35.

Prilleltensky, I. and Fox, D. (1997) Introducing critical psychology: Values, assumptions, and the status quo. In D. Fox and I. Prilleltensky (eds), *Critical psychology: An introduction* (pp. 2–20). London: Sage.

Prilleltensky, I. and Gonick, L. (1994) The discourse of oppression in the social sciences: Past, present, and future. In E. J. Trickett, R. J. Watts and D. Birman (eds), *Human diversity: Perspectives on people in context* (pp. 145–77). San Francisco: Jossey-Bass.

Prilleltensky, I. and Gonick, L. (1996) Polities change, oppression remains: On the psychology and politics of oppression. *Political Psychology,* 17, 127–47.

Prilleltensky, I. and Nelson, G. (1997) Community psychology: Reclaiming social justice. In D. Fox and I. Prilleltensky (eds), *Critical psychology: An introduction* (pp. 166–84). London: Sage.

Prilleltensky, I., Peirson, L. and Nelson, G. (1997) The application of community psychology values and guiding concepts to school consultation. *Journal of Educational and Psychological Consultation,* 8(2), 153–73.

Prilleltensky, I., Peirson, L., Gould, J. and Nelson, G. (1997) Planning mental health services for children and youth: Part I – A value-based framework. *Evaluation and Program Planning,* 20(2), 163–72.

Prilleltensky, I., Rossiter, A. and Walsh-Bowers, R. (1996) Preventing harm and promoting ethical discourse in the helping professions:

Conceptual, research, analytical, and action frameworks. *Ethics and Behavior, 6*, 287–06.

Projekt Automation und Qualifikation (1987) *Widersprüche der Automationsarbeit. Ein Handbuch.* Berlin: Argument.

Radford, J. and Holstock, L. (1996) The growth of psychology. *The Psychologist*, December, 548–50.

Redfield, R. (1959) The anthropological study of man. *Anthropological Quarterly, 32*(1), 4.

Richardson, F. and Fowers, B. (eds) (1998) Social inquiry: A hermeneutic reconceptualization. [Special issue]. *American Behavioral Scientist, 41*(4).

Rieff, P. (1966) *The triumph of the therapeutic.* Harmondsworth: Penguin.

Rieff, R. (1968) Social intervention and the problem of psychological analysis. *American Psychologist, 23*, 524-531.

Riley, R. (1997) *From inclusion to negotiation: The role of psychology in Aboriginal social justice.* Perth, Australia: Curtin Indigenous Research Centre.

Ring, K. (1967) Experimental social psychology: Some sober questions about some frivolous values. *Journal of Experimental Social Psychology, 3*, 113–23.

Rodrigues, A. (1975) *Psicología social.* México: Trillas.

Rogoff, B. (1990) *Apprenticeship in thinking: Cognitive development in social context.* New York: Oxford University Press.

Rose, N. (1985) *The psychological complex: Psychology, politics and society in England, 1869–1939.* London: Routledge & Kegan Paul.

Rosenwald, G. and Ochberg, R. (eds) (1992) *Storied lives: The cultural politics of self-understanding.* New Haven: Yale University Press.

Ross, A. (ed.) (1996) *Science wars.* Durham, NC: Duke University Press.

Rossiter, A., Walsh-Bowers, R. and Prilleltensky, I. (1996) Learning from broken rules: Individualism, bureaucracy and ethics. *Ethics and Behavior, 6*(4), 307–20.

Rudinesco, E. (1990) *Jacques Lacan and company* (J. Mehlman, trans.). Chicago: University of Chicago Press. (Original work published 1986.)

Said, E. W. (1996) *Representations of the intellectual.* New York: Vintage Books.

Sampson, E. (1983) *Justice and the critique of pure psychology.* New York: Plenum Press.

Sampson, E. E. (1996) an article in T. Cordero, I. Dobles and R. Perez (eds), *Dominación social y subjetividad.* San José: Editorial Universidad de Costa Rica.

Sanson, A., Augoustinos, N., Gridley, H., Kyrios, M., Reser, J. and Turner, C. (1998) Racism and prejudice: An Australian Psychological Society position paper. *Australian Psychologist, 33*, 161–82.

Sarason, S. B. (1981) *Psychology misdirected*. New York: Free Press.

Sartre, J-P. (1963) *Search for a method*. New York: Knopf.

Sayers, J. (1982) *Biological politics*. London: Tavistock.

Scarry, E. (1985) *The body in pain: The making and unmaking of the world*. New York: Oxford University Press.

Schraube, E. (1998) *Auf den Spuren der Dinge. Psychologie in einer Welt der Technik*. Berlin, Germany: Argument.

Sedgwick, P. (1982) *Psychopolitics*. London: Pluto Press.

Segall, M. H., Dasen, P. R., Berry. J. W. and Poortinga, Y. H. (1990) *Human behavior in global perspective*. Elmsford, NY: Pergamon.

Serpell, R. (1993a) Interaction of context with development: Theoretical constructs for the design of early childhood education programs. In L. Eldering and P. Leseman (eds), *Early intervention and culture* (pp. 23–43). UNESCO.

Serpell, R. (1993b) *The significance of schooling: Life-journeys in an African society*. Cambridge, MA: Cambridge University Press.

Serpell, R. (1994) An African ontogeny of social selfhood. *Cross-Cultural Psychology Bulletin, 28,* 17–20.

Shawver, L. (1980) *The politics of helping psychology grow*. Paper presented at the California State Psychological Association Convention, Sacramento.

Shawver, L. (1983) Harnessing the power of interpretive language. *Psychotherapy: Theory, Research and Practice, 20*(1), 3–11.

Shawver, L. (1987) On the question of women officers in male prisons. *Corrective and Social Psychiatry, 33*(1), 154–9.

Shawver, L. (1993) *Homosexuals in the military: Issues of privacy and morale*. Paper presented at the American Psychological Association, Toronto, Canada, August.

Shawver, L. (1994) *American modesty secrets and the etiquette of disregard*. Paper presented at a special symposium of the American Psychological Association, Anaheim, CA, August.

Shawver, L. (1995) *And the flag was still there: Straight people, gay people, and sexuality in the US military*. Binghamton, NY: Haworth Press.

Shawver, L. (1996) Privacy, modesty and the ban against gays in the military. In J. B. Jobe, G. M. Herek and R. Carney. *Out in force: Gays in the military* (pp. 226–44). Chicago: University of Chicago Press.

Shawver, L. (1996) What postmodernism can do for psychoanalysis: A guide to the postmodern vision. *The American Journal of Psychoanalysis, 56*(4), 371–94.

Shawver, L. (1998a) Postmodernizing the unconscious. *The American Journal of Psychoanalysis, 58*(4), 329–36.

Shawver, L. (1988b) On the clinical relevance of selected postmodern ideas with a focus on Lyotard's concept of 'differend'. *Journal of the American Academy of Psychoanalysis, 26*(4).

Shawver, L., Clanon, T. L. and Kurdys, D. (1982) Less insanity in the courts. *American Bar Association Journal, 68*, 824–27.

Shawver, L. and Dickover, B. (1986) Exploding a myth. *Corrections Today, 48*(6), 30–4.

Shawver, L. and Dokecki, P. (1970) A Wittgensteinian analysis of the role of self-reports in psychology. *Psychological Records, 20*, 289–96.

Shawver, L. and Kurdys, D. (1987) Shall we employ women guards in male prisons? *Journal of Psychiatry and Law, 15*(2), 277–95.

Shawver, L. and Sanders, B. (1977) A look at four critical premises in correctional views. *Crime and Delinquency, 23*(4), 427–33.

Sheehan, P. (1996) Anticipations ahead for psychology: Looking from past to future. *Australian Psychologist, 31*, 183–90.

Shields, C., Wynne, L. and Gawinski, B. (1994) The marginalization of family therapy: A historical and continuing problem. *Journal of Marital and Family Therapy, 20*, 117–39.

Shweder, R. (1991) *Thinking through cultures: Expeditions in cultural psychology.* Cambridge, MA: Harvard University Press.

Sloan, T. (1990) Psychology for the Third World? *Journal of Social Issues, 46*(3), 1–20.

Sloan, T. (1996a) *Damaged life: The crisis of the modern psyche.* New York: Routledge.

Sloan, T. (1996b) *Life choices: Understanding dilemmas and decisions.* Boulder, CO: Westview.

Spears, R. (1997) Introduction. In T. Ibáñez and L. Iñiguez (eds), *Critical social psychology* (pp. 1–26). Thousand Oaks, CA: Sage.

Stam, H. (ed.). (1998) *The body and psychology.* Thousand Oaks, CA: Sage.

Stam, H., Lubek, I. and Radtke, L. (1998) Repopulating social psychology texts: Disembodied 'subjects' and embodied subjectivity. In B. M. Bayer and J. Shotter (eds), *Reconstructing the psychological subject: Bodies, practices, and technologies* (pp. 153–86). Thousand Oaks, CA: Sage.

Stern, W. (1900) Die psychologische Arbeit des neunzehnten Jahrhunderts, insbesondere in Deutschland. *Zeitschrift für Pädagogische Psychologie und Pathologie, 2* (6), 413–36.

Suleiman, S. R. (ed.) (1985) *The female body in western culture: Contemporary perspectives.* Cambridge, MA: Harvard University Press.

Sullivan, E. (1977a) *Kohlberg's structuralism: A critical appraisal.* Toronto, Ont. OISE Press.

Sullivan, E. (1977b) A study of Kohlberg's theory of moral development. *Human Development, 20*, 253–76.

Sullivan, E. (1983) Computers, culture and educational futures: A meditation on mindstorms. *Interchange* (16, vol. pp. 1–18).

Sullivan, E. (1984) *Critical psychology: An interpretation of the personal world.* New York: Plenum Press.

Sullivan, E. (1987) Critical pedagogy and television. In D. Livingstone (ed.), *Critical pedagogy and cultural power*. New York: Bergin and Garvey.

Sullivan, E. (1990) *Critical psychology and critical pedagogy*. New York: Bergin & Garvey.

Syme, G. J. and Bishop, B. J. (1993) Public psychology: Planning a role for psychology. *Australian Psychologist, 28*, 45–51.

Tape, G. (1993) *Milieu Africain et développement cognitif: Une étude du raisonnement experimentale chez l'adolescent Ivorien*. Paris: L'Harmattan.

Taylor, C. (1992) *Multiculturalism and 'the politics of recognition'*. Princeton University Press.

Teifer, L. (1991) Commentary on the status of sex research: Feminism, sexuality and sexology. *Journal of Psychology and Human Sexuality, 43*(3) 5–42.

Teo, T. (1986) *Moralisches Urteil: Struktur und Inhalt. Eine vergleichende Untersuchung an adoleszenten Schülern* [Moral judgment: Structure and content. An empirical investigation on adolescents]. Unpublished Master's thesis, University of Vienna.

Teo, T. (1993) *Theoriendynamik in der Psychologie: Zur Rekonstruktion von Wissenschaftsentwicklung am Fallbeispiel von Klaus Holzkamp* [Theory dynamics in psychology: The reconstruction of science development using Klaus Holzkamp as a case example]. Hamburg: Argument.

Teo, T. (1996) Practical reason in psychology: Postmodern discourse and a neo-modern alternative. In C. W. Tolman, F. Cherry, R. van Hezewijk and I. Lubek (eds) *Problems of theoretical psychology* (pp. 280–90). Toronto, Canada: Captus.

Teo, T. (1997) Developmental psychology and the relevance of a critical metatheoretical reflection. *Human Development, 40*(4), 195–210.

Teo, T. (1998a) Klaus Holzkamp and the rise and decline of German critical psychology. *History of Psychology, 1* (3), 235–53.

Teo, T. (1998b) Prolegomenon to a contemporary psychology of liberation. *Theory and Psychology, 8*(4), 527–47.

Teo, T. (1999) Functions of knowledge in psychology. *New Ideas in Psychology, 17*(1), 1–15.

Throgmorton, J. (1991) The rhetorics of policy analysis. *Policy Sciences, 24*, 153–79.

Tolman, C. (1994) *Psychology, society, and subjectivity: An introduction to German critical psychology*. London: Routledge.

Trevarthen, C. (1980) The foundations of intersubjectivity: Development of interpersonal and cooperative understanding in infants. In D. R. Olson (ed.), *The social foundations of language and thought* (pp. 316–42). New York: Wiley.

Triandis, H. C. and Brislin, R. W. (1984) Cross-cultural psychology. *American Psychologist, 39*(9), 1006–16.

Trickett, E. J. (1996) A future for community psychology: The contexts of diversity and the diversity of contexts. *American Journal of Community Psychology*, 24(2), 209–35.

Turkle, S. (1995) *Life on the screen: Identity in the age of the internet*. New York: Simon and Schuster.

Tyler, F. B. (1998) *Cross-cultural psychology: Is it time to revise the model?* Paper presented at the Fourteenth International and Silver Jubilee Congress of International Association Cross-Cultural Psychology, Bellingham, WA.

Tyler, F. B., Pargament, K. I. and Gatz, M. (1983) The resource collaborator role: A model for interactions involving psychologists. *American Psychologist*, 38, 388–98.

Ussher, J. M. (1989) *The psychology of the female body*. London: Routledge.

Ussher, J. M., and Baker, C. (eds) (1993) *Psychological perspectives on sexual problems: New directions for theory and practice*. London: Routledge.

Ussher, J. M. (1991) *Women's madness – misogyny or mental illness?* Hemel Hempstead: Harvester Wheatsheaf.

Ussher, J. M. (1996) Premenstrual syndrome: Reconciling disciplinary divide through the adoption of a material-discursive epistemological standpoint. *Annual Review of Sex Research, 7*, 218–52.

Ussher, J. M. (1997a) *Fantasies of femininity: Reframing the boundaries of sex*. London: Penguin.

Ussher, J. M. (1997b) *Body talk: The material and discursive regulation of sexuality, madness and reproduction*. London: Routledge.

Ussher, J. M. (1997c) *Doing feminist research: Issues of competition, discontent and dissent*. Paper presented at the European Congress of Psychology Conference, Dublin, Ireland, July.

Ussher, J. M. (1999a) Women's madness: A material-discursive-intra psychic approach. In D. Fee (ed.), *Psychology and the postmodern: Mental illness as discourse and experience*. London: Sage.

Ussher, J. M. (1999b) Doing feminism: A personal narrative of twenty years of feminist research on PMS. Manuscript submitted for publication.

Ussher, J. M., & Nicolson, P. (eds) (1991) *Gender issues in clinical psychology*. London: Routledge.

Vance, C. (1985) *Pleasure and danger: The politics of sexuality*. London: Routledge and Kegan Paul.

Walkerdine, V. (1997) Postmodernity, subjectivity and the media. In T. Ibáñez and L. Iñiguez (eds), *Critical social psychology* (pp. 169–77). Thousand Oaks, CA: Sage.

Walsh-Bowers, R., Rossiter, A. and Prilleltensky, I. (1996) The personal is the organizational in the ethics of hospital social workers. *Ethics and Behavior, 6* (4), 321–35.

Weisz, J. R. (1978) *Transcontextual validity in developmental research. Vol. 1: Perspectives.* Boston, MA: Allyn & Bacon.

Wexler, P. (1983) *Critical social psychology.* New York: Routledge & Kegan-Paul.

White, S. H. (1996) Foreword. In M. Cole (ed.), *Cultural psychology: A once and future discipline* (pp. iv–xvi). Cambridge, MA: Belknap Press.

Wicker, A. (1989) Substantive theorising. *American Journal of Community Psychology, 17,* 531–547.

Wilson, B. (1997) The postmodern paradigm. In C. R. Dills and A. J. Romiszowski (eds) *Instructional Development Paradigms.* Englewoods Cliffs, NJ: Educational Technology Publications.

Wilson, B., Teslow, J. & Osman-Jouchoux, R. (1994) The impact of constructivism and postmodernism on ID fundamentals. In B. Seels (ed.), *Instructional design fundamentals.* Englewood Cliffs NJ: Educational Techology Publications, 1994.

Winner, L. (1989) *The whale and the reactor: A search for limits in an age of high technology.* Chicago: University of Chicago Press.

Winner, L. (1992) *Autonomous technology: Technics-out-of-control as a theme in political thought.* Cambridge, MA: MIT Press.

Wishik, H. and Pierce, C. (1995) *Sexual orientation and identity.* Lacona, NH: New Dynamics.

Wittgenstein, L. (1965) *Philosophical investigations* (G. Anscombe, trans). New York: Macmillan.

Wober, M. (1974) Towards an understanding of the Kiganda concept of intelligence. In J. W. Berry and P. R. Dasen (eds), *Culture and cognition.* London: Methuen.

Young, M. (1991) *Justice and the politics of difference.* Philadelphia, PA: Princeton University Press.

Zizek, S. (1990) East European Republics of Gilead. *New Left Review, 183,* 51–2.

Zizek, S. (1991) *Looking awry.* Cambridge, MA: MIT Press.

Zukow, G. P. (1989) Communicating across disciplines: On integrating psychological and ethnographic approaches to sibling research. In G. P. Zukow (ed.), *Sibling interaction across cultures: Theoretical and methodological issues.* New York: Springer.

Index